Fighting the Unbeatable Foe

Howard Metzenbaum of Ohio
The Washington Years

Tom Diemer

The Kent State University Press

KENT, OHIO

© 2008 by The Kent State University Press, Kent, Ohio 44242
ALL RIGHTS RESERVED
Library of Congress Catalog Card Number 2008014197
ISBN 978-0-87338-914-3

Manufactured in the United States of America

Library of Congress Cataloging-in-Publication Data
Diemer, Tom.
Fighting the unbeatable foe : Howard Metzenbaum of Ohio :
the Washington years / Tom Diemer.
p. cm.
Includes bibliographical references and index.
ISBN 978-0-87338-914-3 (hardcover : alk. paper)∞
1. Metzenbaum, Howard M. 2. Legislators—United States—Biography.
3. United States. Congress. Senate—Biography. 4. United States—Politics and
government—1945–1989. 5. Legislators—Ohio—Biography.
6. Ohio—Politics and government—20th century. I. Title.
E840.8.M48D54 2008
328.73092—dc22
[B]
2008014197

British Library Cataloging-in-Publication data are available.

12 11 10 09 08   5 4 3 2 1

This book is dedicated, in memoriam,
to my brother Dave Diemer, a "Metz fan," and to my former
colleague Robert E. Miller, a mentor.

Contents

Preface

Shortly before Howard Metzenbaum retired as one of the most improbably successful senators in Ohio history, my wife's parents met him at an event in Zanesville, Ohio, where they once lived. Bob and Pat Zimmer introduced themselves and mentioned that their son-in-law, Tom Diemer, was a newspaper reporter in Washington, D.C. Senator Metzenbaum's smile disappeared and his face scrunched up. "Diemer! That SOB! Why, I . . ." Then he grinned. Of course he knew Diemer. "A nice fella," he said and then engaged my in-laws in other pleasantries.

That was Metzenbaum: gruff, irreverent, sarcastic. He couldn't really tell a joke, but he sure could act. He'd feign anger and threaten chaos to get his way in the Senate. He would practice scowls in the mirror, and then trade dirty looks with cabinet secretaries sitting across from him in a hearing room. Yet, inside the hard-boiled exterior, he had a good heart.

As his health failed and his memory faded in the months before his death at 90 in 2008, he would often tell family members, "I have a great wife. I've got great kids. I'm a lucky man."[1]

In my first experience covering him in his 1976 race against Senator Robert Taft Jr., I never dreamed he would one day become the scourge of Capitol Hill or that his career would amount to book material. It was a lackluster campaign, overshadowed by Jimmy Carter's bold bid to carry Ohio in the presidential contest. Metzenbaum, a two-time loser, seemed headed for another defeat—surely his last hurrah—and a one-way ticket to obscurity as the "millionaire Cleveland businessman" in residence near Erie's shores. Taft owned the most famous name in Ohio politics; he was a decent enough senator and had already beaten this guy six years earlier. Metzenbaum was too liberal, too rich, and too annoying. His act had grown old.

How wrong I was. Whatever his weaknesses—and he had his share—Howard Metzenbaum was also brilliant, tenacious, well-financed, and yes, lucky. He understood the media much better than the typical mid-1970s Ohio politician, and he ran a campaign against Taft that flouted the conventional wisdom of the day. He operated only a rudimentary field operation, aided by union volunteers, and put most of his money into strategic planning and television advertising. The clincher was a thirty-second spot featuring his comely wife, Shirley, assuring viewers that Metzenbaum was a warm, caring family man. "He always sees the good in people," Shirley Metzenbaum liked to say of her husband.

He came to the United States Senate late in life, and his ways were set. He was nearing sixty when he took the oath of office for his first full term after ousting Taft. He had always played hardball in business and in politics. He wouldn't change in Washington. In a town where "go along to get along" was considered sound advice, he declared, "I'm too old to go along for the ride."

I don't know if Metzenbaum understood what a polarizing figure he was in Ohio. When I first contemplated telling his story, one of his old rivals said in exasperation, "Oh geez, don't write a book about him." Metzenbaum's personality just rubbed some people the wrong way. He thought being a nice guy was overrated. Many in the business community disliked him intensely and resented his unceasing efforts to take away their tax advantages, squeeze them with workplace regulations, and strengthen their adversaries in unions. Conservative activists considered him a "limousine liberal," who played down his leftist leanings during campaigns. Right-wingers thought he was evil incarnate—quite possibly a onetime "communist."

But to labor leaders, the consumer movement, the gun-control lobby, children's advocates, migrant workers, and the liberal intelligentsia, he was a hero. He was their knight in shining armor, albeit one who was not always able to slay the dragon, or even tip the windmill.

Was he effective? Did all of the bluster and roar, the delaying tactics, the taste for combat, the class warfare accomplish anything?

If you fed your baby infant formula, Metzenbaum was the guy who established standards to ensure the food's safety and healthfulness. If you wondered about the nutritional content of the products on grocery shelves, he was the one who passed a law requiring ingredient labels on soup cans and cartons of yogurt. If you worked at a plant threatened by a shutdown, he gave you some comfort when he forced manufacturers to give two months' notice before closing a factory. He was on your side, whether you toiled for minimum wage at a fast food joint in Cleveland, picked tomatoes in northwest Ohio, tried to meet utility bills on a fixed income in Youngstown, or worried about your pension in Dayton.

One commentator called him the "last of the New Deal liberals." But his legislative achievements did not rise to the level of a Humphrey, Kennedy, or Mitchell. In his nineteen years on Capitol Hill, he never chaired a full committee or held a top leadership position within the Democratic caucus.

Republican leader Bob Dole gave him a title. Dole called him the "Commissioner," because all significant legislation had to cross his desk for an okay or else risk being sidetracked by a Metzenbaum maneuver on the Senate floor. His power to stop legislation reached beyond his station because he was willing to make enemies, ignore legislative courtesies, and camp out on the Senate floor when others wanted to go home. He was impatient by nature, but patient by his own discipline—he would wait you out, or walk away from the deal if he didn't get what he wanted.

He is remembered more in Washington for what he stopped—the water projects, the timber deals, land giveaways, and tax breaks—than for what he pushed forward. He was a master filibusterer when filibustering wasn't cool, well before Republicans threatened to change the rules to keep Democrats from blocking President George W. Bush's nominees.

In Ohio, his name will always be linked with John Glenn, a man with whom he had little in common and ran against twice, going 1–1. Glenn, the personification of white-bread Americana, was raised in a small Ohio town, instilled with a protestant ethic, and destined for heroism. Metzenbaum, however, was marbled rye, a scrappy Jewish kid who was willing to break rules as he fought his way up from near poverty to financial and political success.

Many books have been written about Glenn, the astronaut turned senator, but this is the first book, as far as I know, about Metzenbaum, a parking lot entrepreneur who became known as "Senator No." Glenn was honored and celebrated for his pioneering feats, and rightly so. A NASA research center in Cleveland and an institute at Ohio State University bear his name, as do a number of public schools. Metzenbaum saw little of that sort of public adulation. He never ran for president as Glenn did, or experienced the adventures of an astronaut, even if many critics would have liked to launch him into the stratosphere. Yet Metzenbaum overcame more obstacles and had a far more interesting Senate career.

So, yes, Metzenbaum is book material. I have tried to do two things here: explain how an abrasive, ultraliberal Democrat won consistently in the affable, moderate Ohio of the late-twentieth century and show how his no-holds-barred tactics made a difference in Washington. My take suggests the Metzenbaum's years in the Senate netted out as a positive contribution for taxpayers, although I hope this books lets readers come to their own conclusions.

In this accounting, Metzenbaum's remarkable story starts with his childhood during the Great Depression and covers his highly success-ful business ventures in the postwar era and his unique Senate career spanning five presidents. This book presents new information from his personal diaries, his official Senate Papers, exclusive interviews with forgotten friends and foes, and fresh reporting on his gaffes, such as the infamous $250,000 phone call that helped sell a hotel. Although I've not attempted to produce a cradle-to-grave biography (the emphasis is on his Senate career), Metzenbaum's early years and his colorful business career are covered here in detail.

In the interest of full disclosure, a little about my personal relation-ship with him is probably in order. When I covered Capitol Hill for the *Plain Dealer* during Metzenbaum's second and third terms, he seldom griped about critical stories. So that was a plus, as far as the press corps was concerned. But he made us work harder and, of course, that was a minus. "Headline Howard" in action might cheap-shot a political ad-versary, usually a Republican, pick a fight with an obscure bureaucrat over some arcane topic, or introduce far-fetched legislation to advance some liberal cause.

But, oh, how we missed him when he retired in 1995. He created buzz. He was the sound bite. Whether squaring off with an imperious Robert Bork, taking on the National Rifle Association, or filibustering to keep a lid on natural gas prices, Metzenbaum made national news. He would get you on the front page more often than not.

And truth be told, reporters didn't see his hard side very often in personal encounters. Get him away from business and he could be charming. He would occasionally entertain other senators, personal friends, and reporters at receptions in his artsy Capitol Hill office. Guests of honor included entertainers and artists. At these little soirees, I met people like painter Robert Rauschenberg (in a loud orange tie and rumpled suit), composer Marvin Hamlisch, and folk singer Mary Travers.

Also, for the record, Metzenbaum once contacted me about a possible job as his press secretary. It was in 1983, I believe, and I was still working in Columbus as the *Plain Dealer*'s bureau chief. We didn't know each other that well, so it's unclear why he considered me for the position. But we had a couple of phone conversations and a meeting one Saturday morning at his Lyndhurst, Ohio, condominium. I thought about the job for a few days and then withdrew. It was fleeting, and neither of us ever mentioned it again. I wasn't ready to give up reporting and didn't think I could return to it had I worked for a partisan figure.

After Metzenbaum left the Senate, he stayed in touch, calling me every couple of months from his part-time office on 16th Street in Washington at the Consumer Federation of America. He knew I was writing a book and welcomed it, although he also knew all of his blemishes would be on display as well as his hard-earned triumphs. A typical telephone conversation went like this:

"Diemer? Metzenbaum here!"
"Oh, hi, Senator, how are you?"
"Want to have lunch Tuesday at the University Club?"
"Tuesday? Let me check. Yeah, that'll work."
"By the way, Tom, how's that book coming?"
"Well, I'm working on it in spurts. It's awfully busy here at the newspaper. I'm about two-thirds done, I guess."

"Oh, well, I was just wondering." And then, the needle: "Do you think it will sell better after I'm dead?"

Under the Capitol dome, on the House side, there is an atrium filled with statuary, larger-than-life images of statesmen, all dead, from the fifty states. Ohio is represented by William Allen, a little remembered mid-nineteenth-century senator from Chillicothe. I have always thought our state would be well served if Congress one day added statues of Glenn and Metzenbaum standing side by side. Those two men dominated the state's political landscape over the last twenty-five years of the twentieth century.

Sincere thanks go to John Hubbell and Joanna Hildebrand Craig, my editors at the Kent State University Press, for their patience with this long-running project. Also thanks to fellow reporters, past and present, for their insights and reminisces, particularly former *Plain Dealer* colleagues Joe Rice, Bill Carlson, and Brent Larkin. Institutions like the Western Reserve Historical Society and the Cleveland Press Archives at Cleveland State University provided historical context. I deeply appreciated the cooperation of the Metzenbaum family—his four daughters, Barbara, Susan, Shelley, and Amy—and also his extended family of former staffers and business associates. Harold Stern, Juanita Powe, Peter Harris, and Joel Johnson were especially helpful. My wife, Judy Zimmer, Bob and Pat's oldest daughter, inspired me to see it through. Judy always believed.

Acknowledgments

I would like to thank all of the hardworking reporters who, over the course of more than half a century, told the story of Howard Metzenbaum's public life and private endeavors to Ohioans and Americans. I drew heavily on their first drafts and want to acknowledge in particular the reporting and writing of the late Thomas J. Brazaitis of the *Cleveland Plain Dealer* and Dick Feagler of the *Cleveland Press*, who has a second career as a television commentator and columnist for the *Plain Dealer*.

I also thank the Metzenbaum family for cooperating in extraordinary ways, even though this was not an authorized biography. Metzenbaum's extended family of former staffers, friends, and business associates were also invaluable to my efforts. And the senator himself gave generously of his time in numerous formal and informal interviews. He knew my undertaking would include all of his warts, but he also knew I would spell his name right.

The Cleveland State University Special Collections Library was helpful as I pored through old clippings and photos from the *Cleveland Press*. And the Western Reserve Historical Society, the repository of Metzenbaum's official Senate papers, was equally accommodating.

I also wish to thank the Plain Dealer Library for its help with my research of old stories and photos, especially Dave Jardy and Carl Matzelle.

Lastly, I wish to thank my family—my wife, Judith, and my daughters, Jenny and Marie Claire—for their patience and support during the lengthy course of this project.

The Early Years

In later years, he would call it one of his worst moments. But as he waited in the rear of the Senate and listened to other men questioning his character and worthiness to join the world's most exclusive club, Howard Metzenbaum was oddly amused. "That didn't bother me. I stood back there and I said, 'Incredible. Howard Metzenbaum's the subject of a Senate debate. Isn't that great?'"[1] In truth, it did bother him. Metzenbaum always thought the odds were stacked against him, and this was yet another example.

It was January 21, 1974, and Richard Nixon would soon be gone from the White House. In the previous year, U.S. troops pulled out of Vietnam; American Indian militants occupied Wounded Knee, South Dakota; the energy crisis pushed the price of gasoline above $1 per gallon; Spiro Agnew was forced to resign as vice president; David Ben-Gurion, the father of modern Israel, died at the age of eighty-seven; and Aleksandr Solzhenitsyn's *The Gulag Archipelago* was published in Paris as the Cold War dragged on between East and West. On the home front, the nation was in a state of high anxiety, fearful that the American system was coming apart.

Metzenbaum, out of electoral politics for more than two decades, was appointed to the United States Senate by Ohio governor John J. Gilligan after the embattled Nixon chose the state's senior Republican senator, William B. Saxbe, as attorney general to succeed Elliot L.

Richardson. Richardson resigned rather than accede to Nixon's order that he fire Archibald Cox, the Watergate investigator.

When Metzenbaum's big day arrived, the Senate gallery was packed with his family and friends from Cleveland. Senator Carl T. Curtis, a conservative from Nebraska, tried to qualify Metzenbaum's seating as a senator, making it contingent on the outcome of an investigation of a dispute with the Internal Revenue Service. Curtis's intent was clear. In the event that Senate investigators—or the IRS—dug up enough dirt, Metzenbaum could be removed more easily from the Senate if his status were conditional. The IRS had audited his tax returns for 1967 and 1968 and questioned the bona fides of Metzenbaum's $3.4 million purchase of a methane plant in Louisiana. Metzenbaum challenged the finding but agreed to deposit $118,000 to be held in escrow for the IRS until the argument was settled.

Metzenbaum's seating was the only item of substance on the Senate calendar that January day, the first meeting of the 1974 congressional session. The opening session was customarily a time for ceremony, routine business, and long-winded speeches about the agenda for the new year. This was anything but routine. Two Democratic titans—senators Sam Ervin of North Carolina and Mike Mansfield of Montana—rose up in Metzenbaum's defense, and an intense partisan debate tied up the Senate for much of the day. When Ervin finally moved to table Curtis's motion, as well as a compromise offered by Mansfield, the vote went in Metzenbaum's favor 53–22. As the roll call ended, Vice President Gerald Ford, presiding over the Senate, became confused and announced the outcome in reverse, making it appear to some that Metzenbaum's opponents had prevailed. Another indignity. Ford quickly corrected himself and prepared to administer the oath of office to the new senator from Ohio.

Senator Robert A. Taft Jr., who defeated Metzenbaum in the 1970 Senate race in Ohio, voted "present" in the seating of his old rival, fearing the appearance of a conflict because of their home state connection. But as Metzenbaum's swearing in approached, Taft escorted him grandly arm in arm down the aisle of the Senate chamber.

Metzenbaum, who was not a religious man, laid his right hand on an open Bible. His wife, Shirley, had marked Proverbs 22:22–25: "Rob not the poor for the Lord will plead their case and spoil the soul of those that spoiled them. Make no friendship with an angry man, lest you learn his ways and set a snare for yourself." It was official. His friends from Cleveland cheered and whooped from the gallery despite an admonition from Ford.

Metzenbaum was fifty-six years old. He had served in the state legislature in Columbus with distinction, raised a family, and made millions of dollars in business ventures. Yet he yearned for acceptance and respect in public life. His triumph was at hand.

Aside from personal wealth, Metzenbaum had little in common with Senator Taft of Cincinnati, who carried one of the oldest, most revered names in Ohio politics. One could argue that Metzenbaum had little in common with a majority of the people he would represent for nineteen years in the Senate. He was a nouveau riche Jewish businessman from Cleveland with a clunky-sounding last name, left-wing political views, and a taste for avant-garde art. A perennial outsider, Metzenbaum would become one of the most dominant politicians in the history of Republican-leaning Ohio, a place where the conservative, stately Taft family had prospered for generations.

Throughout his Senate career, Metzenbaum confounded his rivals, the media, and political scientists. Despite his wealth and a willingness to hire nonunion workers at his various enterprises, Metzenbaum emerged as organized labor's best friend in the Senate. And even though he expresses hostility toward tax loopholes for the wealthy, he used write-offs to avoid paying any federal income tax in 1969, the year before his first Senate campaign, a fact he revealed, cunningly, after his contentious seating in 1974. An early opponent of the war in Vietnam, he identified with the youth-oriented New Left, which rose in the late 1960s. But he was conservative when it came to his personal habits, eschewing the longish hair and informal attire in favor when he first ran for the Senate in 1970. He was sober and disciplined in lifestyle and appearance, peering sternly through thick glasses and usually wearing business suits. During most of the 1950s and 1960s, he favored a close-cropped crew cut.

Howard Metzenbaum was cantankerous, impatient, abrasive, hated by the business community, feared by his own staff, and the devil incarnate to Republicans. He always said he loved children. "It's the adults I have problems with," he once said. He fed on resentment. "Of course, I wasn't one of them," he told the *Cleveland Plain Dealer*'s Joe Rice when asked about criticism of his antibusiness views in 1977 at the outset of his first full term in the Senate. "These are the people who said I couldn't belong to the Union Club. They wouldn't let me in their circle at the Growth Association. They made every effort to exclude me. I've never been very comfortable with them, and they've never been very comfortable with me."[2] When his name surfaced on Richard Nixon's "enemies list," he called it a "mark of distinction."[3] He reveled in the attacks of the Christian Right and the National Rifle Association, which called him "our biggest foe."[4]

Metzenbaum confided to his staff that he knew he had an advantage when he got the other guy angry. "Find out what a man's frustrations are and you have the key to what makes that man tick," he once said.[5] His scowl, whether feigned or an honest expression of rage, could wilt an unwary staff member or a blustery bureaucrat. One top aide swore his boss told him that as a young defense lawyer Metzenbaum would stand in front of a mirror practicing that menacing look. "It can be just icy cold," said Cleveland lawyer James Schiller, who worked for Metzenbaum during his second campaign against John Glenn. "I remember one time I said something [personal] to him in a crowded elevator and he turned and said, 'this is hardly the time for this.'"[6]

In early 1982, as Metzenbaum prepared for what could have been a classic matchup against ultraconservative Republican congressman John Ashbrook, an unsigned memo crossed his desk in his first-floor Russell Office Building suite on Capitol Hill. It was written in large type.

> ON OUR SIDE Cares about improving health care. Ending unemployment; senior citizens, education; hopes and dreams of the American Family.
> Equal rights and fairness for all.[7]

Of course, those had been Metzenbaum's themes all along. Never mind all of the liberal buzzwords, the futile attacks on oil companies, legislation to change the name of the FBI building as a way of discrediting J. Edgar Hoover. Put aside his unrelenting fights against school prayer or his resistance to bills banning desecration of the American flag. He would talk directly to Ohio families about the problems they customarily discussed around the kitchen table: utility bills, the cost of groceries, the state of public schools. Let Ashbrook wallow in irrelevant ideological muck. It all came together around those three little words: on our side.

Years later David Skylar, a onetime business partner and political aide in Metzenbaum's first Senate campaign, began scribbling on a cocktail napkin after a lunch companion asked him to explain Metzenbaum's extraordinary success in the face of difficult odds. "He's on our side!" he wrote, handing the crumpled note across the table. Milton Wolf, the former U.S. ambassador to Austria and a Metzenbaum acquaintance since their days together at Ohio State University, put it this way: "He has a sense of what people care about. He talked about issues that were important to Ohioans."[8]

After Metzenbaum defeated Taft in the 1976 Senate campaign, his wife told him, "Any person who went to a supermarket to buy food was with you."[9] He built an Ohio coalition of labor unions, minorities, and bread-and-butter Democrats. Nationally, he also counted the liberal intelligentsia and pro-Israel Jews in his camp. He always took care of his base but also honed a populist, proconsumer message to win over middle-of-the-road voters, the key to capturing elections in Ohio.

Near the end of his Senate career, Metzenbaum offered this remarkably candid advice to Senate newcomers: "If I've learned one thing in the Senate, it is that you can take positions that don't sit well with the majority of your constituents and still thrive politically. I've always felt it was my obligation to vote based on my own values and to accept the judgment of the voters on election day. . . . You should let your constituents know exactly where you stand on the issues and why."[10]

They knew where he stood—or did they? He frequently took positions on controversial issues that he realized were not popular back in Ohio. But he was careful not to highlight the same issues during election years. In a 1984 University of Akron survey, a hypothetical matchup between Metzenbaum and future foe George Voinovich showed the two running even among self-identified conservatives and voters favoring Ronald Reagan. This not uncommon perception of Metzenbaum as a conservative infuriated and energized right-wing activists, yet the wily Metzenbaum avoided their snares.

He could be shameless. "I'm a product of the free enterprise system," he said in 1976 while running against Taft. "Good government is really nothing more than good business. . . . I'm a businessman."[11] But he didn't believe that for a minute. To Metzenbaum, government was not a bottom-line undertaking but an instrument to battle against corporate greed, and to make life a little more comfortable, safe, and secure for the poor and middle class. The businessman in him often cut corners in amassing a personal fortune, but in the political world, he was an unabashed redistribution-of-wealth liberal. His critics liked to say, "Howard doesn't think anyone should have any money but him."

To say he was disliked by many of his colleagues during his early years in the Senate would be an understatement. For years, John Glenn, a fellow Democrat from Ohio, despised him. Senator Ernest "Fritz" Hollings, a conservative South Carolina Democrat, once referred to him as "the senator from B'nai B'rith" when Metzenbaum kept interrupting him during a debate on school prayer. When Senator Ted Stevens of Alaska called Metzenbaum a "pain in the ass" after the Ohioan gleefully blocked sixteen pork-barrel projects, including a whopper for the forty-ninth state, Metzenbaum knew he was winning the game on his terms. He killed many more bills than he passed. "I don't mind being called a pain in the ass if that's the price I have to pay for protecting the people of this country and this state," he said in 1982 at a labor rally in Cleveland.[12] Orrin Hatch, a Mormon and committed conservative, said it was relatively easy to succeed as Metzenbaum had "if you don't care what your colleagues think."[13]

An unidentified Capitol Hill veteran told a reporter in 1988 that Metzenbaum was a "knee jerk liberal, with an emphasis on 'jerk.'"[14] With grudging respect, Republican leader Howard Baker once said, "The Senate needs someone like Howard Metzenbaum—but only one!"[15]

"I never thought I was going to be the May Queen," Metzenbaum said shortly after defeating George Voinovich and winning reelection to a third Senate term in 1988.[16] This was bravado. He wanted it both ways—to be feared and loved. He eventually gained respect and even a degree of affection from other senators for his tenacity and conviction. Hatch observed that nothing seemed to bother the Ohioan. Senator Alan Simpson, Republican of Wyoming, called Metzenbaum "an unthreatened man."[17] In time, both Hatch and Simpson would say they genuinely liked the hard-edged senator, and Ted Stevens became a tennis partner.

Metzenbaum was rarely embarrassed and almost never afraid. He remained a paradox to the end—"Pappa" to his nine grandkids, "Senator No" to his colleagues, and an unrepentant Stalinist to right-wing foes.

The Metzenbaum story started in the Jewish quarter of a neighborhood on Cleveland's East Side. In an old snapshot, a stern-faced little boy in a sailor suit, short pants, and high-button shoes stares straight at the camera. His arms are held stiffly at his side; his ears stick out a little; one foot is planted ahead of the other. But it is his expression—penetrating, almost intimidating from a boy of no more than seven—that hints at what is to come. The vintage black-and-white photo appeared in the 1961 *Plain Dealer Sunday Magazine,* with a caption noting the "look of extreme concentration" on the "lad."[18]

Howard Morton Metzenbaum grew up somewhere between poor and lower middle class in the Glenville section of what would later be called the inner city of Cleveland. Born in 1917, he lived in a frame house on Chesterfield Avenue with his parents, Charles and Anna, and an older brother, Irwyn. Charles Metzenbaum, a native of Cleveland, was a Jew of Polish and French ancestry. His wife, Anna Klafter, also Jewish, came to Cleveland from Zanesville, Ohio, prior to World War I. Her parents emigrated to the United States from Hungary. As a senator, Metzenbaum seldom spoke of his family life during these lean, early years, and when he did, it was with a curious detachment. "My parents were very laid back, wonderful people," he told interviewers.[19]

Charles scraped and scrimped during the height of the Great Depression, trying to "eke out an existence," Metzenbaum said. He was a wholesale jobber, who bought and sold merchandise at rough-and-tumble bankruptcy auctions. For a time, he operated out of what a family friend called a "junk store," or second-hand shop, on East 105th Street. Eventually, he went bankrupt. Anna got a job, earning $13 per week in a no-frills department store called Bailey's. Dinner was often sardines or creamed peas on toast.

Irwyn Metzenbaum spoke of the years on Chesterfield Avenue with a fondness and insight that his younger brother could not—or would not—express. He described their father, the son of a Polish immigrant, as a serious, hardworking man and a decent provider. "Pop struggled to make a living, but we always had food on the table, and good food," Irwyn said in a 1995 conversation on the front porch of his cluttered University Heights home.

Charlie Metzenbaum was affable and slow to anger, a man who refrained from using profanity, even when he was provoked. He had little education but possessed a determination and inner toughness that ran in the family. "I never saw my father get mad," Irwyn said. "But once he was fixing a tire—in those days you fixed a tire yourself—and some big fella called him a son of a bitch. My father, who was about five feet two inches tall, grabbed the tire iron and chased the guy down the street."[20]

Charles Metzenbaum's younger son would be called an SOB many times over the years, but it didn't bother him nearly as much. From an early age, Howard was thick skinned and single minded. By the age of ten, he was a budding entrepreneur, hauling neighbors' groceries in his red wagon from a neighborhood market for tips. "I was born knowing how to make money," he often boasted.

At Patrick Henry Junior High School, Howard met Alva "Ted" Bonda, a classmate who would become his lifelong friend and business partner in a parking lot empire that made them both millionaires. Except for Metzenbaum's moneymaking schemes, their coming of age was typically middle American and marked by the austerity of the times. "They were relatively poor people—damned poor people—so it was just a matter of surviving," Bonda said of Metzenbaum's family. "His father had no education. There was no television. We didn't go out anywhere. We stayed in our own neighborhood. We didn't know what was going on."[21] But Metzenbaum knew more than most. He understood at a very early age the importance of transportation and mobility in a world that, even in the 1930s, was going through rapid change. The little red wagon was soon put aside for a 1926 Essex, which he used to take his neighborhood pals to the airport for air shows put on by barnstorming daredevils. The kids jammed into the old car—some even on the running boards—paid Metzenbaum one or two cents per mile for gasoline and then sold peanuts at the air shows. Bonda was recruited to drive even though he didn't know how and had an accident on one of his first trips to the movies. "Howard comes running up, but doesn't say anything to me. Instead, he goes to the other guy and says, 'It's your fault.' He does those things on instinct and he also does it as a friend." The adventures in the Essex ended abruptly when Metzenbaum woke up one morning to find it gone. His father had sold it without asking to make a mortgage payment on their home.

In junior high school, Metzenbaum participated in basketball and ran track. He played sandlot baseball during the summer when he wasn't doing odd jobs. He was not physically imposing or exceptionally athletic, but the towheaded boy with glasses loved competition. "We played softball every Sunday, and Howard would come by, and if he would bring the ball he could get in the game," Bonda laughed. His buddies called him "Bunny"—mispronouncing it as "Boony"—a mocking reference to his protruding ears. He didn't mind. He already had been called worse.

The two friends went on to Glenville High School, where Metzen-baum proved to be an excellent student and served as treasurer of the student council. He ran sprints for the Tarblooder track-and-field team and claimed to have once competed against the great Jesse Owens of rival East Technical High School. In 1935, the year of their graduation, Metzenbaum and Bonda planned to sell class rings to other seniors, but their inventory was stolen from a locker. "The person we bought them from bothered us for payment for years. I think that's why Howard became a lawyer," Bonda said.[22]

Metzenbaum was bound for Ohio State University, paying his own way through enterprise and sacrifice. He considered pledging the pre-dominantly Jewish Tau Epsilon Phi but decided Greek life was not for him. Young Howard Metzenbaum was no good-time Charlie. Let others go to the big game, join fraternities, and horse around at campus beer joints; Howard would work and get ahead. He wanted to major in ac-counting, but chose psychology instead because he could schedule all of his classes in the morning, leaving the afternoons free for work that paid. He was tapped for a scholastic honorary group his first year, but he also kept up a fast pace outside the classroom. He sold chrysanthe-mums outside of Buckeye football games on Saturday afternoons and gardenias at High Street restaurants during the evenings. He scalped tickets, making $300 in profits when he had the prescience to buy a hundred Ohio State–Michigan tickets a year in advance of The Game. He was the campus sales supervisor for the *Saturday Evening Post,* oper-ated a bike rental for a quarter a ride, and played slide trombone for fifty cents an hour in a dance band called the National Youth Orchestra.

In the summer and during breaks from school, he and a friend drove from town to town, selling razor blades, sundries, and condoms out of the trunk of Metzenbaum's car. Through the dusty Midwest, they rolled into Fremont, Findlay, Terre Haute, Kokomo, and Battle Creek. Metzenbaum would whip out a razor blade and split one of his own straw-blond hairs in an instant. Sold. Condoms were another matter. They were legal but still an unmentionable, and the police often hassled Howard and his friend when they tried to sell the contraceptives.

Metzenbaum was no goody-goody in college. With a friend from Youngstown, Paul Stevens, he founded the Independent Men's Associa-tion, a males-only social club offering an alternative to fraternity life. His vices were poker and pool. "There was a guy by the name of Herbie Copeland that I used to shoot pool with. We would shoot for rather considerable stakes. I was a good poker player and a bad pool player," said Metzenbaum, who organized poker and crap games, sometimes backing the action with a pot of money.[23] When a professional gambler approached him, offering to back him in a high-stakes game with big-timers, he demurred. Metzenbaum usually knew where to draw the line, even if it did come right to the edge of illegality.

The young Howard graduated in 1939 with a Bachelor of Arts degree and was admitted to OSU's law school that same year. By then, his interest in politics had blossomed. He was a strong supporter of Franklin Delano Roosevelt but also a budding antiwar activist. Without consulting his parents, he turned down the opportunity for a partial scholarship to Harvard Law School. His future would be in Ohio. He was drafting bills part time for state lawmakers at the Legislative Service Commission at the statehouse in downtown Columbus. He got $1 per document produced. And he was active in law school activities, serving as president of the Professional Interfraternity Council and vice president of the legal fraternity Tau Epsilon Rho. He was also treasurer of the Peace Mobilization Committee, which opposed U.S. entry into World War II during a period in which Nazi Germany and the Soviet Union shared a nonaggression pact. He fell in with Bill Halloran, another antiwar leader, who was an officer of the Newman Club, the campus Catholic organization. It was the beginning of an attachment to left-wing causes that would be used against Metzenbaum throughout his career in public office. "In retrospect, we were wrong," he said in a 1994 interview when asked about his early opposition to the war against fascism. "I don't think we appreciated the threat . . . We were 100 percent wrong."[24] For someone who was respected by his adversaries for an uncanny ability to plot the future, this was a stunning lack of foresight. His naïveté in international affairs would recur, bloodying him politically each time. He came to appreciate the "threat" on December 7, 1941, when Halloran was killed in the air raid at Pearl Harbor; he was the first Clevelander to die in the war.

Metzenbaum graduated from law school in 1941 and went back to Cleveland to enter politics and practice law as a labor attorney. He was not drafted due to poor eyesight. After such friends as Bonda and Halloran signed up to go overseas, Metzenbaum was understandably sensitive to his touchy political situation in civilian life. Clearly, staying home had its advantages, but it was not a political plus and took an emotional toll. News clippings from the era quote Metzenbaum—the emerging politician—as insisting he tried more than once to enlist but was rejected.[25] It was just one more thing he had going against him. "In much of his career, he was not an acceptable person," said Bonda, a witness to Metzenbaum's determination to overcome any obstacle.

Metzenbaum's fierce determination to succeed might be traced to certain traits that he exhibited early in life: a strong work ethic molded by hard times, resentment of anti-Semitism and class consciousness, and an expectation that nothing in life would come easily. He would have to fight for what he wanted in life. Rabbi Arthur Lelyveld, the late civil rights activist who was Metzenbaum's longtime friend, said in 1995, "I know his upbringing was always along the line of duty and a sense of responsibility." Howard Metzenbaum, Lelyveld said, was focused on one goal: getting ahead.[26] For him, there was never any contradiction between ambition for material success and a conviction that the government should be used to rein in the free market system and benefit the less fortunate. Metzenbaum could be a no-holds-barred capitalist in his personal dealings and an antibusiness liberal in his politics.

Although he respected people like Lelyveld and Halloran, there appears to have been no valued teacher or coach, no transforming experience during the years on the hard streets of Glenville or at OSU, which helped him work toward his goal. Metzenbaum was not introspective; he felt he had little time for guilt, second-guessing, or postmortems. Nothing would stand in his way.

Shortly before leaving the Senate, he was almost at a loss for words when asked the secret of his success. "I cannot explain why I am the way I am. I cannot think of any individual who molded me."[27] No teacher. No mentor. No guru. He did it on his own. But his ambivalence about his parents was a source of discomfort even in later years. "I know my parents wanted to help me," he said in a 1997 interview. He had raised the topic, admitting he was troubled by his terse responses to earlier questions about his humble beginnings. "They were totally supportive. They were wonderful parents, but I don't think they ever particularly pushed me."[28]

Push, push, push. That was the Metzenbaum way. Push until you got to the top of the hill. Then push some more.

On a scroll in Fairmount Temple, the synagogue his family attended in Beachwood, a plaque reads, "In memory of Anna and Charles Metzenbaum, given by Shirley and Howard M. Metzenbaum and their Daughters." The scroll was mounted in 1980, nineteen years after his father's death and sixteen years after his mother's.

CHAPTER 1

Starting Up in Politics

"Jimmy made the name."
Irwyn Metzenbaum, 1995

No one thought of James "Jimmy" Metzenbaum as a role model. He was an original—and not one easily copied. Other members of the Metzenbaum tribe made way for the diminutive attorney. He was by turns brilliant, foppish, righteous, egotistical, detached, and yet devoted. The love of his life—the only person that made him truly happy—was his wife Bessie.

At times mistakenly referred to as Howard Metzenbaum's "Uncle Jimmy," he was in fact first cousin to Metzenbaum's father, Charles. One of Jimmy Metzenbaum's eight siblings, Myron Metzenbaum, was a well-known plastic surgeon who invented the Metzenbaum scissors, a surgical device often mentioned on the television program *M*A*S*H*.

Buddy Rand, who in later years would cross paths—and then swords—with Howard Metzenbaum, worked in Jimmy Metzenbaum's law office for three years in the late 1930s. Rand remembers him as a workaholic and a tyrant who kept him as late as eleven PM and then demanded that he accompany him in an old Pierce-Arrow motor car to Lake View Cemetery to drop by his widow's mausoleum. By Rand's account, Jimmy was a publicity hound who pressured reporters to recognize him as a self-effacing citizen-lawmaker. Privately, he betrayed a difficult, eccentric personality that bedeviled associates and subordinates.

"He was a son of a bitch," Irwyn Metzenbaum said bluntly when asked about his combative cousin. By comparison, "Howard had more tact."[1] Politics was James Metzenbaum's second career. His calling was the law, and as befits the profession he was meticulous about his personal appearance. He was partial to bow ties and often wore a tuxedo shirt under his well-pressed business suit for court dates and trips to Columbus, where he served as a state senator. He was a fiend for detail. In a rage, he once denounced a secretary for a misplaced semicolon, Rand said, finally suggesting the poor woman jump out of a window.

Through most of his career, public and private, the dominant figure in James P. Metzenbaum's life was a dead woman—his wife, Bessie Benner. She died during childbirth in 1920 when her husband was an up-and-coming lawyer on the brink of his first big legal and political victory. The baby was lost too. Jimmy was inconsolable. Childless, he devoted the rest of his life to his work, her memory, and other people's children. Not infrequently during business meetings at his Euclid home, he would leap up and rush across the room to kiss a picture of Bessie. "I would work on briefs until ten or eleven PM and then drive out to the cemetery with him," Rand said of his trying experience. During those morbid, late-night vigils, Rand would stand in the background as Jimmy approached the mausoleum. He could hear him mumbling, "Oh, Bessie," and recounting the events of the day. The grieving widower had his own key to the cemetery gate and kept an electric light burning in tribute outside the stone edifice at the foot of a steep hill in the graveyard.

That was the private James Metzenbaum. In Columbus, former representative Charles A. Vanik saw another side of him when both served in the state legislature during the years before the war. "I encountered a real tiger," Vanik said. "He was smart, abrasive, and argumentative. Jimmy was not really a role model. Jimmy was a tough, mean son of a bitch. If they ever say that about Howard, Howard was an innocent compared to his uncle. Some of that runs in the blood. His uncle was a wise guy, very bright and pompous about his knowledge."[2] So that was the impression the first Senator Metzenbaum left with Charlie Vanik. But it was not the total measure of the man.

In 1932, the *Cleveland Press* wrote of a Cleveland school board member who "nearly everybody calls Jimmy, not because anyone depreciates his talents, but because he stands just shoulder high to a man of average stature, and because of the informality of his manner." The same *Press* article—the kind of flattering puff piece that would make any politician's day—told of a man "whose shirt may be a small off-size, but he has never had to stuff it for any job, public or private he has ever tackled, and that's more than can be said for many a fellow who has strutted his way to high position wearing a 19½ inch neckband."[3]

Jimmy never finished high school. But he taught himself the basics and managed to graduate from the Western Reserve Law School without the benefit of an undergraduate degree. He taught at the college for one year before starting his own civil practice in 1905. He made his reputation arguing Ohio's first zoning case on behalf of the city of Euclid before the United States Supreme Court. The brief against the right-to-zone was handled by Newton D. Baker, a renowned trial lawyer and former mayor of Cleveland, representing a real-estate firm. Jimmy was so intimidated by the formidable Baker that he breached Supreme Court protocol after his appearance in Washington and telegraphed an addendum to his oral argument to Chief Justice William Howard Taft, the former president of the United States.

No harm was done. Taft even referred to the postscript when he ruled in James Metzenbaum's favor in 1926. The court decided it was within the scope of the police powers of cities and villages to determine which areas of a community should remain residential and free of industry and commercial development. The case, *Ambler v. Village of Euclid,* was a milestone. For the first time, the highest court in the land established the right of cities across the country to enact zoning laws without being sued by developers for violating property rights. For his successful argument, Metzenbaum was recognized as a zoning expert and went on to author a massive three-volume book called *The Law of Zoning.* He also made his mark on the Cleveland school board between 1931 and 1933 and in the Ohio legislature, where he served three non-consecutive terms in 1935–36, 1941–42, and 1945–46. He didn't accept compensation or even mileage reimbursement, giving his salary to charity. Before he was through, Jimmy ran for lieutenant governor, Congress, and the Ohio Supreme Court, losing all of those races. His behavior bemused the media as well as many of his colleagues.

After his stint with the school board, he headed for Columbus and the statehouse, home to the General Assembly chambers and the governor's office. In 1935, as a freshman member of the Ohio House of Representatives, he earned his bona fides with a suspicious Democratic leadership. Because of his audacity and rebel image on the Cleveland school board, the leaders in Columbus were wary of Jimmy when he banty-roostered his way into the General Assembly in January 1935. He had been a strident critic of the school board's established order. "They had heard alarming reports that he would be a troublemaker and a disturber of the peace in the quiet Senate chamber. The lawmakers' fears were more or less confirmed when he didn't ask for any patronage and didn't ask to be put on any committee."[4]

Strange indeed: a politician who didn't have his hand out. Jimmy bided his time. He familiarized himself with the nuances of parliamentary procedure and guarded against any "steamroller" legislation that might overpower his position. Trust grew between the legislative chieftains and their new man. As the months rolled by, Jimmy "failed to detect any signs of a steamroller. There was no whip cracking. On every occasion he voted regularly with the Democratic leaders, who reached the conclusion that perhaps Metzenbaum wouldn't be a hell raiser after all."[5] Metzenbaum emerged not as a hellion but as a troubleshooter for the majority leadership, and—remarkably for a freshman—he was entrusted with some of the most difficult, complex legislation. He authored the School Foundation Act, a formula for public school funding, which combined state aid with local property taxes and which would remain the law in Ohio for nearly forty years. He also shepherded bills on banking and welfare (called "poor relief" during the Depression) through the legislative maze. For his efforts, the *Columbus Citizen* named him the "Legislature's Man of the Year" in 1935. "You can walk into the Senate chambers early in the morning or late at night, and usually there's the bald little head of Jimmy Metzenbaum poring over a pile of important looking papers at his desk. And Jimmy Metzenbaum, with all this work, signed over his Senate paycheck to charity."[6]

Out of office by choice in 1937, he was selected as special counsel to a state senate committee investigating graft in the administration of Governor Martin L. Davey, a combative partisan who had a role in dividing the Ohio Democratic Party in the late 1930s. (The governor's loyalists in the party were sometimes referred to as "Daveycrats.") In the course of an aggressive investigation, Jimmy struck some as a self-promoter, yet his tediously detailed interrogation of witnesses was hardly designed to make headlines. "He doesn't fit into any of the accepted patterns, so you must take him as he is. He has his peculiarities, but he gets results. He may be too unduly considerate of the other fellow to those who prefer their meat raw, but there isn't anything wrong with his sense of direction."[7] Edgy lawmakers, perhaps nervous about his direction, shut down the corruption investigation, but not before Jimmy made an enemy out of Davey. The governor vigorously opposed him when Jimmy ran (unsuccessfully) for lieutenant governor the following year.

That was the political pinnacle for James Metzenbaum. He came back to the state Senate in 1941 and was elected again to a final two-year term in 1944. The little guy in the bow tie wasn't warm and fuzzy. And he lost every time he sought higher office. He made his last bid in 1950, running as an independent for the Ohio Supreme Court. But in the process, as the *Cleveland Press* reported, he enshrined the Metzenbaum name in the "select circle of politically magic names" in Cuyahoga County.[8] "It was not as powerful as some of the Irish names," said Irwyn Metzenbaum. But with "a name like Sweeney, Corrigan, or Metzenbaum, you could run for anything." In 1942, three Metzenbaums were on the Democratic primary ballot in Cuyahoga County: neophyte Howard running for the Ohio House, Jimmy running for Congress, and Irwyn trying for the state Senate. Only Howard made it, but the Metzenbaum name was becoming familiar to voters in the state's largest county.

Away from politics in the postwar years, Jimmy Metzenbaum maintained a lucrative civil practice and kept up an interest in libraries, gardening, and underprivileged youth. His dream was to establish a model orphanage. In 1946, he acquired an undeveloped 101-acre plot on a hillside in suburban Chesterland in Geauga County. He called it Wisteria Hill—the vine had been a favorite of his wife's—and he went about clearing brush and renovating a ramshackle cabin with his own hands. Administered by the Bessie Benner Foundation, which he created in 1948, it became a day camp for Girl Scouts, disadvantaged children, and youngsters with cerebral palsy. "Jimmy Metzenbaum . . . is a little man with a big heart," *Cleveland Press* columnist Bob Seltzer wrote after touring Wisteria Hill.[9]

The extent of Jimmy's devotion to Bessie was revealed in 1935 when a tax agent discovered that Metzenbaum had never probated her will.

Their home in Euclid was still in her name and $7,591 was scattered in savings accounts, checking accounts, war savings stamps, and a sealed envelope. The wealth included $135 in gold coins, which by 1935 were not accepted as legal currency. The taxman, one H. W. Putnam, got interested in Mrs. Metzenbaum's estate as he nosed around county records to look for unpaid inheritance taxes. Jimmy Metzenbaum, who had never invested his late wife's money or even opened a strong box she left behind, readily paid the $240.34 tax bill. He was still living part time in the suburban home, but he had also taken a room on the tenth floor of the Statler Hilton hotel near his law office in downtown Cleveland. "Love Lives On, Won't Touch Wife's Estate," the *Cleveland Press* headlined in 1935: "After her death, Mr. Metzenbaum maintained the shaded old house at 24000 Euclid Avenue, in Euclid, just as it had been during her life time. He did most of the work himself, save for a caretaker. He pruned his own trees, and the furnishings and other accessories of the house he allowed no one to disturb, living on there alone, with his memories."[10]

N. R. Howard, a reporter, told of his search for the Metzenbaum psyche during an encounter in the early 1920s with an old-line pol, Councilman John Reynolds. "Jack, who is this guy, Metzenbaum?" he asked innocently. "Who is James Metzenbaum? No one knows who he is," Reynolds responded. "He is a lawyer. A fine lawyer. He is a 'loner' who is no one's confidant. He is a strange person . . . He goes with no one. Yes, indeed. Who is James Metzenbaum?" In the same piece, the columnist told of developing a friendship with Jimmy, who first told him, disingenuously, "Oh, you don't want anything of me. . . . Newspapers aren't interested in me. I'm just a nobody."[11]

In fact, Jimmy carefully cultivated relationships with reporters—as did cousin Howard—and late-night visits to city rooms were not uncommon. The *Cleveland Press* described Jimmy Metzenbaum as a full-blooded politician who "has a retentive mind that remembers volume and page and paragraph. He has a logical mind that almost uncannily seizes upon the essentials of a proposition. He has an agile and subtle tongue that wads these essentials up into a hard lump and hurls them with telling effect at the opposition."[12]

Agile, even theatrical, Jimmy Metzenbaum had what critics call the classic liberal disease. He strove for the greater good in the public arena, but had trouble translating that commonality to his private life. This difficulty in relating was compounded by lifelong grief over the death of his beloved Bessie. "He had never learned communication on an informal level with other people, for all his true brilliance at business and law," his reporter friend, N. R. Howard, wrote.[13] An incident in 1959, less than two years before his death, suggests a warmer James Metzenbaum, perhaps known only to a few. The bellmen, maids, and other employees at the Statler Hilton presented Jimmy with a scroll proclaiming him "the most distinguished permanent guest of the hotel" and thanking him for his thoughtfulness and kindness. The old man almost broke down. He had lived alone in room 1048 of the hotel for thirty years.[14]

The First Campaign

Jimmy Metzenbaum was staying weekends at the Statler and serving his second term in the state Senate when his career intersected with his cousin's aspirations. Howard, then the *other* Metzenbaum, took his first tentative steps toward a political career in 1942. Howard had returned to Cleveland from OSU as a committed FDR Democrat interested in labor law. That was fortunate because he found out in a hurry that Cleveland's big firms were not hiring "nice young Jewish lawyers."[15] He was admitted to the bar in 1941 and worked for small law firms in exchange for a desk and telephone. He shared space at the Leader Building in downtown Cleveland with Sidney Moss, an attorney who would become a confidant and one of his closest friends. With Moss's help, Howard started a small business preparing income-tax returns for $1 apiece. His brother, Irwyn, had a similar one-man operation. This was a time when low-income Americans filled out their own tax returns—there was no H&R Block. Soon Metzenbaum and a partner had opened twenty-three offices around the city. Howard then had enough capital to open his own law firm, Metzenbaum and Gaines, with his friend, Sam Gaines.

Howard was also thinking about politics and eyeing his old neighborhood on the East Side for a spot on the Cleveland City Council. But Jimmy Metzenbaum, who was chummy with the Republican incumbent, discouraged his cousin from running in Cleveland and suggested state representative as a better entry-level office. Metzenbaum first got the idea for running for office not from Jimmy, but from Hattie Auerbach, a neighbor and a ward leader, who thought the bright young man from Ohio State University would make a good councilman. Auerbach promised him the support of the Democratic organization. That was fine for the primary, but in the general election his opponent would be incumbent Vincent Cohn, the most popular Republican on the East Side. Metzenbaum decided to take Jimmy's advice and instead run for state rep in an at-large primary. "In those days if you were nominated on the Democratic ticket—people voted straight Democratic or straight Republican—and if you were nominated, you were in," he said of the political calculus.[16]

This time, Metzenbaum would run without the endorsement of the county organization and against the wishes of the powerful county Democratic boss, Ray T. Miller, a prominent attorney. The promised assistance from Jimmy Metzenbaum did not materialize, but Howard looked like a winner anyway. A Miller-endorsed rival, saloon owner John J. Gallagher, finished five votes behind Metzenbaum—nineteenth in a field where eighteen were elected. The Cuyahoga County Board of Election's official count, in the days following the balloting, would decide it. "I am scared shitless that between the unofficial and the official, I'll get lost," Metzenbaum said.

The chairman of the Cuyahoga County Board of Elections, Tom Carey, was handpicked by Miller and was an Irish-American like Gallagher. "Of course, I knew that John Gallagher was not only probably more favored than I with a guy like Miller but he was a [legal] client of Miller's. So I figured count me out," said Metzenbaum. But several weeks later, the young Metzenbaum got a call from Carey inviting him to stop by the Board of Elections. Metzenbaum strode into Carey's office expecting the worst. Carey announced that the official count was in. A tense Metzenbaum, perspiration trickling under his white dress shirt, figured his political career was over before it even started. Metzenbaum described the scene:

> Tom Carey is sitting there at his desk—great big bushy eyebrows, looking down scowling. He is seated here, and I am standing there. And he looks up at me and he says, "Gallagher picked up seventeen votes" and my heart skipped. . . . "You picked up forty-two." I expected to get screwed and I had gotten screwed, I thought. But I didn't. The process worked.

He was twenty-five, one of the youngest men elected to the Ohio House and on his way to Columbus while others his age were off to war.

With the shock of Pearl Harbor still fresh and American casualties overseas mounting, winning the war was a national passion. At the statehouse, Metzenbaum's lack of military service because of poor eyesight—and his flirtation with Far-Left politics—got the attention of veterans' organizations, anti-Communist zealots, and other conservative groups. He remained a lightning rod for them throughout his political career. He was a member of the leftist National Lawyers Guild and the Progressive Citizens Committee and a cofounder and counsel to the Ohio School of Social Sciences, which was created in 1944 with the help of the Congress of Industrial Organizations, the old CIO. Even though the school was located in a Baptist church on Cleveland's East Side, Attorney General Tom Clark included it on a 1947 list of "totalitarian, fascist, subversive groups."[17]

When Ohio lieutenant governor Paul M. Herbert demanded an explanation, Metzenbaum said the attorney general, an ardent anti-Communist, was misinformed. He fired off a letter to Clark, defending himself and other board members and insisting the school's only purpose was to bring organized labor and management together for an exchange of ideas. He got a return letter from assistant attorney general Peyton Ford, who did not back off the claim that the school was subversive, though he did say its listing did not "impugn per se the loyalty of any member thereof."[18]

Not impugned. That was far from a vindication for Metzenbaum—and the issue didn't go away. Twenty-three years later, in the midst of his first campaign for the U.S. Senate, Metzenbaum was forced to all but admit that one of the founding members, a college professor named Hyman Lumer, probably was a Communist. "I later learned some disturbing things about Dr. Lumer," he told reporters in 1970. "I was chagrined and if I had known about them at the time, I wouldn't have gone in with him."[19] In an unpublished 1994 interview, he explained further.

I was never anywhere close to them philosophically or politically. If they supported workers' rights and they happened to be Communists, or left-wingers, then I was just not that sensitive in aligning myself with them. But I never was a part of that group. I was an independent thinker who did have a concern about civil rights, human rights, and free speech. In retrospect, I think I might not have been that [careless] working that closely with them on some issues. I am not sure. I have never feared to identify with a particular cause just because some other people supported that cause, or opposed that cause.[20]

How much Metzenbaum knew at the time is unclear. As he neared retirement from public life in 1994, he acknowledged he was aware during the 1940s that some of his associates were Communists or at least leaned that way. But he also insisted that he had never been a formal, or for that matter informal, member of any Communist organization in Cleveland or anywhere else, or that any of his acquaintances ever asked him to join. Despite the ceaseless rumors and innuendoes, there is no evidence Metzenbaum was ever affiliated with the Communist Party or any other avowedly Marxist group.

Down the Road to Columbus

Far removed from the hurly-burly of big city politics in Cleveland, the Ohio General Assembly was a backwater in the 1940s. Maybe that's why Jimmy wanted Howard in Columbus, out of the way. Cigar smoke, spittoons, and whiskey bottles were commonplace in the Statehouse. At least one determined individualist wore spats on his shoes. Rural Republican representatives and conservative Democrats often united in a "cornstalk brigade," pushing for tax relief for agricultural land and, at times, beating back progressive legislation introduced by urban legislators.

Metzenbaum was a quick study, earning a reputation for his easy grasp of legislation, his hard work, and his utter fearlessness. The Ohio Legislative Correspondents Association picked him as one of the assembly's outstanding members in each of his four terms. He won passage of a consumer credit bill requiring full disclosure by financiers of the terms of installment payments and capping interest and the amount that could be financed. His other triumph was a bill limiting what amounted to kickbacks paid by loan companies to automobile dealers in leasing deals. Metzenbaum, who was raising his own family, understood what mattered to average working folks in Cleveland and the rest of Ohio. He advanced "consumer" issues—topics his constituents discussed around the kitchen table—well before the term became part of the legislative lexicon. One of his biggest endeavors involved trying to establish a Fair Employment Practices Commission (FEPC) to deal with job discrimination complaints related to race, religion, and ethnicity. But in 1949 the bill failed, as did so many of his attempts to pass groundbreaking liberal legislation.

"His worst performance probably was his bitter-end fight for a tough FEPC bill," according to one publication, which suggested that Metzenbaum "could have obtained passage for an 'educational' bill as a start toward his goal, but he may have been on the spot with the people who backed him term after term."[21] His frustration was evident as he told of dickering for the support of Governor Frank Lausche, a conservative Democrat. Lausche was lying on a sofa in the governor's office as Metzenbaum met with him and his intrepid adviser, lawyer James W. Shocknessy, one day in the late 1940s. The governor suddenly rose and slapped his hand on his forehead. "Howard," he said. "I think we can be for that FEPC now that the *Cleveland News* editorial is supporting it." Years later, Metzenbaum recalled thinking how the governor's logic "stuck in [his] craw." Lausche wouldn't back the bill because it was wrong to discriminate but because the *Cleveland News* backed it.[22] The governor eventually supported the bill, but it wasn't enough.

Metzenbaum was one of only four Democrats during his first state Senate term, but with Harry S. Truman leading the presidential ticket, he easily won reelection in 1948, along with a swarm of Ohio Democrats. His party took control of the Senate, holding a 19–14 advantage. Now he decided to make his move—his first great leap forward. Although he was only thirty, he ran for the office of senate majority leader with strong backing from organized labor. He was close to locking up enough votes in the Democratic caucus but dropped out when he learned that five of his colleagues, under pressure from business interests and the American Legion, were ready to back a Republican rather than him. He didn't sulk, but took over the chairmanship of the Judiciary Committee and set up a command post in a corner office two flights above the Senate floor in the old statehouse, emerging as one of the most powerful men in Columbus. The Metzenbaum "hideaway" had been home in previous sessions to James P. Metzenbaum. There was no elevator. Lobbyists were forced to walk up forty-five steps to gain an audience. "Now I can get some work done," Metzenbaum smugly told the *Cleveland Press*. "It takes a strong constitution and plenty of stamina to hike up here." For those too old or infirm to make the climb, the *Press* noted, "Metzenbaum is ready to meet in the more convenient Judiciary Committee hearing room, adjacent to the Senate chamber."[23]

Metzenbaum understood the psychological importance of well-appointed surroundings. During the 1980s on Capitol Hill, he settled into another "hideaway" office, no more than a hundred feet from the front entrance to the Senate chamber. It was one of the best locations in the Capitol—and Metzenbaum still maintained spacious quarters next door in the Russell Office Building.

In Columbus in 1949, young Howard Metzenbaum was at the peak of his powers, even as he privately pondered an early retirement from public life. He pressed for repeal of the 1947 Ferguson Act, a law written by Republicans to bar public employees from striking. And he got the state to increase unemployment compensation benefits. He was closely identified with the interests of trade unions, which gained strength as Ohio-based companies built automobiles and manufactured steel, glass, and machine parts in the postwar boom. A CIO newsletter said, "The nattily-dressed, youthful Cleveland attorney has a swift answer to the question, 'Why do you fight for the worker?' His answer, 'I'm one myself.' And he is. He's had to work hard all his life and he knows, at first hand, the problems that face a worker and his family."[24] That was true, as far as it went. But by the late 1940s, Metzenbaum was already on his way to becoming a wealthy man, and the only time he saw the inside of a steel mill or an auto plant was when he was campaigning.

The Ohio Legislative Correspondents Association, a statehouse reporters' group, offered these comments on the confrontational Cleveland lawyer:

> Brilliant, able, excellent in debate. Effective committee chairman.
> . . . A key liberal Democrat. His Credit Charges Control Act will
> earn praise for entire legislature . . . Probably knows more about
> legislation than any other senator; apparently was sincere in his
> so-called liberal philosophies . . . Outstanding, thorough, actual
> leader of majority . . . He got Democrats out of many a hole. He

has plenty of ability. Hardest working member . . . Better than all, but prejudices handicapped his performance . . . So terrifically smart—dangerous.[25]

Shirley

Prejudiced? So-called liberal? Dangerous? That was not the man Shirley Turoff met one quiet Friday night at the Jewish Community Center on Kinsman Road in Cleveland. It was December 19, 1941, less than two weeks after the shock of Pearl Harbor, and Metzenbaum was social chairman for a mixer at the center.

When Howard met Shirley he barely had two nickels to rub to-gether—or so he said. He was starting a law practice, sharing office space at a small firm, and living alone in a modest second-floor apart-ment on the East Side. War had broken out. And, uncharacteristically, he wasn't quite sure where his life was headed. Then Shirley, nineteen, appeared at the top of a staircase at the community center. As Howard remembered, "This very attractive young lady comes down stairs. We get to talking. I get her number—and it's boy meets girl." The two hit it off immediately and soon were dating. But they were in no rush to marry, and Shirley Metzenbaum remembers "a stormy courtship. We kept breaking up and getting back together."[26]

Shirley worked on his first campaign for the Ohio House in 1942 and clashed with Jimmy Metzenbaum, who was running for Congress. Innocently enough, she was hanging "Metzenbaum for State Repre-sentative" posters on the wall of the ward headquarters while Jimmy addressed a small rally. The distraction annoyed the older man. "Young lady," Jimmy bellowed, interrupting his own speech, "when you are finished, I will continue speaking."[27]

Despite the friction between Jimmy and Shirley, Howard proposed one night on bended knee at the Turoff home. They were married in a Jewish ceremony in Cleveland on August 8, 1946, the year Howard ran for the state Senate. His only explanation for why he waited so long is a vague reference to a romantic rival. "I was sort of reluctant to get married, but I was concerned she was going to marry someone else," he said. "I thought if I lost [her], it would be a major loss."[28]

A major loss, indeed. Shirley Metzenbaum was not only his sweetheart but the one who could smooth out the roughest edges on the prickly young man and tell him when she thought he was making a mistake. According to Irwyn Metzenbaum, "Nobody tells Howard 'no' except Shirley."

Howard and his brother, Irwyn, drifted apart after Howard and Shirley wed, and as the younger Metzenbaum established himself in politics and business, Irwyn was left behind. "Since he got married, Shirley and I don't see eye to eye. It was wonderful until they got married, but when they got married, all of sudden . . . I am on the shit list as far as she is concerned." How it turned sour is unclear. Metzenbaum's daughter Shelley insisted years later that any personality conflict between her mother and Irwyn Metzenbaum was "nothing of consequence."[29] On the other side of the family, Irwyn's son, Terry, simply said that his uncle "went his way, and Dad went his."[30]

Irwyn Metzenbaum, like his father, was entrepreneurial, dogged, and unlucky. He lacked his brother's brilliance for business and his impeccable sense of timing in politics. He ran for public office in 1942, 1946, 1948, 1950, 1953, and 1954, losing each time. He was edged out in a Democratic primary for state representative in 1946 by twenty-six votes. In 1949, he suffered a mild case of polio, which partially paralyzed his left side. But he kept running, capturing a council seat in Ward 27 on Cleveland's East Side that same year as a protégé of council president Jack Russell. But he lost his reelection bid after missing an important vote. "I had a headache and didn't feel well," he said, but, in fact, Irwyn had been working on a client's income tax return on the side. The *Cleveland Press* printed a photo of Irwyn, seen through the front window of Stepko's Hat Shop, doing the tax work.[31]

Irwyn Metzenbaum, married and with two kids, sold real estate, costume jewelry, neon signs, car radios, fountain pens, and novelties. Over the years, he worked as a notary, was once involved in a custom car business, and managed a hotel in Detroit. "I was everything but a pimp," he laughed during a 1995 interview. But the good-natured Irwyn Metzenbaum was a wishy-washy politician, once declaring from the stump, "I want what the people want." During a debate on apartment-leasing regulations, he weighed in with, "I am neither for nor against [rent] decontrol."[32] Ted Bonda, who worked briefly for Irwyn after the war, said Irwyn resented his pushy younger brother, Howard, and blamed him for his disappointments in business and politics. "Howard was something he wasn't," said Bonda.[33] Looking back, eighty-two-year-old Irwyn disagreed, "I always made a decent living. I always drove a Cadillac, and I owned a house here for forty-two years." In his driveway on an early autumn day in 1995 was a 1993 burgundy Cadillac, with a peeling, blue bumper sticker that read: "Metzenbaum for U.S. Senate."

The man Irwyn credited with establishing the family name in politics, Jimmy Metzenbaum, never got to see his cousin Howard go to Washington. He suffered a heart attack while visiting his wife's gravesite on a snowy New Year's Eve in 1960. Stricken as he stood outside the mausoleum in the cold, Jimmy staggered to a home near the cemetery and tapped frantically on a window. As the homeowner peered out, Jimmy toppled backward into the snow.

Howard Metzenbaum had maintained a wary but respectful relationship with Jimmy and regarded him as a member of the "educated wing of the family." After Howard ascended to the United States Senate, he rarely spoke of his parents or relatives from the old days. Few Washington reporters knew he had a brother or even that Howard had served in the Ohio legislature. His personal life was centered on Shirley and his four daughters, Barbara, Susan, Shelley, and Amy. But when pressed, Howard acknowledged Jimmy's political achievement. "He made the name," he said. "He was a giant in his own way. He was extremely well respected."[34] Although Howard never credited Jimmy for being a mentor, Charlie Vanik had no doubt. "From his Uncle Jimmy he learned how to play tough," said the former congressman. For all of his idiosyncrasies, Jimmy Metzenbaum was an unwitting role model.

The parallels between Howard and James Metzenbaum are unmistakable: the work ethic, the combativeness, attention to legislative detail, concern for workers, devotion to their wives, and love of children. Both were smart, tough, restless men, willing to make enemies and showing little patience for glad-handing or bull slinging. They knew where they were headed. Each Metzenbaum was quick to calculate the value of creative use of the media in politics. Jimmy Metzenbaum was hailed as a pioneer in 1931 in a school board campaign when he put on a slide show to illustrate waste in building schools. "The picture campaign is an innovation in Cleveland politics," the *Plain Dealer* reported.[35] Thirty-nine years later, Howard Metzenbaum's slick television ads were seen as a breakthrough in Ohio political campaigns and a key component of his upset of the better-known John Glenn in a Democratic Senate primary.

The following passage from the *Cleveland Press,* written in 1932 about Jimmy Metzenbaum, could easily have been written about Howard a half century later:

> He makes brilliant use of invective rarely and of sarcasm frequently and handles "sob stuff" incomparably. All equally effective in law as logic, and of much more utility in politics. He doesn't hesitate to use a little demagogy to put over what he believes to be a legitimate and worthwhile proposition.[36]

Howard Metzenbaum denied that Jimmy was a significant influence on him and harbored a grudge against the older Metzenbaum for refusing to help him get a job as a statehouse page while Howard was a college student. "He never gave me a pat on the back or a word of encouragement," said Howard.

Farewell to Cow Town

None too convincingly, Howard Metzenbaum followed Jimmy's example in trying to downplay the importance of ideology in his political makeup. Jimmy, of course, was a maverick who once ran for office as an independent and another time as a "nonpartisan Democrat," which may have been an allusion to his ability to work well with Republicans in the Ohio legislature.

Howard Metzenbaum portrayed himself as a pragmatist in an interview with a union newspaper. "Seriously," he said in 1949, "I don't have any ideological view of legislation. My creed is simple. If a bill is good for all the people, in my judgment, then I'm for it. If it isn't good, then I'll fight it and I don't give a damn whose bill it is."[37] But ideology (and anti-Semitism, in Metzenbaum's mind) played a significant role in the first political crisis of his career, the Ohio Senate Democratic leader's contest. He was a man of the left, close to the unions, pressing radical civil rights legislation, when he decided to run for Senate majority leader after the 1948 election gave his party a 19–14 edge. The Democrats were so divided they had been incapable of choosing a minority leader in the previous Senate session. Metzenbaum was the favorite in the leader's race, but he was opposed by business and veteran groups. Governor Lausche, a fellow Clevelander, also appeared to be against him and reportedly played a behind-the-scenes role in the internecine fight. Senators Margaret Mahoney of Cleveland and Clingan Jackson of Youngstown were viewed as formidable challengers to Metzenbaum for the majority leader's post.

Metzenbaum suddenly withdrew from the contest the night before the intraparty vote. He said he was tipped that several Democrats— whose ringleader was real-estate broker William M. Boyd—were prepared to endorse a Republican for majority leader rather than support him. It was a bitter pill he never got over. "In the middle of the night we learned those five were being pressured by the American Legion to vote against me and vote to organize the Senate with a Republican leader," he said. "It was a combination of the lobbyists and the American Legion. They considered me a liberal, no question about it."[38]

Metzenbaum would have been the first Jewish leader of the Senate. The compromise choice, Mahoney, was the first woman in the job. News accounts of the party struggle indicated that Governor Lausche was using his influence to promote a conservative leader like Mahoney. The press credited Metzenbaum, "the tall, scholarly Clevelander,"[39] for graciously stepping aside in the interest of Democratic unity. He kept his bitterness to himself.

Nearly fifty years later, a vengeful Metzenbaum could tick off the names of his betrayers in Columbus without hesitation: "Bill Boyd, Nick Bernard, Arthur Blake, Clingan Jackson, Ed Sawicki. I lived to help see them retired from the Senate."[40] Two of his antagonists, Jackson and Bernard, were mainstays of the Mahoning County Democratic machine. The *Plain Dealer* suggested that Metzenbaum dropped his bid in part because he suspected his foes, including Boyd and the Youngstown duo, "may have been unmanageable," even if he had prevailed as majority leader. Metzenbaum's "biggest weakness has been his failure to recognize that conservative Democrats are entitled to as much representation as rabid left-wingers," the *Plain Dealer*'s Al Silverman wrote.[41]

Although Metzenbaum did not play the Jewish card often, he and Shirley had little doubt that anti-Semitism contributed to his downfall. Nothing specific was unearthed to validate his suspicions of bias, but Susan Metzenbaum said that her father "was confident he lost the election as leader of the Senate because of anti-Semitism."[42] Metzenbaum tried to ignore the prejudice against Jewish people that lingered in mid-twentieth-century America, but he and his family were repeatedly reminded of it as his career moved forward.

Metzenbaum flirted with the notion of running for lieutenant governor the following year but abandoned the idea when the ground failed to swell. The incumbent Democrat, George "Jumpy" Nye, had initially encouraged Metzenbaum to run in his place but changed his mind and decided to seek reelection. In another small betrayal, the Cuyahoga County Young Democrats endorsed Nye over their townsman.

Shirley had had enough of Ohio politics. She talked about her disillusionment in 1988 to a *Plain Dealer* reporter, who wrote,

> Shirley Metzenbaum remembers the years in the state legislature as a time when her ideals about politics and government were shattered. She said she saw powerful state senators not only cheating on their wives, but in some cases, cheating on their mistresses. She saw legislators with their feet up on a desk, chewing tobacco, reading newspapers, not paying the slightest attention to what was going on. Worst of all, she heard lobbyists whisper about her husband as "that Jew."[43]

What's more, Shirley did not like Columbus, which was much smaller than Cleveland, then Ohio's largest city. Columbus had a "cow-town" image with little to offer the young metropolitan couple, beyond the statehouse and university. "We stayed at the old Neil House hotel and he pointed out the ladies of the night in the lobby," Shirley recalled. "These were our lawmakers. I couldn't believe it."

Metzenbaum was unforthcoming years later when asked about his first retirement from political life: "I had no interest. I was a nobody," he said.[44] In truth, it had been a practical decision. Shirley was pregnant with the couple's second daughter, Susan, and firstborn Barbara was still in diapers. His friend and business partner, Sidney Moss, had died. It was a simple equation: Metzenbaum was putting more into Columbus than he was getting back. How could he solve other people's problems when he faced with his own financial uncertainties? He had a family to feed, a law practice to nurture, and parking lots to build.

"We talked about it and decided Howard was either going to be a politician or a father," Shirley Metzenbaum said. "He doesn't do anything halfway. So he tore up the petitions."[45] Good-bye, Columbus. Frustrated that the top spot had eluded him, Metzenbaum retired from the Ohio legislature when his second Senate term ended in 1950. Shirley believed anti-Semitism had blocked her husband's advancement in politics. He was thirty-two, and twenty years would pass before he would again seek public office.

———— ⚡ ————

CHAPTER 2

Making Money

The Entrepreneurial Years

"The two growing giants meet at the parking lot."
Howard Metzenbaum

It's been said that mud and foresight made Howard Metzenbaum a millionaire. But a gimmick and nonunion labor helped him get started. "It was a hunch that Sidney Moss had—a hunch that the rent-a-car business might be a good business to get into after the war," Metzenbaum said.[1] Moss, his law partner and close friend, figured that the postwar era would launch a travel boom unprecedented in American history. Automobiles, virtually out of production during the war, were again rolling off assembly lines and back on the market in limited numbers. And air travel was gaining in popularity.

With only two cars at their disposal, Metzenbaum and Moss decided to open a rental business. They borrowed $2,000 and leased a thirty-space parking lot on Walnut Avenue near East Ninth Street in downtown Cleveland. Metzenbaum's high school chum, Ted Bonda, fresh out of the army, was enlisted to run the newly christened Drive-a-Car Company in January 1946. "It sounded good," Metzenbaum said. "But cars were hard to get. I came up with a gimmick." Wartime price controls were off, and demand for new cars exceeded supply. Even batteries were hard to find. So Metzenbaum and Moss went to the dealers and bargained for a reasonable price for a small fleet. In exchange, they said, "We'll give you a share of the stock in our new company."[2] The dealers bit, waiving any premium for their cars and accepting the stock offer at $5 a share of the rental enterprise. The automobiles didn't come at a discount, but at least they were available in some volume, and the business partners gradually built up their inventory.

At first blush, Bonda appeared to be an unlikely choice for the take-charge type needed to run the fledgling rental car/parking lot business. Often mistaken for Italian because of his last name, he was the Jewish son of an Austro-Hungarian immigrant, a dressmaker named Jacob Bonda. Ted Bonda was brash, industrious, and hungry, a city kid who had never ventured outside of Cleveland before joining the army. "Before the war I sold shoes and I hated it," he said. "When I got out I had zero money. My wife and I had nothing. I sold fountain pens for Howard's brother, Irwyn."[3] Remembering adventures in the old Essex, Bonda jumped at the opportunity to join his friend in the new undertaking, even if he would be little more than a parking attendant at the outset. "During the day, [cars] were parked at meters on the curb and Ted . . . was hired to run along the sidewalk stuffing nickels into the meters," said Metzenbaum.[4] But it went way beyond stuffing meters, according to Bonda. Some cars were parked illegally, and some, driven in by all-day parkers, were brazenly leased for a few hours to rental customers. Space was always a problem. "We had no place to park the cars, so we put them on the street and the police chased me," Bonda said.

Metzenbaum juggled the parking business with his duties as a legislator and a lawyer, representing injured railroaders and union members in workers' compensation cases and other disputes. "He stayed in the office and I shoveled the snow," Bonda joked. Metzenbaum had an office-sharing arrangement with Moss and used a desk and telephone in a suite with two other attorneys, J. C. Luckay and Philip Schwimmer. "When I got out of law school, a member of my faith could not get into a major law firm or any other law firms in town," Metzenbaum said. "I wanted to be a people's lawyer. I wanted to represent unions." But he also wanted to make money and wasn't going to get rich arguing those kinds of cases. "I wanted to make [money] in a way that was compatible with my own philosophy and principles," he said. "I didn't think there was any inconsistency in what I wanted to achieve [in business] and my principles."[5]

The path to wealth would not run through a law firm but through a parking lot, thanks to his prescient understanding of how Americans craved mobility. "Airport Parking was formed through a combination of mud and foresight by two young men," the *New York Times* reported.

In 1947, a 30-year-old Ohio State Senator, Howard Metzenbaum, and his boyhood friend and associate in a small rental car business, Alva T. Bonda, often drove from Metzenbaum's law firm in downtown Cleveland to the municipal airport so the senator could get to the state capitol in Columbus. Frequently, both had to trudge through ankle-deep mud to reach the terminal after parking in a pasture-like field. One day it occurred to them that parking facilities at the airport would make air travel more inviting and could also be profitable and provide additional revenue to the airport.[6]

At the time, Cleveland Hopkins International Airport had no paved lot, no marked spaces, no security, and no charge for parking. All of that was about to change. The business partners decided that the personable Bonda would pitch the parking proposal to Major Jack Berry, the head of the airport authority. In 1949, air travel was still for the well-to-do, and airplanes were seen as novelties compared to the familiar and commonly used trains. Young men often drove to Hopkins, parked at the side of the road, and sat on the hoods of their cars to watch the incoming planes. It was a good show. For them, as for most middle Americans, air travel was viewed as somewhat risky and prohibitively expensive. Metzenbaum and Bonda gambled that it would soon replace rail as the preferred choice of long-distance travelers in the United States.

Berry hesitated at first, saying it didn't seem right for the city to charge the traveling public for parking on municipal property. But he relented and leased the two young entrepreneurs a plot near the terminal in return for a guarantee that the parking concession would return $400 a month to the city. Even then, Bonda said the main motive was to find another locale for the rental car business by breaking into the Hertz monopoly at the airport.

Bonda recalled telling Berry that the duo would organize the airport's parking. "But I didn't care about the parking," he said. "I just wanted to rent my cars . . . In two months, I found out that parking was more profitable than car rental."[7] Metzenbaum and Bonda moved quickly. They paved and fenced the lot, installed lights, provided nighttime security, and hired attendants at fifty cents a day. Parking was no longer free, but it was more convenient.

Metzenbaum and Bonda were on to something. Parking had been a headache for airports from coast to coast. Other airport operators began seeking the partners to ask about parking at their facilities, and within a year Airport Parking of America, known as APCOA, was born. Metzenbaum was chairman of the board and handled negotiation of leases and other financial matters. Bonda, the president, was the day-to-day general manager for operations and expert in layout and traffic patterns. They soon contracted with airports in Columbus, Cincinnati, Akron, Dayton, Indianapolis, and Toledo. Within twelve years, the $400 monthly guarantee at Hopkins had grown to an annual $410,843 for the city from parking. "They were in the midst of the 'travel boom' as we call it today," said David Skylar, a business associate. "They saw cars and airports leading to a transportation revolution."[8]

For Metzenbaum and Bonda, the revolution would occur largely without unions. The lot at Hopkins and many of the others were staffed with nonunion labor, an embarrassment that Metzenbaum swallowed for the sake of business. "We had a business that was nonunion and I ran the business," Bonda said. "Howard was obviously a very strong union man, but in his own business if it was better to be nonunion, that's what he would be."[9] Metzenbaum and Bonda insisted they never tried to bust a union or actively oppose an organizing drive. But critics called Metzenbaum a hypocrite because of his prolabor stand in Columbus and his representation of the AFL-CIO in Cuyahoga County and eventually in the entire state of Ohio. "My view then, as it is now, was that whether you have a union or you don't have a union, it is something the employees should decide," Metzenbaum said in an interview. "It was not the employer's function to force his employees to join a union."[10]

In 1959, APCOA secured a long-term contract at Cleveland Hopkins by underbidding a union-organized company called Systems Auto Parking and Garages, which paid its attendants $2.26 an hour. Metzenbaum and Bonda were paying their guys about $1 an hour less.[11] Metzenbaum's friends looked the other way, but his enemies never let him forget it. "I was a union lawyer, so if the unions had been upset about it, they wouldn't have kept me on. But my attitude was, I am not going to interfere. If the employees want a union, fine with me."[12]

The next year, one of his political opponents, Republican councilman Ralph Perk, introduced legislation requiring the city to pay the prevailing wage—that is, a salary level consistent with the union wage for similar employment in the county. "Howard Metzenbaum was never one to let his friendship with labor unions interfere with his efforts to build up the Airport Parking Company of America," wrote *Plain Dealer* columnist Wilson Hirschfeld. The same article then quoted a 1960 statement from A. C. Helm, president of Teamsters Local 946: "The management of Airport Parking is definitely opposed to the use of organized labor and has done everything it could to keep its men from joining the union."[13]

Bonda, interviewed in 1995, said of policy at APCOA, "If I had to [hire union employees] I would. If I didn't have to, I didn't."[14] Eventually, he did, as the Teamsters succeeded in organizing some of the company's lots. Metzenbaum, for his part, was never close to the Teamsters Union, which had an unsavory national reputation.

In 1960, APCOA went public at $10 a share and the company expanded into the motel business at airports and in business districts. Metzenbaum and Bonda got a lease for the Los Angeles Express Airport, giving them the largest single parking lot in the world at the time—5,000 spaces. The partners were also in Chicago, Detroit, Denver, New Orleans, Tampa, and Hartford—in all, forty-seven lots in twenty-one states.

Metzenbaum understood early that airports would be engines for economic development. He and Bonda built motels in Tulsa, Columbus, and Omaha, some of them on pylons above their parking lots. They formed a partnership with Holiday Inn and put up new motels in Denver, Columbus, and other cities. Looking toward the future, they provided ground transportation from airports to downtowns, built innovative parking decks at the Hartford airport, and placed Avis Rent-a-Car franchises in ten midsize cities. By the mid-1960s, APCOA was the largest Avis franchise. "I knew that we would be in the direct path of a double-barreled expansion," Metzenbaum said. "First, the expansion of automobile usage. Second, the expansion of air travel. The two growing giants meet at the parking lot."[15] He told the *New York*

Times that airports were "becoming important centers of business and industry, as well as travel, with offices, hotels, shops, banks and many other facilities built around the air terminal core."[16]

That same year, 1965, APCOA settled into plush offices in downtown Cleveland, complete with artworks and a waterfall in the lobby. Metzenbaum leased the space in a rundown bowling alley on Euclid Avenue for about thirty cents a foot and put $300,000 into renovation. He subleased office space, offsetting his own rent. By then, APCOA was the largest parking lot company in the world, with 150 lots and 98,000 spaces in sixty cities from San Juan, Puerto Rico, to Honolulu, Hawaii. The City of Cleveland was getting a return of $500,000 annually from APCOA's business at Hopkins.

The next year, the partners added New York's Kennedy International Airport and LaGuardia, and Newark International Airport. Metzenbaum was the king of parking lots, but he was about to relinquish his throne: three days after he publicly denied any plans to merge with International Telephone and Telegraph, which owned Avis, Metzenbaum and ITT announced a $30 million deal. The agreement in 1966 made the parking conglomerate a subsidiary of the communications giant. APCOA's shareholders, including Metzenbaum and Bonda, who owned at least 50 percent of the shares, were paid in blue chip stock. The full compensation package wasn't made public, but each man walked away with a bundle of ITT shares, valued together in 1965 at more than $6 million. Their financial security was assured. Bonda stayed on as APCOA's operations chief while Metzenbaum began pulling back to devote more time to his law practice, politics, world travel, and a myriad of community interests.

Moving On

From his seventh-story law office in the Union Commerce Building, Metzenbaum surveyed the growing social and political turmoil in mid-1960s America. In his business suit and flattop haircut, he was no aging flower child. But he was involved in the civil rights movement and came out against the Vietnam War as American war planes began intensive bombing raids. He assumed important roles in presidential and U.S. Senate campaigns. And he was a familiar figure to newspaper reporters, as well as to the city's movers and shakers. His headquarters was the law firm on Euclid Avenue in the heart of Cleveland's downtown, the command post where he plotted a return to public life.

When Metzenbaum wasn't available, the man to see about politics was Harold Stern, a graduate of Columbia University and Western Reserve College of Law, and also a Navy veteran. Stern joined Metzenbaum's firm when it was still in its infancy in 1953. "There was only Howard and one other lawyer. He had a practice that constituted doing some labor law work, personal injury, and general legal work, mainly for working people," Stern said.[17] For a fellow from McMechen, West Virginia, working for even a small firm in a city the size of Cleveland was a good opportunity. Postwar Cleveland was the seventh largest city in the country, an industrial behemoth with thousands of unionized workers making steel, machine tools, and automobiles.

The Metzenbaum law office, through its many incarnations, was never among the city's elite firms. It seldom employed more than sixteen or seventeen lawyers. But there was plenty of buzz. In addition to its labor practice, the firm delighted in going after the big fish: railroads, country clubs, and the county government. In part due to intervention by Metzenbaum and Stern, Cuyahoga County's blue laws were struck down after the two attorneys persuaded Sidney Axlerod, a discount store operator in Parma, to stay open in defiance of the Sunday closing law.

By the time Byron Krantz signed on with the firm in 1962, it had a reputation for trial work and labor practice—and also for paying young lawyers below the accepted scale of competitive outfits. However, times had changed. Krantz, a graduate of Dartmouth and Western Reserve University School of Law, turned down offers at the more prestigious Squire, Sanders, and Dempsey and at Calfee, Halter, and Griswold. Metzenbaum won him over after agreeing to give Krantz the freedom to work on nonpaying civil rights cases and other public interest projects. "I wanted to do some public service work, long before 'pro bono' was even part of our language," he explained.[18]

The idealistic Byron Krantz, and Harold Stern, a pragmatic liberal, mirrored different facets of Metzenbaum. While he took pride in his legal skills and was named administrative head of the law firm, Stern evolved into Metzenbaum's alter ego in the political world. The phrase "You'll have to talk to Harold Stern about it" was a caution light for ward leaders and cub reporters. Stern was the troubleshooter—a guy tough enough to let Metzenbaum play the "good cop" when it suited his purposes. Meeting the no-nonsense Mr. Stern for the first time was a revelation. Small in stature, courteous, and a meticulous dresser, he didn't look the part of political hardball player as he peered through glasses at a visitor. But in his day, he was fearless, whether his adversary was another lawyer or a county chairman. Often he would sign checks for Metzenbaum and even impersonate him in telephone conversations with political figures. "You can't become Howard Metzenbaum's alter ego without being somewhat of a hard-ass yourself, because that is the kind of person he is," Stern said.[19]

Reporter Joe Rice saw the Harold and Howard show from the front row. "Harold Stern would imitate Howard on the phone when county chairmen called. I would ask Howard a question and Harold would answer. I said, 'Howard, who is the candidate?' He said, 'Well, I guess I am.' All right then, I said, 'Harold, shut up.'"[20] Not many people had the nerve to tell Harold Stern to shut up. Yet if Stern was firm and direct, he also advocated for a civil, businesslike approach, preferring to avoid intimidation and confrontation when possible. "Harold didn't make many enemies—very few enemies," Metzenbaum said. "Harold does not antagonize people."[21] So Metzenbaum listened when Stern, in private, argued against a hasty jab at a rival or a slight to a potential ally. Away from the office, the Metzenbaum and Stern families were close personally and traveled together to political conventions and resorts. Their wives shared the same first name, Shirley. Metzenbaum had four daughters, Stern three. "The two people over the years he probably fought with the most, or who tried to smooth out his abrasiveness, were Shirley [Metzenbaum] and me," said Stern. On more than one occasion, he threatened to fire Stern for work that was less than perfect.[22]

Metzenbaum was bullheaded to the point of agitating his closest associates, brushing off sound advice and plowing ahead with a questionable scheme. It was both a strength and a weakness. "He was not the easiest person to work for—very demanding and at times unreasonable," Stern wrote in a memoir.[23] Stern soon found himself more concerned with satisfying Metzenbaum than the firm's clients. "I was stubborn and I think I was single-minded," Metzenbaum said. "I think, frankly, that helped me as a United States senator."[24] His stubbornness was tempered by a healthy dose of common sense, which seldom betrayed him. "Howard has more common sense than anybody I have ever known," Stern said. "And you would be surprised how much common sense makes up for lack of knowledge or experience. He takes nothing for granted. Howard is a person who always asked, 'Why?'"[25]

By the 1960s, Howard Metzenbaum was an important man in Cuyahoga County and he had all the trappings to prove it. He expected deference and most of the time he got it. Above his office door at the law firm was a red bulb, which also lit up on the switchboard. When the light was on, Metzenbaum was not to be disturbed by anyone other than his wife or one of his four daughters. Candy Korn, the switchboard operator, made sure that the other person was waiting on the line before putting "Mr. Metzenbaum" through. He didn't expect to waste time talking to assistants or secretaries, and he wanted the edge in the conversation with his intended party. This made for interesting duels with his friend James W. Shocknessy, the imperious head of the Ohio Turnpike Commission, who had the same protocol for phone calls.

Metzenbaum, the millionaire, flew coach but insisted that his personal secretary, Juanita Powe, book him in the first row, window seat, sunny side of the airplane. He kept a backup reservation in someone else's name to give him flexibility for last-minute changes. From time to time on business trips, he would take one of his daughters along for companionship and as a learning experience for the girl. Once, when she was nine, Susan, his second oldest, worked in the ticket booth at the airport parking lot in Tulsa while her dad did business inside the terminal.

It wasn't all work. In Salt Lake City, Good Samaritan Metzenbaum fell into a fountain outside the Mormon Tabernacle as he tried to help a woman who had slipped into the water. Susan pulled her soggy dad out.

Back in Cleveland, Metzenbaum mixed business with politics and unrelenting crusades against exclusive clubs for golfers, tennis players, and old men having lunch. His family lived in a stately home, complete with a duck pond and tennis court, on what amounted to millionaires' row in Shaker Heights. The *Cleveland Press* once photographed a beaming Metzenbaum mixing a chocolate ice cream sundae at his home soda fountain. He had worked hard for every nickel, but he appreciated his good fortune. Metzenbaum was frequently in the right place at the right time. "He would tell us, 'we are so lucky,'" said Susan

Metzenbaum. "Even when he is being kicked, he feels lucky." When a playmate protested to Susan that "your dad is trying to take the tennis court away from our club"—a reference to one of his legal efforts to open up a private outfit—the Metzenbaum daughter fired back, "If you belonged to a club that allowed Jews and blacks you would not have that problem."[26] Accepting an invitation to address the Masons, Metzenbaum lectured the venerable fraternal order for claiming to foster "brotherly feelings" and then barring "a segment of men solely because of the pigment of their skin."[27] The Masons should have seen it coming; Metzenbaum always backed the rights of an individual over the interests of an institution.

Metzenbaum became almost a surrogate father to the younger Krantz, who, in turn, developed into the partner Metzenbaum most often looked to for help on sticky legal matters. "He had a light above his door. I had a light above my door. I was an absolute clone. I modeled myself after him in a lot of things. I liked the way he did it."[28]

During her first years at the firm, Metzenbaum called Candy Korn "girl," but before long he became a father figure to her too. "He was tough but he was fair," she said.[29] As a United States senator, he would emerge as a champion for the feminist movement, a reliable vote for workplace equality. But his consciousness-raising did not predate that of most other men of his time. In the mid-1960s—before *The Feminine Mystique*, before the Equal Rights Amendment—Candy Korn, Juanita Powe, and other young women at the office would don matching outfits for special events and appear as the "Metz Girls." They helped promote whatever cause Metzenbaum attached himself to.

Metzenbaum always kept his finger in politics, propping up one candidate, trying to bring down another. He once unsuccessfully targeted Congressman Michael Feighan, a conservative Democrat with a base of support from Cleveland's Irish-American community.[30] Feuds energized him. One long-standing antagonist was Ray T. Miller, the boss of the Cuyahoga County Democratic Party. In 1960, Metzenbaum and former U.S. senator Thomas Burke were on a Democratic National Convention delegate slate pledged to Ohio governor Michael V. DiSalle. Burke had served as mayor of Cleveland in the 1940s and counted famed crime-fighter Eliot Ness among his defeated Republican opponents. The Miller organization had its own slate in 1960, headed by county engineer Albert S. Porter, a party stalwart. Both groups intended to support John F. Kennedy for president at the convention. But in the meantime, they could knock each other around and probe for weaknesses that might come into play in some future battle. Miller instituted a gag rule that barred "unendorsed" delegate candidates from speaking at Democratic ward meetings. Metzenbaum would have none of it. "Ray Miller doesn't own the Democratic Party, even though he may think he does. The Democratic Party is bigger than he or any other individual."[31]

Amid the jealousies and petty power struggles, Metzenbaum and Burke strode briskly into a ward meeting one cool April night in the suburban University Heights City Hall. They were determined to have their say. As they took their seats near the speaker's rostrum, Miller was winding down a speech denouncing a flyer put out by the DiSalle camp as "scurrilous and libelous." As he left the podium, Miller turned to Metzenbaum and Burke, and with a tight smile, said quietly, "You can't speak here. You know the rule." The rule was this: at a county party meeting, only the organization's anointed candidates would get the platform. Metzenbaum didn't care who owned the microphone. He shot back, "You are not going to tell me when I'm going to speak, or where, or about what." Miller ignored the outburst and walked away. But Metzenbaum and Burke were eventually introduced informally and managed to get in a few words.[32] So Metzenbaum had the last word— he had gotten his way again—but he also hardened his enemies. "He has left a trail of people who do feel he was less than gentlemanly with them," said Moses Krislov, a lawyer who was his adversary on more than one occasion.[33]

The dustups never seemed to bother Metzenbaum. He trusted his instincts. If he was wrong, he was willing to pay the price. "There's something in my brain that puts things together and puts it in order . . . I'll do it in my head—that gives me a little bit of a jump on you," said Metzenbaum.[34] His daughter Susan said her father "does not look back. He looks forward." His view is, "If you said all day 'should I do this?' you would not do it."[35]

CHAPTER 3

The Activist

"I think you have come to the right door."
Bernard E. Rand

Buddy Rand was riding high when he first met Howard Metzenbaum. But by the end of their relationship, Rand was embittered, fading from the limelight, and under investigation by the Securities and Exchange Commission. Yet by his own admission, he was also a wiser and wealthier man for the experience.

In 1949, Rand was on top in the Cleveland sports world, mentioned in the same breath as Paul Brown, the revered founding coach of the Cleveland Browns, and the legendary Bill Veeck, owner of the Indians, winners of the 1948 World Series. The *Cleveland Press* called Rand one of the "Big Three of Cleveland pro sports" after he became president of Crown Investment, owner of the Cleveland Arena and Ice House and the American Hockey League Cleveland Barons, the arena's prime tenant.[1] Rand, the *Press* said, "mixed business acumen with showmanship."[2] He was a Renaissance man: a radio personality, civil war buff, snappy dresser, and husband of art aficionado Gertrude Sherby Rand, a much-admired community activist.

Like Metzenbaum, Bernard E. Rand's early life had been a struggle. He grew up outside of Youngstown with a widowed mother and worked at an early age to support the family. "I have a great overriding sympathy for poor people. I was brought up poor and I never knew I was poor," he said.[3] Rand toiled at his late father's dairy farm, washed cars, and later sold shoes and magazine subscriptions. "I had a hundred jobs by the time I graduated from law school," he recalled.

Rand came to Cleveland during the Depression to attend law school at Western Reserve University,[4] working his way through as a radio announcer. After he graduated in 1932, he practiced law, toiling briefly for Jimmy Metzenbaum. He didn't cherish law the way Jimmy did and quickly grew restless writing briefs and researching the Ohio Revised Code. Ambitious and headstrong, he looked for opportunities to go into business. "I always had an aptitude for making deals, not so much for spending my time in the law library," he said.

Rand turned to professional sports, which grew in popularity in the postwar era as Americans enjoyed more leisure time. "I wanted out early and tried to make a buck and moved toward sports. I guess it was my ego when I was young." He joined a partnership that ran Thistledown Racetrack in Northfield, Ohio, becoming secretary-treasurer and general manager of the thoroughbred track. From that perch, he engineered the sale of the Cleveland Arena from its creator, builder Al Sutphin, to a new corporate ownership group, Crown Investment.

Rand, named Crown's president, wanted to promote events other than hockey and college basketball at the arena. With a seating capacity of more than 13,000 and a choice location on Euclid Avenue and East Thirty-sixth Street, the arena was a short hop from downtown Cleveland and the West Side and an easy drive from the prospering suburbs to the east. Rand's partners were satisfied playing landlord to the status quo and eventually ousted their rambunctious front man. So Rand tried to buy the facility in 1952 but came up short in the takeover bid. The arena's general manager, Jim Hendy, dismissed a subsequent proposal as a "phony offer."[5]

It was a rude awakening. Rand complained to Herman Goldstein, the sports editor of the now-defunct *Cleveland News,* urging Goldstein to write a story about the raw deal that Rand thought he got from the arena owners. The crusty sports writer put him in his place. "Bud," he said, "as far as the public is concerned you are nothing but a big shit. They don't care about you. They want the sports. You are nobody." So much for the Big Three. "That rang in my ears and it is still there," Rand said. "It was a great thing to me—not to think you are important."

Rand changed course again. He joined with hairdresser Jo Portaro and opened a string of successful beauty salons in 1954 called Lady Beautiful. But the enterprise ended in a messy $10 million lawsuit over a struggle for control of the salons. By the time the case was settled in 1962, Rand had left the beauty parlor business. He drifted to newspapering, buying the Printing Company of America, a letterpress that began operations in 1907. Before long, Rand started getting telephone calls from Howard Metzenbaum. "He kept bugging me. He said, 'Look, we can make a big thing with these newspapers.'" Rand had met Metzenbaum through Cleveland's legal fraternity and he was aware of his high public profile. "I knew Howard mostly through the publicity he was getting. I remember him walking down the street with Harry Truman. He got up at six AM and when Truman came to Cleveland, Howard was there. Howard had chutzpah." Rand was impressed—and also a little put off—by Metzenbaum's boldness.

But Rand was interested. He, too, was considering a partnership. Once, waiting for an appointment with Metzenbaum at his law firm, he overheard the businessman shouting into the telephone behind closed doors: "Goddamn it, judge, I am not asking you, I am telling you." That conversation left an impression. "I have never met anybody that had that kind of chutzpah," Rand said. Friends warned him that he was not ready for Metzenbaum's brand of hardball, suggesting he was "too aggressive" and "too sharp for you."

So Rand and Metzenbaum began slowly, purchasing the *Parma Post* in 1965 when it was little more than a shoppers' paper filled with ads. They built it into a respectable news weekly and in 1967 added four West Side papers and upgraded them. Two years later, Metzenbaum and Rand teamed up to buy the Sun Newspaper chain from Harry Volk and Milton Friedlander, and also Berea Publishing Company from James C. Toedtman. A media empire was born. The partners owned seventeen weekly papers, with a combined circulation of 280,000. Rand remained wary of Metzenbaum but continued to be impressed with his vision. "I said, 'Howard, I am concerned about our relationship. This has got to be a fifty-fifty deal. If you and I don't agree on something, then we don't do it. It has to be unanimous between you and me.' I wanted to make sure that that's the deal. And we shook hands, [but] he never kept his word."

In the heady days of 1969, Rand forged ahead with Metzenbaum. The partners borrowed $1 million from Society Bank "on our signatures," according to Rand. More staff was hired, and the company was renamed ComCorp, with Volk staying on as editor in chief. Toedtman became a vice president, and David Skylar, an advertising agency executive, was selected as president of the new corporation.

Metzenbaum was a tough manager. "When we lost $109,000 in the first quarter, I thought that was pretty good," Skylar said. "When I told him about it, he looked at me and said, 'We are going to show a profit at the end of the first half, aren't we?' I said, 'Yes, sir.'"[6] "He had great confidence in everything he said and did—and he said it in a very strident way," Rand said of his partner.

In 1969 ComCorp went public, offering 210,000 shares at $12 per share. Metzenbaum and Rand already owned 183,000 shares each and Skylar was cut in for 108,700 shares. Things started to turn sour within months of Skylar joining the company. His approach, Rand said, was, "Let's drink a little whiskey and talk this over." Rand didn't care for this style and, more importantly, often found himself outvoted by Metzenbaum and Skylar on business matters. "Howard packed the executive committee with David Skylar," he said. "Skylar was his boy."

Rand suspected that Metzenbaum, a potential Senate candidate, intended to use the newspapers as his personal political vehicle. He was not alone in his suspicions as Metzenbaum edged toward his first confrontation with John Glenn in the 1970 Senate primary. "Contrary to some reports, my involvement doesn't mean I'm trying to get support for any political activity I may become involved in," Metzenbaum said when he and Rand acquired Berea Publishing in July 1969.[7]

Rand soon felt like a bit player. What most annoyed him, according to Skylar, was the media constantly referring to "Howard Metzenbaum's newspapers."[8] Feeling betrayed, Rand began secretly acquiring stock through a second party in April 1970. Allegedly guaranteeing his straw purchaser against any loss, Rand bought more than 13,000 shares. The Securities and Exchange Commission exposed the scheme in 1973, saying Rand sought to manipulate the value of ComCorp stock by buying it at inflated prices through a front man. "I innocently got involved," Rand insisted years later. "I didn't fully realize there was any implication of SEC violations. It was a small amount of stock out of hundreds of thousands of shares." Rand never admitted wrongdoing but accepted a settlement that barred him from doing business with securities brokers or dealers.

It was no innocent misstep to Metzenbaum. He was enraged, and the already-fractured relationship came apart completely. "He and I had bad blood,"[9] Metzenbaum said. Negotiations to buy out Rand began, but Rand, unrepentant, demanded $9 per share for his stock and backed up his bravado by hiring the formidable Moses Krislov as his lawyer. If Metzenbaum overpowered Rand, he met his match when he sat down across a desk from Mo Krislov, a chain-smoking trial lawyer who had represented accused mobsters. Big Mo was eight years younger than Metzenbaum, talked just as tough, and outweighed his rival by at least 150 pounds.

Years before his confrontation with Metzenbaum, Krislov's automobile was bombed as it sat in the driveway of his Shaker Heights home. The blast, reportedly dynamite, tore a hole in the pavement, blew the two front hubcaps off his new Cadillac, and broke three windows in his home. Krislov, his wife Lois, and their three children were asleep inside, but, having earlier received an anonymous threat by phone, he believed the blast was meant for him.[10] Krislov insisted the 1962 incident had nothing to do with his representing organized crime figures or his hitches for Teamsters union officials. Instead, he suspected a company that had refused to withhold garnished wages from one of his cases. But the incident remained unsolved. In later years, he downplayed the entire matter, saying the explosive was nothing more than a cherry bomb.

Shaker Heights police were familiar with the Krislov home. Five years earlier, he held officers at bay when they attempted to arrest his wife for a string of unpaid parking tickets. It turned out Krislov was the one who had accumulated the tickets, but the car was registered in his wife's name. The *Plain Dealer* reported that "police said Krislov used offensive language and tried to get his wife to hide in the house next door."[11] Lois Krislov paid the tickets, and Krislov sued police for false arrest but lost.

Krislov described Metzenbaum and Rand as "two very strong people [who] each wanted to have his own way. . . . Howard is a tough man to be a partner with. He's a very hard guy when it comes to the question of little nitty-gritty things. He fights. He is not a compromiser. I won't say he's mean-spirited, but there's a saying in business: when you get the better of a deal, leave a dollar on the table" to mollify your opponent. "Howard wouldn't leave the dollar on the table."[12]

Byron Krantz, Metzenbaum's former law partner and political troubleshooter, represented Metzenbaum in the negotiations. Krantz had a different perspective on the Rand-Metzenbaum relationship. According to Krantz, Rand's misguided business ideas (like hiring off-duty police to deliver the newspapers) alarmed Metzenbaum and damaged the partnership. Rand's attempt to gain control of the company by manipulating the price of the stock for his own benefit further damaged the relationship. Krantz, an elegant, low-key man, worshiped Metzenbaum and was turned off by Krislov's rough-and-tumble manner. "He was bluster and bluff," Krantz said of the big man. "He was one of the early [lawyers] that just threatened."[13]

Rand's legal team was bolstered by the addition of Howard Markham, a respected Cleveland lawyer who helped negotiate a settlement in 1972 after months of bitter wrangling. Rand got his price: $9 a share— a $1.7 million buyout by Metzenbaum and an investors group. Rand resigned as ComCorp board chairman, treasurer, and executive committee member, saying little to the media. Some twenty-five years later, however, he said with satisfaction, "You can't shout a mountain down. You have to erode it. And that's what we did."

Krantz said Metzenbaum was simply glad to be rid of Rand and didn't make any money on the transaction when he later resold most of the stock. "Buddy Rand said to me, if you can't take a pig out of the front door, take a ham out of the back," Krantz said. "That was Buddy Rand."[14]

"With Howard, it was like a Faustian opera"

While Metzenbaum feuded with Rand, he and his company, ComCorp, resisted attempts by the Newspaper Guild, Local 1, to organize the suburban newspapers. George Condon Jr., then a reporter at the *Plain Dealer*, said, "We also thought naively that a person who is the counsel for Cleveland's AFL-CIO would not stand in our way. We were wrong. He crushed us."[15]

Metzenbaum did not acknowledge he was behind any move to stop the guild, but there is no doubt he was in charge—and ComCorp did not want its employees unionized. "I tried to stay out of it," Metzenbaum insisted in a 1995 interview, but in another conversation, he conceded that the newspaper guild was angry with him.[16]

The guild sought recognition at ComCorp's seventeen newspapers in 1971. Jack Weir, executive secretary of Local 1, said he expected Metzenbaum and ComCorp management to "live up to the principles of the labor movement." Metzenbaum, Gaines, Finley, and Stern represented the Cleveland AFL-CIO and had been the guild's legal firm until the organizing drive was launched. "After all," Weir said, "Metzenbaum has made his living through the labor movement."[17] Metzenbaum countered, "I have said over the years as an employer that if the union has the people and the people want the union, the corporations in which I have an interest will recognize the union and will bargain collectively."[18] Skylar took the point for Metzenbaum and insisted that the work force, for purposes of guild representation, be defined as all employees—down to stringers, part-timers, and spot photographers. The guild wanted only full-time reporters and photographers to vote on certification, believing they would be most sympathetic to a union since they had the most to gain.

Metzenbaum's standing with the labor movement was so strong and enduring that Weir was denounced that summer at an AFL-CIO meeting. Metzenbaum had always been with the unions—in courthouses as their lawyer, in Columbus through every legislative battle, even on picket lines. Weir made the mistake of making the organizing struggle personal by needling Metzenbaum and suggesting that he was a hypocrite for seeming to put his business interests ahead of his principles as a labor lawyer. The unions pooh-poohed the charge. Delegates at the Cleveland area meeting passed a resolution to support organizing drives of all the unions at ComCorp but did not mention the newspaper guild by name, a slight of Weir. To this day, Skylar maintains that ComCorp's determination to make it tough on the guild was "100 percent my call." Yet, he also allowed, "If we defined the union, they can't win, and I think [Metzenbaum] understood that."[19]

On July 8, 1971, the Sun newspapers editorial employees voted against guild affiliation 76–58. The newspaper guild—"an elitist union," in Skylar's view—was shut out. Once again, similar to the flap over his nonunion parking lots, Metzenbaum distanced himself from the dispute. If he had chosen to set a tone, Skylar agreed, the boss could have said at the outset when he bought the chain, "These are going to be guild newspapers." That he did not was no surprise to his intimates. "With Howard, it was like a Faustian opera," said Skylar.[20] Bonda said his friend was a man of conviction and a true believer in the American labor movement, but "if there was a subject that interfered with making money—not a vicious subject but a subject—he would go to the part of making money."[21] Self-interest would come first, then the greater good.

But the greater good, as Metzenbaum saw it, would be served. By the time he got into newspapers, he was already a millionaire several times over and a force for social change. He had always been an activist—a gadfly and irritant to the vested interests—but now he had more time to devote to his causes. In 1959 Metzenbaum sued Society for Savings as it converted from a mutual bank to a for-profit national institution owned by its depositors. Metzenbaum, arguing that the depositors were getting shortchanged on stock being issued, ultimately got a better deal for the new stockholders at the reorganized Society Bank. He was urged to settle but took it to trial, arguing the case personally before the Court of Common Pleas judge Daniel Wasserman. "I am not settling this goddamned thing, because these guys are trying to steal the bank," he told Wasserman in a private conversation.[22]

Metzenbaum was not finished with Society, which he regarded as a bastion of Cleveland's Waspish old guard. He kept his eye on the huge institution, which owned three other banks and had assets exceeding $819 million by 1968. Nine years after intervening on behalf of Society's depositors, Metzenbaum and his partner in the parking lot business, Ted Bonda, launched what had all the markings of a takeover bid.

Mervin B. France, Society's chief executive officer, accused Metzenbaum and Bonda of engaging in a "stock raid" as they quickly increased their holdings to 25,000 voting trust certificates, paper that would be converted to stock shares. The two men controlled the largest single block of shares. Bonda was already a member of the bank board. Yet Metzenbaum was denied a seat on the corporate and bank boards of directors. France said Metzenbaum had little experience in banking and was not "entitled to a major voice in this corporation."[23]

Not entitled? Those were fighting words. In fact, Metzenbaum was experienced, winning election to the board of directors of the Cleveland-based Capital Bank in 1962. He threatened to sue in an attempt to force Society to open its books and to block it from increasing the authorized number of common and preferred shares. Metzenbaum, wishing to protect the interests of small depositors and questioning the bank's loan policies, wanted to see a complete list of common stockholders. "We do not seek control," he said, but later admitted it was an "assault"—a takeover bid—that nearly succeeded.[24] Metzenbaum was troubled by the lack of diversity on the board of directors, whose members included only one Jew and no blacks. And he was still irked that "these so-called high-and-mighty country club big deals were taking over this mutual bank, which belonged to the depositors, and [they] still had not shown any evidence of concern for the depositors." Besides, Metzenbaum said, "We thought it was probably a good business investment to be able to take control of a national bank in downtown Cleveland."[25]

The crisis passed as Society relented and expanded the corporate board by one to add Metzenbaum as a director. "Howard . . . we're happy to have you aboard," France said, meaning he would rather face his formidable foe in the boardroom than in the courtroom.[26] The adversaries were now on a first-name basis, but, just in case Society had not gotten the message, Metzenbaum and Bonda increased their holdings to some 57,563 trust certificates, worth about $5 million.

France had reason to be nervous. Metzenbaum's law firm handled labor law cases on behalf of workers, fought Sunday blue laws that kept discount houses closed one day a week, and battled to open private clubs. "Howard is a very formidable opponent," said Krislov. "He is smart. He thinks things through. He knows where he wants to go."[27]

Knocking Down Barriers—
"You came riding into court on your white horse"

Metzenbaum wanted to go for a drink one steamy day in 1955 after watching play in the Carlings Open golf tournament at the Manakiki Golf Course in suburban Rocky River. He was a duffer and often joined in a foursome with Bonda and two other well-to-do pals, Max Friedman, an automobile dealer, and doctor Sid Peterman. "We bet some serious money on those games. We used to struggle an awful lot," said Friedman. "If you thought [Howard] was a great filibusterer in the Senate, he was greater on the golf course. When he lost, he wasn't always that gracious."[28]

Nor was he gracious when a Manakiki bartender refused to serve him because the clubhouse was "members only." Manakiki, though owned by Cuyahoga County Metropolitan Park Board, was a private club. Metzenbaum was reminded of the public ownership as he exited the clubhouse and noticed a stone monument that had been donated to the park board. When the deeply offended Metzenbaum returned to his office, he began researching the club's real-estate history. Law partner Harold Stern told Metzenbaum he was "going to tee off every judge in the community" if he pursued legal action, because many prominent judges and lawyers were members of a similarly leased club called Sleepy Hollow. Howard replied, "Yeah, but it isn't right. The public should have this."[29]

Metzenbaum first complained to the park board then went to court and argued that the 220-acre Manakiki and the Sleepy Hollow Golf Club were publicly owned and should not be privatized in any way. He and Stern had done their homework. Manakiki was given to the park board during World War II with the stipulation that it be put to public use, Metzenbaum said. Instead, it was leased to the operators of a private club for a paltry $9,000 a year. The park system had purchased the 188-acre Sleepy Hollow property in 1929. "Both of these courses were obtained by a public body for public use. I don't see any logic in their operation as private clubs," he told the board. "What enjoyment and benefit does the public receive when the club is under private lease?" The park board said it would probably lose money on the courses if it gave up the private leases. Besides, said board chairman Stephen H. Hazelwood, "These are difficult courses for the average golfer."[30]

Nevertheless, Metzenbaum won the case on behalf of all average golfers when the court ruled that a lease to any private interest was illegal. His firm, Metzenbaum, Gaines, Schwartz, Krupansky and Stern, had handled the litigation without fee. A gleeful Metzenbaum had his payback while serving a higher cause. He said he was sorry if members of the two clubs were about to be inconvenienced. His opponent, representing the park board, was Jim Davis, a top lawyer at Squire, Sanders, and Dempsey, a firm so prestigious in the legal fraternity that it was known as Squire, Sanders, and God. "You came riding into court on your white horse," a bemused and beaten Davis told Metzenbaum.[31] It had not been easy. Metzenbaum had received threatening telephone calls during the dispute and at one point hired an off-duty Shaker Heights police officer to keep watch at his home. He took the threats seriously, but they didn't stop him. His commitment to civil rights and social justice went beyond the golf course.

Eventually, it took him all the way to Selma, Alabama. After his rabbi, Arthur Lelyveld, was beaten up in Hattiesburg, Mississippi, during the freedom summer of 1964, Gerry Wedren (a friend) contacted Metzenbaum and urged that they head south to get involved in the voting rights movement. Metzenbaum was shaken by the incident involving Lelyveld. The rabbi, until his death, bore scars under his right eye and on the back of his head from the assault with iron bars. "Look at the white niggers," two toughs yelled at Lelyveld's racially mixed group before attacking them near railroad tracks in Hattiesburg.

The following March, Metzenbaum and Wedren joined Martin Luther King Jr. and a host of other activists, celebrities, and politicians for the well-publicized march from Selma to Montgomery. Two weeks earlier, on "Bloody Sunday," the marchers were thwarted from reaching their goal by a violent mob. Metzenbaum's family, at home in Shaker Heights, was in a near panic worrying about his safety at the second protest. "I was scared to death," said daughter Susan Metzenbaum. "I thought my dad might be killed. 'Do you have to go?' we asked him."[32] But this time President Lyndon B. Johnson federalized the Alabama National Guard to make sure the civil rights demonstrators were protected, and Metzenbaum marched without incident. He was not subjected to any personal abuse and telephoned home to assure Shirley and the girls that everything was okay. "I was not frightened," he said. "I was concerned."[33]

Afterward he contributed $10,000 to the Lawyers Constitutional Defense Committee, which recruited attorneys to handle voting rights cases pro bono. He was soon named the group's chairman. That same year, President Johnson appointed him to a commission overseeing enforcement of the new civil rights law.

Back in Cleveland, he dabbled in less weighty matters and invested in professional sports. But here his genius for making money failed him. He lost $100,000 in the Cleveland Indians while Bonda was president of the baseball club in the early 1970s. He and Bonda also lost money on the Cleveland Stokers, a failed soccer franchise, and the Cleveland Crusaders, a member of the old World Hockey Association. "Soccer, I got clobbered," Metzenbaum admitted. "Hockey, I got clobbered."[34]

Sports were a pastime, but politics was his passion. He was still a familiar figure in Columbus, roaming the statehouse as the top lobbyist (and chief counsel) for the Ohio AFL-CIO. Nine years after leaving the

General Assembly, Metzenbaum was "the most powerful voice around legislative halls," according to the *Cleveland Press*.[35] He was credited with helping install Toledo labor leader Frank King as Senate majority leader, but his political horizon was not limited to the flat landscape along I-71, the highway connecting Cleveland and Columbus. He had become a world traveler, taking particular interest in the affairs of Israel and Africa. Having met Pope John XXIII briefly in Rome, Metzenbaum considered him the "most forward-looking religious leader of almost any person who has lived in this century."[36]

Metzenbaum also made the rounds in Washington, D.C. In addition to people he met through Ohio congressmen, he had personal ties to the Kennedy family dating back to 1959 when, while vacationing in Florida that year, he was recruited to run John F. Kennedy's state operation in Ohio's Democratic presidential primary. Ted Kennedy, in his mid-twenties and just out of law school, was dispatched to drive Metzenbaum to a political planning meeting at the Kennedy family's Palm Beach mansion. And so the connection was made, even though, as events unfolded, JFK did not face a primary in the state in 1960 and Metzenbaum's services were not needed. In the fall, Ohio governor Mike V. DiSalle was picked to chair Kennedy's campaign against Richard Nixon.[37]

Metzenbaum stayed active in the campaign by offering advice and helping behind the scenes. After Kennedy's election, Metzenbaum had hoped to be named assistant secretary of state for African affairs, but the post went instead to Mennen (Soapy) Williams, the former Michigan governor. Resilient as always, Metzenbaum nurtured his relationship with Ted Kennedy, meeting privately with him in Cleveland in 1965 after Teddy's election to the Senate.

That same year, former attorney general Robert F. Kennedy followed his younger brother to the Senate, representing New York. With antiwar sentiment growing, Kennedy was soon under pressure to run for president. Metzenbaum was an early supporter and was going to be "Bobby's man in Cleveland" if RFK got the nomination, according to the *Cleveland Press*.[38] His involvement with Robert Kennedy's campaign brought him closer still to Ted Kennedy and also to Kennedy in-law Sargent Shriver, who kept in close phone contact with his Cleveland friend.

Events moved quickly in 1968. The day after Martin Luther King Jr. was shot, a time of crackling racial tension, Metzenbaum arranged for Robert

Kennedy to appear in Cleveland at the City Club. The city had endured rioting in the largely black Hough and Glenville neighborhoods in 1966 but stayed calm after the King assassination. "It was national news," Stern said of the appearance of Kennedy, who reached across racial lines.[39] But two months later Bobby Kennedy was gunned down in Los Angeles. Metzenbaum, in disbelief, attended his funeral at St. Patrick's Cathedral in New York City and the burial at Arlington National Cemetery. He was shocked by the assassinations and deeply troubled by events that August at the Democratic National Convention in Chicago, which he attended as an uncommitted delegate. Breaking with the Democratic establishment, he blamed Mayor Richard Daley personally for the strong-armed tactics of police in dealing with demonstrators.

By then, Metzenbaum, practically a household name in Cleveland, had established powerful contacts in Columbus and Washington. His four girls were nearly grown and his fortune made. If Howard Metzenbaum had a master plan for going to the United States Senate—as his friends had long suspected—now was the time to carry it out. On September 17, 1968, at the relatively tender age of fifty-one, Metzenbaum grandly announced his retirement from the business world. "I have spent twenty-seven years in meeting business challenges. I would now like to invest a similar amount of time and energy in the challenges facing the nation and the rest of the world," he said.[40] He resigned as chairman of the board of ITT Consumer Services Corporation, the former APCOA. He regarded the newspaper business as a sideline, albeit an important one, and continued as a senior partner at his law firm.

The Cleveland media loved him. He was quick with a quote, frequently shot from the hip, and always returned telephone calls. Elaborating on his retirement, he told Dick Feagler of the *Cleveland Press* that he would "spend several hours each week thinking about how I can crack open the Union Club," downtown Cleveland's premier power-lunch destination for aging WASPs. "It's shameful that a club, which hosts a lot of visitors to this city, restricts Negroes and Jews from membership. I have never set foot inside it, and I won't." Metzenbaum, Feagler said, recounted earlier battles to open up the private golf clubs "with relish, like an old general."[41]

Howard Metzenbaum had established himself as a man who wouldn't take no for an answer, but who could say no to others with a firmness that discouraged further inquiry. He made his share of enemies—and they would haunt him. "He was not a man of his word. He sold me a bill of goods," Buddy Rand complained. "We shook hands and he never kept his word."

Rand took his revenge in 1974 when John Glenn knocked on his door, looking for a contribution at the outset of his second Senate primary campaign against Metzenbaum. Rand told the former astronaut he'd "come to the right door" and gave him $5,000, one of Glenn's biggest contributions in the primary contest against Metzenbaum.

Despite the grudge Rand held against Metzenbaum, Rand eventually came to respect his abilities as a public servant and contributed to Metzenbaum's subsequent campaigns, saying, "I think the good he has done for those that don't have anything far outweighs the harm he has done to those he has bested in business."

CHAPTER 4

Glenn Wars I

Battle Plan for an Upset

"If it looks like John Glenn is going to walk into
the Senate seat unopposed, I just may run. . . .
It could be interesting."
Howard Metzenbaum

T he roots of Howard Metzenbaum's dispute with John Glenn go
back to a man named Steve Young, an Ohio senator who was more
cantankerous than Metzenbaum though not as smart. In 1964, Colonel
Glenn, still glowing from his historic 1962 orbital flight and encouraged by the Kennedy family to try politics, decided to shoot for the U.S.
Senate in his first political venture. The startling decision of a political
neophyte, albeit a world-famous one, to challenge an incumbent senator split the Democratic Party. Even one of Glenn's aides marveled in
later years at the "arrogance of climbing into a U.S. Senate race" against
a sitting senator, and one who was a minor hero in his own right, for
Steve Young had toppled a Republican once thought invincible.

Glenn's audacious bid for Young's Senate seat drew Metzenbaum
into the fray. It was the beginning of a twenty-year cold war between
two titans of the Ohio Democratic Party. Metzenbaum had engineered
Young's huge upset six years earlier over John W. Bricker, a nationally
prominent conservative who also served as Ohio's governor and ran
for vice president on Thomas Dewey's ticket in 1944. "Honest John"

Bricker opposed the New Deal and fought against the expansion of presidential power during his two terms in the Senate. He once denounced Social Security as socialism and opposed the censure of Senator Joseph McCarthy. Shortly after taking office, Bricker survived an assassination attempt—"two wild shots" in a Senate subway—which only enhanced his stature.[1]

Of Steve Young, a former Cleveland congressman, Metzenbaum said, "We were not real close, but I thought John Bricker was the antithesis of everything I believed in."[2] Bricker represented a status quo that Metzenbaum detested: privilege, unchallenged power, and rigidly conservative values.

Harold Stern knew Bricker would be formidable. "He looked like a senator, being a large man with flowing white hair. He acted like a senator, and had been his party's candidate for vice president."[3] Metzenbaum agreed. "He was a stately man. He looked like God had come down to earth. And he thought he was."[4]

"You should be the candidate"

Approaching the 1958 election against Young, John Bricker recognized the peril in a ballot initiative that would have sharply curtailed the ability of trade unions to organize in Ohio. But he was unable to distance himself since the incumbent Republican governor C. William O'Neill embraced the right-to-work proposal with gusto. This constitutional amendment, placed on the ballot by business interests through a petition drive, barred union shops, where workers were required to join unions immediately after being hired. Organized labor saw the proposed change as a serious threat to the union movement in Ohio. But advocates argued it was needed to curb the power of union bosses and the "forced" political contributions they collected from union members. One thing was certain: by mid-October State Issue 2 had galvanized union sympathizers, many of whom were likely to vote Democratic as they cast ballots against the right-to-work amendment.

Metzenbaum, with Stern's help, had to build a statewide campaign almost from scratch—a new challenge for both men. "There was no significant campaign organization," Stern said. "We were on a very fast learning curve."[5] Metzenbaum already knew most of the Democratic county chairmen, and he was about to become acquainted with the rest. He coordinated the efforts of the Democratic bosses with the grassroots work of the AFL-CIO to build Young's field operation. Stern hired a public relations man and a driver to get the candidate around the state. While Young campaigned, Metzenbaum hit the phones, tapping his influential contacts to raise money for the candidate. He also took Young for interviews with the editorial boards of Ohio's major newspapers, making a case for change in the U.S. Senate.

Former president Truman even came to Cleveland for appearances on Young's behalf, including a $100-per-plate fund-raising dinner. Metzenbaum also entertained Truman and Democratic contributor Leonard Bernstein at his Shaker Heights home. Local papers ran a photograph of Truman campaigning on the streets of Cleveland, with Metzenbaum, Young, and Stern trailing close behind. "Give 'em Hell Harry" was showing "Give 'em Hell Howard" how it was done.

Young, then sixty-nine, was a World War I veteran who began his political career in 1913 as a state representative. He was in and out of public office over the next forty years. The perennial candidate got beat when he took on Governor Martin Davey in a Democratic primary in 1936. Young was fearless and resilient, but he still had rough edges. Two years before the Bricker campaign, he lost a statewide race for attorney general.

Going into the fall campaign, the myth of Bricker's invincibility was intact. Only the *Toledo Blade* endorsed Young, who struggled for attention in the press. But as Ohioans turned against the right-to-work ballot question, Young linked his campaign to the emerging groundswell. And he effectively peppered Bricker with criticism on several other fronts. "He scored especially well with his attack upon Bricker's vote in 1954 against the Saint Lawrence Seaway [funding]," Richard O. Davies wrote in his biography of Bricker. "Despite the overwhelming popularity of this project along the shores of Lake Erie, Bricker stoutly defended his opposition as an effort to protect the taxpayers from unnecessary expense."[6] Cities like Cleveland and Toledo expected the seaway would bring a boom in business at their ports. But Bricker said it would not be self-supporting financially and would weaken the nation's "system of essential transportation," an apparent reference to the railroads. What the senator did not say—but Young charged without contradiction— was that Bricker's law firm, Bricker, Marburger, Evatt, and Barton, had received nearly $400,000 in legal fees from the Pennsylvania Railroad, a powerful foe of the seaway.

Metzenbaum and Stern had worked hard at making the unpredictable Young a better candidate, rewriting his speeches and rehearsing him for debates. His handlers saw the Cleveland City Club debate as an opportunity for Young to finish strong since the debate was traditionally staged the week before the November election. To appeal to working-class voters, the Democratic team made a big deal of the Bricker law firm ties to the Pennsylvania Railroad, which Metzenbaum saw as a symbol of the failures of corporate America. "We spent hours just prepping [Young] to get the points across that Metzenbaum wanted him to get across," said Stern. "He was like a rabbit jumping out the starting gate when the debate opened."[7] The hard work paid off. Steve Young held his own with the imposing Bricker.

The results on Tuesday were catastrophic for the Ohio Republican Party, which lost Bricker's Senate seat by 155,000 votes and every statewide office except secretary of state, where Ted Brown survived. The right-to-work issue went down by more than 800,000 votes, a 63 percent margin. The turnout of nearly 3.4 million voters, including many prolabor Democrats, was the second largest in Ohio history, topping the 1954 midyear election by 732,000. Michael V. DiSalle of Toledo became governor, the first elected to a four-year term. And a crotchety little guy named Stephen M. Young succeeded the elegant Bricker, who returned to his Columbus law practice.

Along the way Metzenbaum received unsolicited encouragement for his own political ambitions. Early in the campaign, he telephoned Paul Block, the mercurial publisher of the *Toledo Blade,* asking for a meeting to introduce him to Young. Block responded that "there wasn't any point in it because neither [Young nor Bricker] was worth anything." But Metzenbaum persisted, and the three men chatted for three hours in Block's office in the Blade Building overlooking Maumee Bay in downtown Toledo. As the two visitors got up to leave, Block pulled Metzenbaum aside and blurted out, "You should be the candidate." So Young picked up the *Blade*'s backing that year, and Metzenbaum got a strong signal from a powerful opinion maker. Block's words "may have planted some small seed," Metzenbaum said.[8]

Young was off to the Senate, where his unswerving liberalism and undiplomatic ways became legendary. He was known to fire off rude responses to critical letters from constituents, telling one in particular, "Some SOB wrote me this stupid-ass letter and put your name on it."

"He was a real curmudgeon of a guy. Drank, chased women," said Byron Krantz, the Metzenbaum law partner who worked on Young's subsequent 1964 campaign. "I loved him . . . Steve was probably the most liberal man I have ever known." Young was close to majority leader Lyndon B. Johnson, who escorted him down the aisle for his oath of office in 1959 after Young brushed off Senator Frank Lausche's offer to accompany him. Young, who was mindful that Lausche had not helped him in his campaign, didn't give a damn about the opening day custom of walking arm in arm with the senior senator from his home state.

As president, Johnson would drop by Young's Senate office to gain insights on the mood on Capitol Hill. Young, admired for his honesty and candor, drank blended whiskey during these sit-downs. The president stuck to root beer. The friendship soured when Young came out against the Vietnam War. "He was one of the original doves, and that was the end of his relationship with Johnson," said Krantz.[9]

As the 1964 election year approached, Young was regarded as beatable: an unattractive liberal Democrat running in a Republican-leaning swing state. Bricker had retired from electoral politics to devote his full attention to his law firm, renamed Bricker and Eckler. But Congressman Robert Taft Jr., from Ohio's foremost Republican family, was preparing to run on the Republican side. John and Robert Kennedy, meanwhile, were grooming Glenn for a career in politics as a Democrat. The Republicans, thinking that military men tend to favor the GOP, wanted the new hero on their side, but in truth Glenn's family roots were planted with the Democratic Party. His father, a plumber and car dealer in New Concord, Ohio, was an admirer of Franklin Delano Roosevelt.

John Kennedy wanted Glenn to join the Democratic Party and announce his candidacy for federal office in the fall of 1963 for several reasons, according to authors Scott Montgomery and Timothy R. Gaffney. "Kennedy had lost Ohio to Richard Nixon in the 1960 presidential race, and with Kennedy's civil rights position likely to cost him dearly in the South he could not afford to lose Ohio again in 1964," say the authors. "Running side-by-side with Glenn would have been ideal. Also, the sitting senator, Stephen M. Young, looked vulnerable to the expected Republican challenger [Taft]."[10]

Wayne Hays, the outspoken congressman from eastern Ohio coal country, and a few other party regulars signed on with Glenn. But Metzenbaum and most of the Democratic organization stayed with

Senator Young. Then, lightning struck. Kennedy's assassination on November 22, 1963, changed the political landscape across the nation. The Democratic Party was looking for stability, and Johnson, the new president, would be its nominee for a full four-year term. The Republicans were split, with the emerging conservative wing determined to take the party away from the eastern establishment and its likely presidential candidate, New York governor Nelson A. Rockefeller.

Young, still friendly at that time with President Johnson, was mad as hell at the nervy Glenn. He had no intention of stepping aside, even if it meant going against the Kennedy family. With John Kennedy gone from the White House, any hope that Young could be bought off with an ambassadorship disappeared. The rationale for a Glenn campaign in terms of national politics was also gone. Johnson considered Young an ally, was not close to Glenn, and didn't need his help in Ohio.

Glenn procrastinated. "I talked to Bobby about it, but he felt it was too late, that there was not enough time to really put the whole thing together," Glenn said of his situation. "I decided to go ahead and run anyway."[11] Glenn's decision to run owed as much to his sense of entitlement than to any missionary zeal for carrying out the Kennedy legacy of idealism in public service. After announcing his candidacy on January 17, 1964, he quickly learned that heroes were legitimate targets in an American political campaign.

Striking an above-the-fray pose, Glenn refused to get involved in the give-and-take of campaigning. He was reluctant to say where he stood on issues before his retirement from the Marine Corps was official. Young wasn't worried about the colonel's dignity. He attacked, even ridiculing Glenn's accomplishment in space. During one campaign stop in February, Young sarcastically paid tribute to "America's first space heroes," and then ticked off the names of Able, Baker, Ham, and Enos, the first monkeys in flight.[12] That same month, Glenn's foes tried to capitalize on his vagueness on issues by suggesting he was a closet conservative with ties to Barry Goldwater, a leader of the GOP's growing right wing.

Glenn "felt very strong that the electorate and interest groups should elect him as a U.S. senator and then trust him to use his good judgment," said Don Oberdorfer, a frustrated campaign aide. "I tried to explain to him that under the democratic system people felt they had a right to know where the person stood when they decided whether or not to give him support." But Glenn refused to accept that common-sense premise.[13]

The aura of glamour surrounding Glenn still had strong appeal. Three days after his formal announcement, the Ohio Democratic Party, meeting in convention at the Neil House Hotel on High Street in downtown Columbus, denied the incumbent Young the party endorsement. Neither man would be anointed, but Glenn had captured a majority of the votes cast on the convention floor. He rejected an overture from the Young camp for support in a campaign for congress at large if Glenn would drop out of the Senate race. He was now in the contest to stay, or so he thought.

What happened next became part of Ohio political lore, an incident from *The Twilight Zone.* John Glenn, a man who successfully circled the globe three times just two years earlier, slipped on a bathroom throw rug while trying to adjust a sliding cabinet mirror. Glenn went crashing into the porcelain edge of the bathtub. It happened in a Columbus apartment loaned by a campaign backer, who still resided in Houston. As Glenn fell to the floor and the mirror landed on top of him, the crashing sound alerted Oberdorfer, who had been waiting for him in the living room. The former newspaper reporter found Glenn, bleeding from the head, in a heap in the steamy room. "Call for help," a dazed Glenn whispered. He had to be carried out of the place and was taken to the emergency room of a nearby hospital.

The impact damaged his left ear. "Whenever I moved my head a little too fast, the whole world would spin," Glenn later recalled. "It would take me ten minutes just to work my way from the bedroom downstairs to the couch. For nine months, I was afraid that I'd have to live the rest of my days like that."[14] Glenn suffered a concussion and buildup of blood and fluid in his left inner ear, damaging the vestibular system, his balance mechanism. He was nauseous and wobbly—symptoms he would struggle with for most of the remaining year.

Except for the pain, it was not unlike the woozy feeling Glenn experienced in 1998 when stepping off the space shuttle *Discovery* after living in weightless conditions for nine days. Glenn was back to normal after a couple of days following this second mission in space. But in 1964, the hero was flat on his back and hospitalized for weeks. The diagnosis was traumatic vertigo, but Glenn called it "probably the low point of my life."[15] His slow recovery from what seemed like little more than a household accident fed the rumor mill. Was Glenn suffering aftershock related to his mission in space? Was he just looking for a way out of a losing campaign? How could an athletic ex-Marine, still in top shape, get knocked out of commission slipping in a bathroom?

Glenn was inactive but still a candidate, so Young and Metzenbaum stayed on the attack. In a highly publicized letter, Metzenbaum wrote to Glenn's campaign manager, Bob Voas, who was also a NASA psychiatrist.

> Col. Glenn now has two platforms, a conservative position as related in the *Saturday Evening Post* and in some newspaper stories, and a liberal platform carried in other newspapers. . . . Ohio voters are entitled to know and in some detail, what your true position is. . . . It is quite possible that neither you, a Texan, nor Colonel Glenn, who has not lived in Ohio for twenty-two years, understands the degrees to which Ohio voters insist on having a candidate's views made clear. . . . If this confusion persists, we Ohio voters may well wind up needing your professional psychiatric services.[16]

The notion that the inscrutable Glenn was driving Ohio voters nuts was a reach, but his campaign *was* tottering. Annie Glenn, afflicted with a stammer from childhood, and Rene Carpenter, spouse of fellow *Mercury* 7 astronaut Scott Carpenter, hit the campaign trail in Ohio on behalf of the felled candidate. Glenn held on as the favorite in some quarters, and Young and Metzenbaum saw the peril in making a martyr out of the bedridden marine. But Glenn was discouraged and in pain, and his doctors urged him to quit the contest.

It went against his grain, but he didn't want to be an absentee candidate, so he took their advice. He made his withdrawal statement with his wife, Annie, by his side from a hospital bed at Wilford Hall Air Force Hospital in San Antonio on March 30. He sounded like his critics: "I do not want to run just as a well-known name. No man has a right to ask for a seat in either branch of Congress merely because of a specific event, such as orbiting the Earth in a spacecraft, anymore than he would have the right to just by being a lawyer and having tried a few cases at the local courthouse."[17]

Wayne Hays, acerbic and outspoken, had lobbied Glenn not to drop out. When he did, Hays was angry and suggested Glenn had been looking for an escape hatch from a tough campaign. Embarrassed by his political misjudgment, Hays took it out on Glenn. "He claimed he fell in the bathtub. Hardly anybody believed him. I didn't argue with him. I talked to him earlier and he talked about dropping out, and I just finally said to myself, 'to hell with him.' . . . He had that goddamn psychiatrist [Bob Voas] around him all the time, and he wouldn't do anything unless he consulted him. Everybody in the party was getting fed up," Hays said.[18]

Most people in the party had stuck with Young. But it was too late to get Glenn's name off the primary ballot and he drew almost 207,000 votes that spring to Young's 520,641. It should have been a warning to the Young camp. But with Glenn out of the way, Metzenbaum, perhaps overconfident, lost interest in the looming confrontation with Taft. Unlike his law partner, Byron Krantz, he was not fond of Young and regarded his 1958 victory over Bricker as almost a fluke, attributable to the right-to-work initiative and Metzenbaum's own political guile.

That summer, Chuck Baker, a Toledo-based consultant who was managing the day-to-day activities of the Young campaign, pleaded with Metzenbaum to take charge. His laissez-faire attitude ignored the reality that Taft's organization was quickly gaining a tactical and financial advantage, Baker cautioned.

"When we let the opposition get so far ahead of us in organization, planning and money, I was not surprised. The fact that no awareness of this fact appears to have penetrated the top echelon startles the hell out of me," Baker wrote in an angry memo to Metzenbaum. "The heart of a campaign is policy and planning. There is no discernible policy, and if any planning has been done beyond my own, it is so well hidden that is escapes my vision. . . . My frank evaluation is that you have done so little homework in the policy-planning area that we cannot talk the same language at the moment."[19] Two days later, Baker told Metzenbaum, "It seems to me you are so concerned about your personal role that you aren't taking a cold look at what is needed. . . . You exercise the right to make a decision off the top of your head, without doing enough homework to make the right decision."[20]

Metzenbaum was busy developing a national profile with Democratic Party insiders through his work on behalf of Senator Young and his political fund-raising prowess. He was one of the better-known Ohioans at the 1964 Democratic National Convention in Atlantic City. "Metzenbaum certainly knew a fair number of people from the national scene," said Stern, who accompanied him to the convention.[21] Back in Ohio, Metzenbaum jumped into the fray just in time to salvage the Young campaign. The incumbent senator benefited from a huge Democratic year as voters in Ohio and other states leaned toward Johnson rather than take a risk on the right-wing policies of Republican Barry Goldwater. His views were so controversial that Metzenbaum and other Young advisors tried to dream up ways to link the moderate Taft with Goldwater or other right-wing groups.

Meanwhile, the struggle inside the campaign was to control the blunt-talking Young, who did not take well to political handlers. Again, Baker vented his frustration with Metzenbaum. "I personally do not believe SMY [Young] will ever agree to follow orders. . . . I don't believe he'd do it for any man."[22] At one point, Krantz said, a rumor circulated that Young had died. "Reports of my death were premature," Young said after getting off a plane, alive and well, at Washington National Airport.[23] Harold Stern devised a signal meant to stifle Young when he went off on one of his rambles. "When I would take out my handkerchief and blow my nose, he was supposed to shut up. He didn't pay attention to that. It didn't work."[24]

Metzenbaum, Stern, Baker, and Byron Krantz rallied the campaign that fall, finally taking advantage of the momentum created by Johnson's surge ahead of Goldwater. "We felt the only way we could be comfortable and win that campaign was to hang on to Johnson's coattails as strongly as we could," said Stern.[25] Metzenbaum had spent $45,000 in campaign money managing Young's five-point victory over Bricker in 1958. This time, he poured more than four times that amount into the contest, helping Young win by 16,827 votes, less than 0.5 percent.

On election night, with a slow tabulation at Secretary of State Ted Brown's office, Taft led into the early morning hours, apparently overcoming the Democratic tide. Krantz, following the count at Young's headquarters in Cleveland, walked out in disgust shortly after midnight, flinging the office keys into the street. He was awakened at four AM by a telephone call from Stern at the board of elections. A computer error in Columbus had skewed the earlier results. Returns from Cuyahoga, Lucas, and Hamilton counties were still being counted. A Taft victory in Hamilton, which included his hometown of Cincinnati, was a forgone conclusion. But it could be more than offset by a big Democratic vote in the other two counties, which included Cleveland and Toledo.

Krantz immediately phoned Metzenbaum, rousing him in his Shaker Heights home. "Howard told me exactly who to call in those three counties to make sure the election wasn't stolen," Krantz said. By daybreak, Young had pulled ahead to stay. But the senator, a notoriously early riser, had already left by car for Washington, a seven-hour drive from Cleveland. Krantz called the Ohio Highway Patrol in an effort to flag him down with the good news. No luck. Complicating matters, the young lawyer was locked out of the campaign office after his tantrum with the keys. Krantz set up shop in his own office at the Metzenbaum law firm and mulled over what to do next.

Krantz later recalled receiving a phone call from someone who claimed he was the president. "Of what?" asked Krantz. "Of the United States," said the voice on the other end. President Johnson, a good friend of the senator, had called looking for Steve. Krantz gave the president the election news but said he still had not tracked down the senator. Then, still stunned by the phone call, Krantz hung up. The highway patrol eventually located Young, so by the time he got back to Washington, he knew it would be his home for another six years.[26]

By 1968, Lyndon Johnson's presidency was in ruins. It was a year of bloodshed, not only in Vietnam, but also in Memphis, Los Angeles, and Chicago. Metzenbaum could see some of the changes blowing through society in his own teenage daughters and their friends. The oldest, Barbara, went to the University of Wisconsin "in plaid," and "came out a hippie" by her own account. Barbara became a student activist. She let her short blond hair grow out, dressed in bellbottom jeans, and listened to rock and "farout" jazz. Metzenbaum tolerated the lifestyle changes of the late '60s and supported his daughter's political activity. He advised Barbara not to follow the crowd but to understand the issues and make her mind up based on her own understanding. And "under all circumstances," he said, "keep the lines of communication open between us."[27]

Back in Shaker Heights, the Metzenbaum daughters threw large, interracial parties around the family's backyard swimming pool. Metzenbaum, more comfortable in business attire than in jeans, didn't smoke and rarely drank alcohol. "He would walk through just to let us know he was there," said Susan Metzenbaum.[28] He was also strongly antidrug and let his daughters know it. "He was very worried about sex, drugs, and rock and roll," said Barbara.[29]

On the political front, debate in the presidential campaign centered on the Vietnam War and past rioting in major cities like Detroit and Cleveland. Robert Kennedy was assassinated in June 1968, and Eugene McCarthy's antiwar candidacy faded over the summer months. At their raucous convention in Chicago, divided Democrats nominated Vice President Hubert H. Humphrey. Metzenbaum, though opposed to the war and horrified by the police brutality in dealing with demonstrators, supported the nominee, a man he had respected for years.

In Ohio, another battle was raging. Conservative Democrat Frank J. Lausche of Cleveland was in the political fight of his life against Congressman John J. Gilligan, an upstart from Cincinnati. A *New York Times* article by reporter Jim Naughton set the scene.

> If Lausche gets dumped it will be less because of his opponent's campaign than because of the mood of the sixties. Growing ranks of young voters are showing concern for, of all things, issues. They are looking for stances on Vietnam, crime, poverty, taxes, civil rights. They respect fresh ideas. They like liberal Jack Gilligan.
>
> But there are a lot of their elders left in Ohio as elsewhere. Less liberal in outlook, they are still impressed with the traditional fist-banging oratory. They respect Frank Lausche's flag-waving style, like his loud shouts for economy in government, and identify with his self-engineered rise from the old ghetto—the ethnic East European immigrant neighborhood—through the governorship to the United States Senate.
>
> Most politicians in Ohio do not think the new breed is yet numerous enough to take charge by electing a Jack Gilligan. Tuesday will tell.[30]

Tuesday told. Lausche, once a popular governor with a strong ethnic base and crossover appeal to Republicans, was seeking his third Senate term. But he had worn out his welcome with Ohio's powerful labor unions and offered little to younger voters—danger signals in a Democratic primary. Metzenbaum, still simmering twenty years after Lausche's belated and reluctant support of his fair-employment bill, backed Cincinnati's Gilligan over the senator from Cleveland.

Lausche, who had won reelection by twenty-three points in 1962, recognized the peril too late, handing Gilligan a huge upset. In November, Gilligan lost the general election to popular Ohio attorney general William Saxbe by a slim 114,000 votes out of the more than 3.7 million ballots cast. But the Democrat used his strong showing as motivation for a governor's race two years later. The moderate Saxbe managed to reclaim the Republican votes that had belonged to Lausche in previous elections and stole some union votes from the Democrat.

"At each stop I'd put a plug of Mail Pouch chewing tobacco in my cheek before I left the bus, and it became my calling card with the plant workers," Saxbe said in a postmortem. "They seemed to love it when I directed a stream of juice into a nearby trash bin. I became one of them; they began to listen to what I had to say, and I listened to them, too." Saxbe later said that the two main campaign issues were the Vietnam War and crime. "The voters wanted an end to both, and I promised I would do what I could do to get that accomplished in Washington," he later wrote.[31] But Metzenbaum saw positives in Gilligan's narrow defeat: a modern-day liberal had a chance in Republican-leaning Ohio. All he had to do was put together the right coalition, a variation on Lausche's formula.

Taking on a Legend

The next year Metzenbaum let it be known that he was available if Steve Young, then eighty, decided not to run for reelection in 1970. Figuring that Glenn was also again eyeing Young's seat, Metzenbaum offered himself as the seasoned, dues-paying Democrat—an alternative to an interloper.

That was good enough for Maynard E. "Jack" Sensenbrenner, the God-and-country mayor of Columbus. Jack Sensenbrenner was no liberal. Almost always bedecked in an oversized American flag lapel pin, he was antagonistic to antiwar students who demonstrated on the OSU campus, just two miles from the mayor's office. But he was a loyal Democrat and a party builder who created a "Kennedy Room" at City Hall and surrounded himself with an "Irish Mafia" of Dorrians and O'Shaughnessys. The Sensenbrenner organization established a foothold for Democrats in Franklin County.

Sensenbrenner's affection for Metzenbaum was an early example of the Cleveland liberal's ability to appeal to conservatives. And so after a routine meeting with Metzenbaum at city hall overlooking the banks of the Scioto River, Sensenbrenner emerged with an unexpected announcement. "If Howard Metzenbaum decides to run for the United States Senate, I intend to support him," he told reporters, who had no idea an endorsement was in the offing.[32]

Days passed, busy days. Metzenbaum ferried back and forth between Cleveland and Columbus, meeting with party regulars and identifying contributors. He was gaining confidence. "If it looks like John Glenn is going to walk into the Senate seat unopposed," he said, "I just may run against him. Of course, I'm no longer Howard Metzenbaum, boy legislator, but it could be interesting."[33]

Early in 1970, Metzenbaum got his chance when Young announced his retirement from the Senate. Glenn and Metzenbaum declared their candidacies in swift succession. But Metzenbaum was regarded as an afterthought, an unrecognized face to most voters and running against Ohio's homegrown hero. He was far behind in the early polling.

About a month after the official announcement, Glenn sought a confidential face-to-face meeting with Metzenbaum. The two sat down in a hotel room in Mansfield, Ohio, midway between Cleveland and Toledo. Glenn, in later years, said he didn't recall the get-together, but Harold Stern, who was with Metzenbaum, described it this way: "John Glenn said to Metzenbaum, 'You should withdraw from the race. You're not going to win it and it's not good for the party. You haven't got a chance.'" Metzenbaum refused on the spot but did not appear offended by Glenn's presumption. "It was a matter-of-fact thing. We were more confident that Howard could win, obviously, than Glenn was. It didn't rattle us," Stern said.[34]

Metzenbaum knew Glenn had a lot of friends in high places, including the compound at Hyannisport. But Glenn's relationship with the Kennedy family did not extend to Senator Ted Kennedy, a friend of Metzenbaum for more than ten years. Thanks to the Teddy connection, Metzenbaum hired media specialist Charles Guggenheim to produce television commercials—ads of a quality and quantity never before seen in Ohio. Glenn, trying to micromanage his campaign, did his own TV ads, standard fare featuring him sitting at a desk, speaking directly to voters. By contrast, Guggenheim introduced cinema verité, slices of life that were meant to dramatize the need for change in Ohio.

He portrayed Glenn as a military man, out of touch with the lives of everyday people in the state. "We mapped out a strategy," Stern said. "What we thought was that Glenn didn't get it."[35]

By springtime, Metzenbaum, the former "Howard Who?" of 5 percent name recognition, began to smell victory. The county chairmen knew who he was and the rest of the state was finding out, even if it seemed like "millionaire Cleveland businessman" was part of his name. The state had never elected a Jew as senator or governor.

"In newspapers of the 1970s, Cleveland Jewish businessman precedes Howard Metzenbaum's name a very large number of times," said Cleveland political consultant Bob Dykes. "The press would defend themselves by saying, well, no one knows who this guy is, so we need to give him a shorthand."[36] He wore an oversized lapel pin for the benefit of downstaters, announcing, "Hi! I'm Howard Metzenbaum." Everywhere he went, he rallied "Metz fans," borrowing from the New York Mets' improbable World Series victory the previous October. "I have to let people know who I am and what I stand for," he said.[37]

Maybe Howard Metzenbaum couldn't run against an American hero, but he could run around him. "Glenn could not escape marginally valuable autograph sessions with school children well below voting age; Metzenbaum had no such time-wasting troubles," noted *Time*.[38] He would shake voters' hands while Glenn signed autographs. When a heckler at OSU threw marshmallows at him, Metzenbaum caught a few and threw them back, to a roar of approval from a rally crowd.

Metzenbaum, quick with the needle, almost always referred to his rival as "Colonel" Glenn, a not-so-subtle way to introduce the Vietnam War into the campaign. After U.S. troops were accused of massacring civilians in My Lai, Vietnam, Glenn said blame should rest with higher-ups who permitted the area to become a free-fire zone—that is, shoot anything that moves. Metzenbaum agreed the GIs involved should not be made scapegoats. But he skipped the nuances in framing the larger picture. "How can I condemn an eighteen-year-old boy who was taught to hate, taught to kill, taught to destroy, by the best military machine in the world?" he asked. "War makes men animals—barbaric, cruel, cunning animals, whose only objective is to keep alive."[39]

When President Nixon invaded Cambodia on April 30, Metzenbaum sharply criticized the move and demanded a date for the withdrawal of

U.S. troops. Glenn also questioned the war, but he held back criticism of the so-called incursion, not wanting to do anything that would harm American soldiers or morale in wartime.

Senator Young also piled it on, trying to make an issue of Glenn's work as an executive for New York–based Royal Crown International, parent company of RC Cola. Even though the soft drink company was headquartered in Columbus, Glenn and his wife lived for a time in a well-appointed apartment near Royal Crown International's corporate offices on Madison Avenue in midtown Manhattan. Glenn and his family, Young said, "have never lived in Ohio. He has never helped any Ohio Democratic candidate for county, state, or national office."[40]

At a debate in Dayton, Glenn lost his cool after Metzenbaum charged that he was inconsistent on gun control and the appropriateness of government subsidies. "When you say I go around the state saying one thing in one place and another thing in another, you lie, Howard. You're a liar." Metzenbaum had been called a liar before. It didn't shake him. "When you said I lie, sir, you lie about that, sir," he replied calmly.[41] Glenn, infuriated, rose quickly from his chair ready to challenge Metzenbaum, but a Democratic Party functionary held him back and eased him into his seat.

What enraged Glenn more were the rumors of trouble in his marriage to the former Anna Castor. Scandal sheets hinted that Glenn had had trysts with Ethel Kennedy and actress Claudine Longet during ski vacations in Vail, Colorado. His marriage was said to be on the rocks. Glenn came to believe that Metzenbaum's right-hand man, Stern, was behind some of the rumors. Stern always denied it, but Glenn blamed him for many of the hard feelings. After the campaign in Columbus, Glenn ran into Stern in the Neil House lobby and pinned the smaller, bespectacled man against a wall. "The next time I walk into the room, you walk out," Glenn told Stern. "And anytime you see me, walk away from me because I'll hit you."[42] In subsequent years, Glenn said he didn't threaten to slug Stern, but he did not deny other aspects of the incident.

Glenn still thought he should be immune from the rough and tumble of politics. And for his part, he would not hype or distort—much less lie—because, after all, he was the good Presbyterian, the war hero, the astronaut. It was a self-fulfilling attitude among some politicians that the *Columbus Citizen-Journal* columnist Joe Dirck would later refer to as "the tyranny of the good."[43] In 1970, "Glenn still had not shed the naive concept that heroism entitled him to public office. That so many other Ohio Democratic politicians seemed to agree only set Glenn up for the difficulties that lay ahead," Frank Van Riper wrote in *Glenn: The Astronaut Who Would Be President*.[44]

At the entry level, Glenn had good political instincts that set him apart from the other *Mercury 7* astronauts, even before his orbital flight in 1962. He was eager for the limelight and knew when to speak up and "toot my own horn" in a modest way. Throughout his political career, he maintained the image of a moderate, even though he was in the liberal mainstream of his party.

All of this was to Glenn's advantage. He was capable of taking the superficial first step but had difficulty implementing the make-it-work second step. Metzenbaum raised more than $800,000—including several hundred thousand dollars in donations from family members—and aired the most sophisticated television advertising campaign ever seen in Ohio. Glenn's campaign was amateurish by comparison. According to author Frank Van Riper, Glenn analyzed his botched campaign this way:

> My supporters told me the primary would be a snap. I was taking nothing for granted, but I had trouble convincing them I needed a war chest for the primary. They didn't think I would need much money until the fall and what promised to be a tough general election fight against the likely Republican senatorial nominee, Robert Taft. When the polls tightened during the primary campaign, it was too late. Metzenbaum was better funded and better organized. He ran well-produced TV spots and had 15 offices around the state. Toward the end of the campaign, he was outspending me by four to one.[45]

Metzenbaum targeted his vote, building a coalition of union members, blacks, Jews, antiwar students, and liberal activists who found him more in tune with the times than bland Colonel Glenn. Metzenbaum was usually on the offensive: more ardent in his opposition to the war and more eager to get the federal government involved in such matters as aid to education and controlling pollution in Lake Erie. "I didn't give Howard much of a shot. I think it was in Canton, about ten days out, he told me, 'Joe, I think I'm going to win it,'" political reporter Joe Rice recalled.[46]

While Metzenbaum cultivated the grass roots, Glenn acted as if he were due another promotion. He was soft on issues, and he did little to reach out to the Democratic Party base. He was outspent two to one, even though he had the potential to raise money all over the country. Political scientist Richard F. Fenno Jr. said candidate Glenn "lunched with Rotarians instead of Democrats, and he hardly campaigned in Cleveland's heavily Democratic black wards. . . . He paid little attention to the party's allies in organized labor."[47]

Metzenbaum eventually picked up newspaper endorsements from the *Dayton Journal-Herald* and the *Akron Beacon Journal,* which said he "pioneered in the areas of civil rights and consumer protection" during his time in the Ohio legislature. The *Plain Dealer* and the *Cleveland Press* backed Glenn. And in the final weekend of coverage, the *Press* predicted Glenn's triumph on its news pages but warned, "Watch out for an upset."[48]

Then, the day before the primary, May 4, 1970, Ohio National Guardsmen, dispatched by Governor James A. Rhodes, shot and killed four students during an antiwar rally at Kent State University. The tragedy may not have hurt Rhodes politically with the GOP base—many Ohioans were fed up with unruly antiwar activists—but the two-term governor lost the Senate Republican primary to Taft, who edged him by 0.5 percent. On the Democratic side, the tragic incident galvanized antiwar sentiment, bringing out voters who trusted Metzenbaum with the issue more than Glenn.

On election night, Glenn carried seventy-six of Ohio's eighty-eight counties, but Metzenbaum prevailed in the large population centers, including Cleveland, and came away with the upset victory by just over 13,000 votes. To the shock of much of the nation, Ohio voters had passed over Glenn. It turned out to be the only election he would ever lose in his home state. Glenn said he didn't know whether the Kent State tragedy had made the difference but observed that "Metzenbaum was vocally against the war, while my questions had focused mainly on its conduct." In the aftermath, feeling like he had been sucker punched, Glenn said he "toted up the political lessons I still had to learn." One, he soon decided, was that "politics was sometimes a waiting game." His moment would come.[49] Metzenbaum, in a matter-of-fact analysis of his victory, attributed much of his success to his use of television, calling it a "powerful medium."[50]

Taking on a Taft

Metzenbaum went right to work on the fall campaign against Robert Taft. Knowing he would have difficulty winning newspaper endorsements in Columbus, Cincinnati, and perhaps even in his hometown, he went back to Toledo, a Democratic base. This time he met Paul Block in Dyer's Chophouse, a white-tablecloth restaurant that had once been an all-male bastion in downtown Toledo. Metzenbaum fully expected Block to endorse him, but Block hedged. "You know, Howard," he said during the meeting, "with some families there is just sort of a dynasty. And that's how it is with the Tafts."[51] Metzenbaum walked out, shaking his head.

In a parallel political universe, Taft's heavyweight championship match against Rhodes had energized Republicans, who were not used to contested primaries. Republican voters came out in droves—940,000 strong. The party, alerted to the liberal threat posed by Metzenbaum, united behind Taft, who slipped past Rhodes by a mere 5,270 votes. The race between the two GOP giants enticed nearly one million Republicans to the polls and "helped dad win the race in November," said Taft's son, Bob Taft, the onetime Ohio governor.[52]

Metzenbaum preferred Taft as an opponent to Rhodes, whose populism transcended the country club and drew in Democrats and independents. Rhodes was a mainstream Republican, but no ideologue. His emphasis was always "jobs, jobs, jobs." He bashed federal government spending but spread the wealth when it came to state tax dollars during his two terms as governor. Rhodes delighted in going over the heads of union leaders, promising jobs to blue-collar workers and pay raises to teachers. Metzenbaum had observed Rhodes's success with bemused admiration ever since the onetime Columbus mayor upset Democrat Joseph "Jumping Joe" Ferguson in the 1952 state auditor's race. Arguably, Rhodes was getting votes from so-called Reagan Democrats before Ronald Reagan gave them a name in the 1980 presidential election.

Stretching the point a little, perhaps, *Cleveland Press* political writer Roy Meyers said Metzenbaum "dreaded the thought of running against Rhodes, or Saxbe, because they were so much like him"[53]—blunt, plain-talking populists. No, Metzenbaum wanted to take on the cautious, lackluster Taft, heir to a stubborn brand of midwestern conservatism that still played well in doughty old Cincinnati but seemed out of sync with a society in transition. Taft still had the name—son of Mr. Republican, grandson of a president—and Metzenbaum was still Metzenbaum, the millionaire Cleveland businessman, who, by the way, was Jewish.

"Bob Taft had narrowly lost [to Young] in 1964 in the Goldwater landslide, and Howard was running for the first time. Now arguably," said Bob Dykes, "Bob Taft had run before, had a fabulous political name, and it wasn't 1964 again, so he figured to win that race."[54]

Ohioans, it seems, like to get comfortable with candidates before voting them into office. There are many examples of politicians who went on to successful careers in statewide office after their first loss in an all-Ohio general election. Gilligan, Saxbe, Mike DiSalle, and now Glenn had been snubbed before later winning. Rhodes was trounced by Lausche in a 1954 governor's race, although he had won statewide two years earlier in the auditor's contest. So the odds were against first-time candidate Metzenbaum, the parking lot entrepreneur from Cleveland.

He got no help from Glenn. Summoned to the Neil House for a public endorsement of Metzenbaum, Glenn tried to back out, telling Democratic Party stalwart Pete O'Grady, "I just can't do it."[55] O'Grady took him to a private room in the hotel, preached about being a good Democrat, pleaded with him not to embarrass the party, and finally turned Glenn around. He offered Metzenbaum a tepid endorsement and then disappeared for the rest of the campaign.

Glenn's stature—not his political advice—would have been helpful to Metzenbaum, who wanted credibility in a contest against what Paul Block and others saw as a political dynasty. Of course, he knew Taft's record and felt he had already beaten him once as Young's campaign manager in 1964. He portrayed the incumbent as an out-of-touch, do-little congressman who missed key votes and opposed higher spending on popular programs like veterans' medical care.

After the Kent State shootings, there was no way to keep Vietnam out of a contest for the U.S. Senate, a body with power to provide or withhold money for waging war. Taft tried to defuse the war as an issue, depicting himself as a peace candidate nudging his president, Richard Nixon, toward a "just and peaceful conclusion" of the conflict. Taft avoided Vice President Spiro Agnew, who had been critical of a commission investigating the Kent State shootings. H. R. Haldeman, in a published diary of his years as Nixon's chief of staff, noted the president's displeasure when Taft skipped a dinner honoring Agnew in Cleveland that June. Presidential assistant Bryce Harlow pressured Taft to reconsider. This "ended with Taft calling Harlow and refusing to go, really stupid. P[resident] really furious about his attitude and says he won't help him campaign," wrote Haldeman.[56]

But Metzenbaum, too, was hitting some bumps in the road. Three years before the U.S. Supreme Court legalized abortion, he accused Taft of favoring a "liberal New York abortion law."[57] Taft took what would later be regarded as a pro-choice position, saying there should be no federal law on abortion. Privately, Metzenbaum's teenage daughters were aghast at their father's position.

More embarrassing from a liberal perspective, since it was not a new issue, was Metzenbaum's stance on gun control. He did not support it and backed the right of anyone to own a firearm.[58] This was only two years after gunmen cut down Martin Luther King Jr. and Robert F. Kennedy and after Congress passed the landmark Gun Control Act of 1968. Metzenbaum did, however, advocate a three-day waiting period for the purchase of a handgun. And in later years, as a champion of gun control and abortion rights laws, Metzenbaum would be unsparing in his denunciations of his opponents on those divisive issues.

Two weeks before the election, the *Cleveland Press* reported ominous poll findings for Metzenbaum. Taft trailed him by fewer than seven percentage points in his home base of Cuyahoga County, a Democratic stronghold where the party's candidate was expected to win by more than 100,000 votes to offset losses to Republicans downstate. "I grew up with Metzenbaum and I don't like him," the *Press* quoted an unidentified Euclid voter as saying.[59]

Metzenbaum had been put on the defensive by revelations about his past connections with leftist groups, such as the Ohio School of Social Sciences and the National Lawyers Guild. Confronted in Columbus by a right-wing radio reporter, he lost his temper and angrily insisted he didn't owe anyone an explanation about something that occurred twenty-five years earlier. "He just flabbergasted me with the question. I guess I so much resented that red-baiting that I think I reacted more strongly than I needed to. I don't think that cost me the election."[60]

But Metzenbaum always maintained that the difference between victory and defeat in a close race could be traced to the week before the election when the issue of anti-Semitism surfaced in his campaign against Taft. It came twenty-two years after the rejection of his bid to become the first Jewish majority leader of the Ohio Senate. On October 28, 1970, Sargent Shriver spoke to Metzenbaum partisans at the old Statler Hilton hotel in downtown Cleveland. In his speech, Shriver decried personal attacks against Metzenbaum, linking the Ohio broadsides to a "Republican tactic all over the country." The former Peace Corps director never accused Taft of anti-Semitism but said, "After this election, no one will think anything of a Jewish person running for the Senate from Ohio."[61] For his part, Metzenbaum said the campaign proved the American electoral system worked when, "in Ohio, with a name as difficult as Metzenbaum, you can run for the U.S. Senate against a famous name like Taft and still be neck and neck."[62]

A name as "difficult" as Metzenbaum? How did you spell it? Was he Jewish? German? Metzenbaum was, in fact, trying to become Ohio's first Jewish senator, but he had not emphasized his religion any more than he stressed his liberalism. He had, after all, started the campaign against Glenn as "Howard Who?" and despite the media's capsule of him as rich and Jewish, his background was not widely understood by the average voter. "Nobody knew," he said, years later. "I didn't make an issue of it. I didn't run around the state and say, I'm Jewish."[63] He didn't campaign in a yarmulke, but neither did he hide his religion. Anyone who was around Metzenbaum for any length of time came to understand that his Jewishness was an important part of him, even if his outlook was secular. Many of his closest advisors and law partners were Jewish; he counted rabbis among his confidants, and he had a long-standing relationship with the Fairmount Temple, a reform synagogue in Beachwood.

It is apparent that Metzenbaum and his family had their share of run-ins with anti-Semitism over the years. But he downplayed it because, as his daughter Shelley said, "He never let the bad stuff get in his way."[64] The family was not particularly observant, but, said Susan Metzenbaum, "We were very aware of being Jewish." Well into adulthood, Susan and her sisters remembered disturbing incidents: armed guards appearing for brief spells at their Shaker Heights home following vague threats and concerns about suspicious packages that turned out to be harmless. Susan said she was spit at and called a "Yid" while campaigning for her father in 1970 in Parma, a conservative, blue-collar Cleveland suburb.[65] And Amy Metzenbaum recalled anonymous telephone calls denouncing her father as a "Commie kike."[66]

It is highly doubtful that Shriver or Metzenbaum knew then of the anti-Semitic comments attributed to Richard Nixon in the early 1970s. And Shriver's references to anti-Jewish smears at the Statler Hilton were only a part of his speech. But the *Plain Dealer* reported in its story that Shriver "implied" Taft was "responsible" for anti-Semitic attacks.[67] Metzenbaum was enraged by the newspaper's account, believing it gratuitously raised an issue that had been kept in the background. Now Taft had cover. He could knock down a straw man and highlight Metzenbaum's religion while sanctimoniously denying any hint of anti-Semitism in his campaign. "It wasn't a major focus point of his speech, but Shriver did bring up anti-Semitism, not accusing Taft, but in a generic sense," said Harold Stern, who attended the speech with Metzenbaum. "The *Plain Dealer* made a bigger thing out of it than was justified from a straight news story, which then played into Taft's hands. At the time, we felt it was a very bad hit to take, you know. And it was something we couldn't do anything about."[68]

A few days earlier Taft had disavowed a newspaper advertisement that tried to make an issue of Metzenbaum's religion. But at the annual preelection City Club debate in Cleveland, the day after Shriver's speech, Taft did exactly what Metzenbaum and Stern had feared, using newspaper accounts of the speech as a wedge. A phantom smear of Metzenbaum became a "shameful" smear of Taft. After all, his father, the late senator Robert Taft, was an early and ardent supporter of the struggle to establish Israel as a Jewish nation-state. "The attempt to smear me as anti-Semitic is a reflection upon the record of my father and his efforts in behalf of the State of Israel," Taft huffed.[69] Third-party candidate Richard B. Kay also went after Metzenbaum, questioning $480,000 in gifts contributed to Metzenbaum's campaign by members of his own family, including one of his daughters. When Kay said Metzenbaum had yet to explain his affiliation with groups once listed by the Justice Department as subversive, the red-baiting drew a smattering of boos from the luncheon crowd. But the damage was done.

Metzenbaum was certain Taft had exploited his Jewish faith by needlessly renouncing statements he had not been directly accused of making. Taft and his aides denied it, and Taft never behaved in a way suggesting he had any tolerance for anti-Semitism. Stanley Aronoff, a Taft campaign advisor who was Jewish (and later president of the Ohio Senate), called the assertion ludicrous. But Metzenbaum was so angry about the *Plain Dealer*'s coverage that he sought revenge by complaining personally to S. I. Newhouse of the Newhouse publishing house, which owned the Cleveland paper. It seemed Newhouse and Metzenbaum were neighbors at Casabriasa, an Acapulco resort they both frequented.

On election day, Taft beat Metzenbaum by just over two percentage points—76,000 votes out of more than 3 million cast across the state. Metzenbaum carried Cuyahoga County, but only by 61,000 votes, well under the 100,000 margin that Democrats expected would offset Republican advantages downstate. He didn't blame anti-Semitism for his low total in Cuyahoga County, which has strong Jewish voting blocs. But one had to wonder. Metzenbaum's margins in Lucas (Toledo), Summit (Akron), and Montgomery (Dayton) counties were also disappointing, given their Democratic majorities. Taft carried Hamilton (Cincinnati), Franklin (Columbus), and most of the Republican-leaning rural and suburban counties.

Taft put more than $1 million into his winning campaign, slightly outspending his Democratic opponent. In all, Metzenbaum spent more than $1.6 million in 1970 on the general election and the primary against Glenn, a huge sum for that period. Yet he ended up losing. But he was no longer "Howard Who?" He was a player who came within two percentage points of beating the Taft name after starting his campaign as a little-known candidate in most of the state. "When I ran in 1970 I had a difficult time convincing myself I would have a chance of winning even a primary over John Glenn. I told myself, you're nobody in the state of Ohio. Who's Howard Metzenbaum?"[70] That question had been answered. Metzenbaum was an established politician. And Shriver turned out to be right about the future for Jewish candidates: Metzenbaum's religious affiliation was not an issue in his subsequent races for public office.

Similar to his reaction after failing to capture the Ohio Senate leader's post twenty years earlier, he didn't retreat to the weed patch after coming up short in 1970. He wasn't discouraged. He became an active voice in national Democratic politics and an ally of the brash new governor, John J. Gilligan, who had defeated Republican state auditor Roger Cloud. For practical purposes, Metzenbaum kept right on campaigning. He hit the rubber-chicken circuit, crisscrossing the state for county dinners and fund-raisers for other candidates. He was solidifying his contacts outside of Cleveland. Metzenbaum knew running against

Republican Bill Saxbe in 1974 would be tough duty, but, if necessary, he could wait until 1976 for another shot at the Taft dynasty.

During the 1972 presidential campaign, Metzenbaum embarrassed himself on the Sunday before the Ohio primary. He endorsed Democratic presidential candidate George McGovern while sharing the stage at a Cleveland Heights shopping center with McGovern's rival, Hubert Humphrey. The former vice president had already given a peppery speech to the crowd of 3,000, mostly young marchers for the Jewish Welfare Fund Appeal. With no warning of what was to come, Humphrey sat nearby, staring at his shoes as Metzenbaum declared, "I have today publicly endorsed the candidacy of George McGovern." Explaining afterward, Metzenbaum said, "the accelerated pace of the war in Vietnam had made it crystal clear to me I can no longer remain inactive."[71]

Metzenbaum's belated activism in the presidential race didn't matter in the larger scheme of things. Humphrey won the Ohio primary without his help. But some Democrats were furious with Metzenbaum for the slight of the "Happy Warrior," a revered figure in American politics. "After voting in the last election for Howard Metzenbaum for senator, I am now thrilled he lost," said one enraged letter writer to the *Plain Dealer.* "Anyone who is so callous as to verbally slap a presidential candidate in the face, as Metzenbaum did to Humphrey, deserves failure if that is an example of his political savoir-faire."[72]

Embarrassed for one of the few times in his life, Metzenbaum wrote his own letter to Humphrey and released it publicly. "My humble apologies to you! The decision to appear at the rally Sunday was a last minute one—since I didn't decide to endorse Sen. McGovern until that morning. I owed you the courtesy of advising you. Then, I added to the discourtesy by making public my endorsement from the platform instead of just reading McGovern's statement."[73]

Metzenbaum got clobbered, so he apologized. Humphrey accepted with a gracious response. Metzenbaum was fifty-four, but far from a finished product. Ohio is not New York; rudeness is not attractive in the Midwest. He could still overstep the fine line in politics between aggressiveness and crassness—and it would cost him dearly in his next campaign. Not everyone was as forgiving as Hubert Horatio Humphrey.

Glenn Wars II

The Astronaut Strikes Back

"I have held a job, Howard."
John Glenn

O hio governor John Joyce "Jack" Gilligan, an urbane liberal, once
sized up his two would-be senators with a patented wisecrack.
He was dealing with a "two-platoon system," Gilligan said. "Howard
Metzenbaum is the most offensive politician I ever met, and John
Glenn is always on the defensive."[1] Poor Gilligan was on the defensive
himself in 1973 in what initially looked like a serendipitous situation
for Ohio Democrats.

Although William B. Saxbe once questioned whether Richard Nixon
had "left his senses" with the Christmas-season bombing of North
Vietnam in 1972, Saxbe was the choice for U.S. attorney general after
Elliot Richardson resigned on October 20, 1973. Richardson and his
number-two man, William Ruckelshaus, quit rather than carry out
President Nixon's order to fire independent counsel Archibald Cox,
who had gone to court to compel the release of the White House tapes.
The "Saturday Night Massacre" elevated Saxbe, the gentleman farmer
from Mechanicsburg, Ohio, to the top law-enforcement position in the
land. And it opened a Senate seat to the Democratic governor, who
coveted the spot but couldn't get around Glenn and Metzenbaum.

"Jack wanted to appoint himself," said James Schiller, a Cleveland lawyer who worked for Gilligan before becoming Metzenbaum's campaign manager in 1974.[2] Instead, Gilligan had to deal with competition between two ambitious men with a growing hatred of each other. "I told the governor I thought Howard could be elected," said Cleveland lawyer James Friedman, Gilligan's first chief of staff. "At that point there was no issue about John Glenn. Nobody raised that with me and I was not particularly aware that John was a candidate."[3]

Glenn, who was not used to losing, had gone into a funk after the 1970 campaign. This was worse than being passed over for the space mission in May 5, 1961, when NASA chose Alan Shepard as the first American to rocket into microgravity. Shepard's flight, after all, was suborbital, and he was selected in part as a result of a straw poll of the six other *Mercury* astronauts—a majority preferred a man's man like Shepard to a straight-laced guy like Glenn.

May 5, 1970, was even harder on Glenn's considerable ego. "John Glenn does not like to end up second. I think that's obvious," said the late Stephen Kovacik, his political guru in the 1970s. "But Glenn not only wound up second, he got beat by an unknown. I mean, in Ohio for an unknown Cleveland Jew to beat one of the country's heroes is unheard of. I think that when John woke up and found out he really got clobbered he attributed it not to the fact that he ran a bad campaign, but that Howard ran a dirty campaign. It had nothing to do with Howard being a Jew. If Howard had been an American Indian, John would have hated him."[4] America, Glenn thought, always turned its back on its heroes.

Glenn was zero for two, counting his abortive 1964 effort, and this time he was also stuck with a campaign debt. He settled it for less than the full amount with some vendors and depended on postelection donations to retire the debt. To make matters worse, his mother and Annie Glenn's father died within ten weeks of each other in early 1971. "It was a big disappointment," Glenn said. "I had a few bad days, and I had to remind myself that the rest of my life was ahead. Sometimes, I have learned a failure may be a blessing in disguise. I'm not saying that I got beat the first time because there was some divine plan to give me better experience, but I think those times were very important in helping prepare me to go ahead with what I was able to accomplish later."[5]

Glenn immersed himself in business, investing much of his earnings as an RC Cola executive into Holiday Inns near the new Disney World in Orlando, Florida. But he also established a residence in a Columbus high-rise and began courting some of the political professionals and insiders he had kept at arm's length during his two failed campaigns. "I don't think anyone besides the governor went to more Jefferson-Jackson Day dinners or fund-raising events," Glenn said.[6] He had been named honorary chairman of Gilligan's successful 1970 gubernatorial campaign, and the governor returned the favor, selecting him to head a state environmental task force, associating Glenn with a dynamic new movement. This gave him a platform to use for hearings throughout the state and a share of credit for the eventual creation of Ohio's Environmental Protection Agency.

Glenn learned that running as an American hero was not enough. "He has learned from a bitter primary victory in 1974 that he had to identify himself with the party rank and file in order to win a primary," author Richard F. Fenno Jr. wrote.[7] Glenn's disappointment made him more determined to return to the fray in 1974 when the Saxbe seat was up for reelection. Both Glenn and Metzenbaum felt entitled and neither man wavered. When Saxbe announced his resignation, Glenn and Metzenbaum both lobbied the governor for the appointment.

Metzenbaum surely went to as many county dinners as Glenn. He worked hard cobbling together a coalition of labor unions, blacks, Jews, and McGovern liberals. Still, he watched his money. Once, returning from a dinner in Delaware County, just north of Columbus, he pulled over to stop for gas about halfway home to Cleveland. To the surprise of his passenger, *Plain Dealer* reporter Joe Rice, Metzenbaum purchased only $2 worth, even though he paid only thirty-two cents per gallon. When Rice asked why he did not fill up his Camaro, Metzenbaum said he preferred a station near his Shaker Heights home because he could get a deal there. "If I buy eight gallons or more, I get a free car wash," he told the incredulous writer. "That's how I got wealthy."[8]

Jack Gilligan, who won the Silver Star as a navy lieutenant during a kamikaze attack on a destroyer in World War II, didn't much care for Metzenbaum personally. But this was politics and Gilligan had his own agenda: reelection in 1974 and a possible bid for national office two years later. Naming Metzenbaum, he reasoned, would get Gilligan a big IOU from the Ohio AFL-CIO and the powerful United Auto Workers.

Cincinnati millionaire Marvin Warner, one of Gilligan's most important financial backers, also went to bat for Metzenbaum.

Politically, it was a no-brainer. But columnist Mark Shields, who managed Gilligan's 1970 campaign and was among the few in the governor's inner circle to favor a Glenn appointment, warned Gilligan that Glenn would prevail in any rematch with Metzenbaum in a Democratic primary.

Yet Metzenbaum had won the 1970 Democratic primary against Glenn and had been active in the Ohio Democratic Party for more than three decades. Gilligan expected to be reelected, and, as a big-state governor, might even be considered for the second spot on the party's national ticket in 1976. Why, the pundits asked, would Gilligan help establish "senator" Glenn as an in-state rival? The governor decided to give Metzenbaum the plum while trying to buy off Glenn with the offer of lieutenant governor and support in 1976 when the Taft seat was up for reelection.

Gilligan invited the reluctant Glenn to a closed-door meeting at the drafty governor's mansion on a tree-lined street in suburban Bexley. With Gilligan were union leaders, warning that they would back Metzenbaum if Glenn rejected the governor's offer and ran against the Clevelander. To seal the deal, Gilligan told Glenn he had also lined up Democratic chairmen from about a dozen large Ohio counties—all in favor of the compromise that would keep Glenn out of the Senate race. No dice. "The governor's people evidently thought I was going to knuckle under, but I didn't," Glenn said.[9] At a subsequent meeting of the Ohio Democratic Party executive committee, Glenn roared his defiance. He wasn't born to be lieutenant governor. He would go for broke and the political establishment be damned. No one was going to shove him aside or postpone his political destiny for the convenience of a political party.

Glenn announced his candidacy that December in Cleveland, even before Gilligan made it official and appointed Metzenbaum to the Senate. With the country in turmoil over Watergate and Vietnam, Ohio's own political civil war between the two factions of the state's Democratic Party was now under way. It pitted a self-made Jewish millionaire from the inner city against a Presbyterian boy from Smalltown, U.S.A.—a man of the left, a champion for unions and antiwar activists against America's blue-eyed hero, the fighter jock with the "right stuff."

The campaign simmered during the Watergate summer when concern over ethics in politics was in the forefront of many campaigns. This proved to be to Glenn's advantage. While Glenn and Metzenbaum did not differ sharply on issues affecting the economy, race relations, or foreign affairs, the two men had bad chemistry. They traded broadsides, often acrimoniously. "I don't think he has the slightest grasp of what it takes to function in the United States Senate," Metzenbaum said, highlighting Glenn's inexperience.[10] He also claimed his rival was getting campaign money from the oil industry and from individual Republicans. And he revved up an old charge that Glenn had voted for Richard Nixon in 1960. Senator Metzenbaum was delighted when his name and Bonda's showed up on Nixon's infamous enemies list. He called it a "mark of distinction."

When Metzenbaum held a $100-per-plate dinner and champagne reception at a four-star hotel in downtown Cleveland, Glenn followed the next night with a ninety-nine-cent corned beef dinner at the Flatiron Cafe, an old Irish bar in the Flats, along the Cuyahoga River. His featured guest was Rosie Grier, the ex-pro football player and an intimate of the Kennedy family. Glenn was building support among blacks and white working-class voters, many of them Catholic, in large urban centers like Cleveland, Toledo, and Cincinnati. At last he had a strategy. Glenn went over the heads of party bosses and liberal opinion makers. He depicted Metzenbaum as a candidate of the party elites and labor bosses—and as a man of questionable integrity during a time of disillusionment over political scandals.

The race was nasty and at times ridiculous. Both candidates fended off waves of accusations, including charges that they "lived in houses built with non-union labor."[11] Metzenbaum's money, not his mansion, gave Glenn and advisor Steve Kovacik the opening they sought. Metzenbaum's $118,358 bill from the Internal Revenue Service for writing off the failed Louisiana methane extraction plant, a tax shelter, was already a matter of record. Metzenbaum had deposited the full amount with the IRS after getting the 1973 Senate appointment with the understanding that the IRS would hold it in escrow until the dispute was settled. That was bad enough. As detailed earlier, his swearing in as Saxbe's appointed replacement in the Senate was marred by a challenge to his seating stemming from the argument with the IRS. But shortly after taking office, Metzenbaum called a meeting of his new Senate staff and campaign workers to consider an even bigger problem, one that he had so far kept quiet. Monroe W. "Bud" Karmin, a former *Wall Street Journal* reporter who shared a Pulitzer Prize in 1967, was about to be handed a public relations nightmare as Metzenbaum's first press secretary.

"I asked him, 'Do you have any skeletons in the closet?'" Karmin recalled in an interview. "He said, 'Absolutely not, no skeletons whatso-ever.' A few weeks later, we all met in Cleveland for this strategy session and he gets up and says, 'Now, about this tax problem.'"[12] Metzenbaum went on to explain how he had legally sheltered his income in 1969 to the extent that he paid no federal income taxes that year—none. Horri-fied, Karmin immediately recommended full, unambiguous disclosure. Metzenbaum resisted, fearing unfavorable publicity, particularly in the *Columbus Dispatch,* which was owned by the conservative Wolfe family. Karmin drafted two statements, one telling all; the other, obfuscating, as in "the dog ate my tax returns."

When disclosure day arrived, Metzenbaum relented. "We'll do it your way, but George Embrey will have a field day," he said of the *Dispatch*'s Washington bureau chief.[13] Sure enough, Metzenbaum's tax holiday made bold headlines on the front page of the state capital paper—and on most of the other major newspapers across the state.

Typical of his reaction when his financial dealings became public, Metzenbaum seemed unable to grasp why he was pilloried for making an aggressive but legal maneuver to keep as much of his money as he could. He didn't see the irony in the self-professed workingman's friend using the same shelters and loopholes as the oil company executives and wealthy bankers whom he tormented throughout his career in public life. "I had not been a party to any impropriety," he said. "I was getting the short end of the political stick."[14]

The irony was not lost on the media. The *Cleveland Press* editorialized that Metzenbaum "revealed he paid no federal income tax in 1969, a fact understandably resented by those who did."[15] Cleveland mayor Ralph Perk, the Republican Senate nominee, chimed in: "Mr. Metzen-baum's tax payments to Uncle Sam do not seem fair or equitable when you consider that Mr. and Mrs. Joe Citizen pay through their nose on the income tax year after year."[16] The artful tax-dodger issue was a natural for Glenn, who told of growing up as a plumber's son during the Depression, hunting rabbits for food, and selling rhubarb, grown in a family garden. He all but questioned Metzenbaum's patriotism, because he failed to pay taxes.

Glenn released his own tax returns and insisted that his adversary make public all of his financial records. But Metzenbaum offered summaries, and a full accounting only for 1973, the last year before the campaign. He had itemized clothing donated to thrift shops. Between 1967 and 1972, the "millionaire Cleveland businessman" had paid $164,000 in federal income taxes—and nothing in 1969. Glenn crowed about it, saying he too could have sheltered his income but chose not to because he didn't think it was right. "I had paid more in taxes for 1972 than my opponent had paid for 1968 through 1972 combined, and my income was less than a third of his," Glenn said.[17]

The Metzenbaum family had total assets of $6.9 million and a net worth of $3.6 million. With Kovacik egging him on, Glenn even questioned Metzenbaum's $3.3 million in liabilities, demanding to know to whom the money was owed and what Metzenbaum was hiding. "This is just like trying to get Watergate information out of the White House," Glenn said. "If he has nothing to hide, why doesn't he release everything? If there is nothing to be ashamed of why doesn't he bring it out?"[18] A pro-Glenn bumper sticker needled, "Nixon/Metzenbaum Tax Consultants."

Watergate, of course, was about public corruption, not the tax shelters of private citizens. And never mind that Glenn's fame as an astronaut helped him land an executive job with RC Cola and sent him on a path to celebrity that connected him with the rich and powerful. Schiller saw that Kovacik "for the first time put steel in the backbone of John Glenn—who I didn't have much respect for."

The irreverent Schiller, Metzenbaum's campaign manager, decided to respond in kind. He would take the heat and keep his candidate in the background. "I said, it is now apparent that both of these men are very wealthy," Schiller recalled later in an interview. "Metzenbaum started poor, worked his way through Ohio State law school, invested in parking lots, and became a wealthy man through hard work. The simple throwaway for us was: Colonel Glenn, on the other hand, had capitalized on his reputation as an astronaut." Schiller was in Bethesda, Maryland, staying at a friend's house when the statement was released in Ohio. The phone rang at 1:30 in the morning with *Dayton Journal-Herald* reporter Hugh McDiarmid calling to inform Schiller that he had read his entire statement to Glenn. McDiarmid said, "I would suggest, Jim, that you not be around Colonel Glenn in the future. He's furious."[19]

Ten years later, during Glenn's 1984 presidential campaign, the *Washington Post* offered this historical perspective on Glenn's criticism of Metzenbaum.

> In his spirited Senate primary race against Howard Metzenbaum in 1974, Glenn attacked his opponent for using tax shelters to slash his tax liability. He was quoted then as saying, "I haven't used tax shelters even though they may be legal because I don't think it's right. How much of a sense of responsibility can a man have for his country when he diddled it out of taxes?" Glenn makes considerable use of tax shelters now. . . . In his first year in the Senate after beating Metzenbaum, Glenn reported an income of more than $500,000 and charitable contributions of $548. He increased his charitable giving in 1981, when he began to consider running for president.[20]

Metzenbaum took up Schiller's theme, repeatedly calling Glenn an "overnight millionaire" and suggesting that Glenn had traded in on his fame. Talking to students on the OSU campus, he said, "Outside this building, I hustled chrysanthemums. Down the street I rented bicycles for twenty-five cents an hour, and peddled razor blades in front of the Neil House Hotel. I got my money by working for it."[21] That was all true enough, but he was headed in a dangerous direction.

"I have held a job, Howard"

Syndicated columnists Rowland Evans and Robert Novak, critiquing Metzenbaum's television commercials, said they depicted him as a "warm father figure who loves children and hates sin." Off camera, Metzenbaum's love of children was genuine, but he was seldom described as warm and fuzzy. He still had a steely, abrupt persona. He could be charming and effusive, but he had little patience with anyone who couldn't keep up with him as he rode into battle.

The campaign broke Glenn's way during the final weeks. Four years earlier, the tide had moved against him near the end of the campaign, as the incursion in Cambodia and the Kent State tragedy seemed to help the staunchly antiwar Metzenbaum. In 1974, the dynamics in another close race favored Glenn. Voters, disgusted by corruption in Washington, were looking for fresh candidates untainted by scandal. "Glenn's political ideology is not easy to identify and most who are drawn to him are attracted because they see him as being an honest, decent guy, who would be a good, new symbol . . . not because of his political philosophy,"[22] the *Cleveland Press* said in an analysis.

Meanwhile, CBS News correspondent Roger Mudd charged that Metzenbaum was using the Sun Newspapers as a personal vehicle to promote his campaign. Mudd reported that the papers had given their 275,000 readers far more coverage of Metzenbaum's activities—a ten-to-one margin over Glenn in terms of column inches. David Skylar, who ran the company, denied it, arguing that Metzenbaum deserved more ink because he was local. In a May 2 nonendorsement, Skylar told how Metzenbaum had put his Sun holdings in a blind trust to avoid any suggestion of a conflict. "We're not endorsing in this race for national office," the page-one editorial said, "simply because we don't want to kid you."[23] *Cleveland Magazine* said Metzenbaum had lined up the support of just about every Democratic suburban mayor, in part because the towns' fathers didn't want to tangle with his Sun Newspapers. "The fact is the chain was used for personal political purposes by its owner," the magazine concluded.[24]

With the tax problem chipping at him, Metzenbaum couldn't be distracted with nitpicking about the coverage of a suburban newspaper. This was a statewide campaign and a statewide problem. He bought television time for the express purpose of explaining away the tax question—a nothing-to-hide technique used by candidates to give the illusion of full disclosure. He succeeded only in drawing more attention to his plight. "I believe the people will see through the efforts of my opponent to make himself out to be Mr. Clean, riding on a white horse," Metzenbaum said. "They will recognize we have both become wealthy men. But he moved faster than I. I hope they will conclude both men are men of integrity and choose the man who is best able to be an effective United States senator."[25]

In their first TV debate, Metzenbaum accused Glenn of falling behind on his Ohio taxes: "You admit you became a wealthy man in a short time, but you pretend to be holier than thou in connection with your own taxes. The truth is, John, you have used about every tax shelter and tax advantage available."[26] Metzenbaum was the one playing defense this time, but still the contributions poured in from Ohio's political elite: $3,000 from banker Warner; $6,000 from Cleveland industrialist Milt Wolf and his wife, Roslyn; and $1,000 from Cleveland automobile dealer Max Friedman, one of Metzenbaum's closest friends. He ended up spending $930,000 on the primary. Glenn stayed competitive at $670,000.

Glenn had also counted on help from the Kennedy family. Senator Ted Kennedy, who kept up his friendship with Senator Metzenbaum, stayed neutral in keeping with custom for officeholders in a party primary. But Glenn had always been close with the family of Robert F. Kennedy—he had the task of telling some of the kids that their father had died after the shooting in Los Angeles in 1968. Yet Ethel Kennedy turned down Glenn's request for help, saying she feared she would be drawn into a multitude of campaigns if she helped Glenn. Bitterly disappointed, Glenn approached Jacqueline Kennedy Onassis, on the advice of Rosie Grier. Glenn called Jackie himself and she readily agreed to cut a radio commercial. She had heard what they were doing to "our John" out in Ohio. The thirty-second spot was pure Jackie, gracious and warm proclaiming the affection she and President Kennedy had for John Glenn, "an outstanding American." Afterward, she turned to Glenn's media consultant, Jim Dunn, and asked, "Was that good enough, Jim?"[27] It was more than good enough. It added to Glenn's surge in late April, in the closing weeks before the May 7 primary.

Metzenbaum tried lamely to counter Jackie with an endorsement from Leonard Woodcock, president of the United Auto Workers. He also won the endorsement of his hometown *Cleveland Press,* which said Metzenbaum came across "as a candidate who not only has a grasp of the complex issues that face a senator but has a genuine concern and appreciation for the bread-and-butter issues that affect most of us in our daily lives."[28] But then, during a fund-raiser at the Sheraton Hotel in downtown Cleveland, Metzenbaum stepped over the edge of the cliff. He took the suggestion of an informal advisor, Brooklyn mayor John M. Coyne, who urged him to highlight Glenn's inexperience by pointing out that Glenn had never met a payroll or done much at all in the workaday world. In his speech before a partisan audience, Metzenbaum said Glenn had spent much of his life at the public trough. "How can you run for the Senate," he asked, "when you've never held a job?"[29]

Metzenbaum's campaign chief, Schiller, had seen the speech in advance, but the reference to Glenn's job background was not in the text. His reaction was one of horror. "He is a hero, you can't touch him," he said to Metzenbaum. "I know you have very good reasons why you didn't serve, your eyes and all of that, but you can't do that." Metzenbaum's reaction was nonchalant. "So sue me, I made a mistake," he said.

Glenn's campaign recognized the gaffe—repeated by Metzenbaum on at least one other occasion when his rival was not present—and went to work on a response. The parking lot king had declared that a veteran of two wars, a death-defying astronaut, had never held a job. "In the last two elections his campaign had accused me of everything from voting for Richard Nixon over John Kennedy in 1960 to having an affair with Andy Williams's wife, Claudine Longet," Glenn wrote in his 1999 book. "But this was more than just a political sally; this was an assault on everyone who had ever served the country. Metzenbaum had never been in the military."[30] Glenn said he drafted most of the subsequent rebuttal—the famous "Gold Star mother" speech—himself, with help of an aide.

Contrary to Ohio political folklore, the speech was not delivered for the first time at Cleveland's City Club the Friday before the primary. It came a few days earlier in little-noted remarks that were overlooked on a heavy news day that also brought word of Jackie's endorsement of Glenn. "It was so silly that I wasn't even going to respond," Glenn said of Metzenbaum's inflammatory comment. "But then I decided to put it to rest once and for all."[31]

And that he did. At the City Club on May 3, traditionally the site of the last debate of statewide campaigns, supporters cheered their respective candidates and heckled the responses of the other guy. A labor leader called Glenn a liar after the candidate said he was denied the opportunity to speak before a union meeting. Throughout the debate, Glenn waited for Metzenbaum to repeat the insult in front of the audience of 600 Clevelanders. But the exchanges were relatively restrained until the closing minutes. Metzenbaum, forewarned by a newspaper reporter that he had gone too far with the "job" comment, didn't touch the subject. But Glenn did, saying he was hurt by Metzenbaum's attack on his life's work. "Howard, I can't believe you said that," he began in a low, serious tone.

I served twenty-three years in the United States Marine Corps. I was through two wars. I flew 149 missions. My plane was hit by antiaircraft fire on twelve different occasions.

I was in the space program. It wasn't my checkbook, it was my life that was on the line. This was not a nine-to-five job where I took time off to take the daily cash receipts to the bank. I ask you to go with me . . . as I went the other day to a Veterans hospital and look those men with their mangled bodies in the eye and tell them they didn't hold a job. You go with me to any Gold Star mother, and you look her in the eye, and tell her that her son did not hold a job.

You go with me to the space program, and you go as I have gone to the widows and orphans of Ed White and Gus Grissom and Roger Chaffee, and you look those kids in the eye and tell them their dad didn't hold a job.

You go with me on Memorial Day, coming up, and you stand in Arlington National Cemetery—where I have more friends than I like to remember—and you watch those waving flags, and you stand there, and you think about this nation, and you tell me those people didn't have a job.

I tell you Howard Metzenbaum you should be on your knees every day of your life thanking God that there were some men— some men—who held a job.

And they required a dedication to purpose and a love of country and a dedication to duty that was more important than life itself. And their self-sacrifice is what has made this country possible. . . . I have held a job, Howard.[32]

People were on their feet. The applause went on for twenty-two seconds. Glenn's emotionally charged speech remains a singular moment in political history. Metzenbaum was doomed. He tried damage control, insisting he respected Glenn as a national hero, but "Let's be clear, John. I was talking about a job in private employment. I used the context of never having hired anyone, meaning in private employment."[33] But his attempts at placating voters failed. "He tried to respond," Glenn said, "and that only made it worse."[34]

Metzenbaum later admitted, "It was the goddamned stupidest thing I have ever done. It was calculated. John Coyne, the mayor of Brooklyn, who was one of a number of mayors supporting me, had said to me, 'You know, Glenn has never held a job in the private sector, never met a payroll, etc.' So, I used the line in the speech and afterward Joe Rice, a reporter who hated me more than any reporter in Ohio, came up to me and said, 'You know, my father was a career military officer, a colonel in the army, and I don't think he would have appreciated what you said.' I made a big mistake. I should have called Glenn right away and apologized."[35]

Twenty-three years later, columnist Mark Shields remembered being so moved by the speech that "I was all but certain that Glenn would some day become president." Metzenbaum was equally certain he had let the election slip away with a careless comment. "I lost to John Glenn specifically by reason of stupidity. That cost me the election."[36]

In an *Akron Beacon Journal* analysis, political writer Abe Zaidan said Glenn's answer to Metzenbaum was a "knockout punch" that may indeed have decided the closely fought contest. "By Election Day, Glenn was riding a strong tide of public sentiment aroused by his secure image of integrity, heroism and political independence. So much so, it now appears that thousands of Republicans, faced with a hum-drum ballot, crossed over to sweeten his margin of victory." Metzenbaum ran hard on middle-class pocketbook issues, but in a post-Watergate year voters opted for Glenn's brand of political honesty.[37]

When a reporter asked Glenn the weekend before the election, "Do you hate Howard Metzenbaum?" he replied with lawyerly caginess: "I have a strong, personal dislike for the things he has said about me, but I don't hate anybody."[38] He didn't "hate" anybody, but he could carry a grudge with the best of them.

Glenn's patriotic rebuke of Metzenbaum was in the headlines and on the air throughout Ohio—and the sound bites were all going his way. Glenn said his campaign team sensed immediately that momentum had swung to his side. "It was on the front page of just about every newspaper in the state, I think."[39] That last weekend, Glenn's media team combined Jackie's words with excerpts from his stirring speech and aired a sixty-second radio commercial all over the state. It was over, and Metzenbaum knew it. On election night, May 7, Glenn won by 95,000 votes and went on to a one-million-vote victory in November over Republican Ralph Perk, the mayor of Cleveland. Metzenbaum endorsed Glenn as the "Democratic nominee" but didn't offer him any financial help.

Gilligan lost that year by fewer than 12,000 votes to Rhodes, who returned to the governor's office after sitting out for four years. After his defeat was confirmed by a recount, Gilligan went home to Cincinnati and later told friends the Metzenbaum appointment was one of the worst political mistakes he ever made. It didn't cost him the election— he had lost on his own with an inept campaign—but he had snubbed a national hero.

Metzenbaum's flip remark and Glenn's powerful comeback lived on in urban legend. Decades later, accounts of the confrontation, often exaggerated or incorrect, continue to be debated.

The Lively Lame Duck

It wasn't finished for Metzenbaum in the Senate. Similar to 1948, when double-dealing cost him the Ohio Senate leadership post, he moved forward without sulking or self-pity. He went right back to work with gusto. "My activity as a lame-duck senator doesn't have that much politics in it," he told a reporter, holding his thumb and forefinger a hair apart. "I'm keeping busy because I'm an active guy and there are still all these problems. I could say what the heck, and sit back until my term runs out. But if I felt that way, I'd tell Governor Gilligan I was quitting now."[40]

Metzenbaum instructed his aides to work even harder and said he didn't intend to "just piddle along" during his remaining months.[41] His staff called him the lively lame duck, lowest in the Senate in seniority but pressing on with a sense of urgency. He took telephone calls from the public every morning between 8:30 and 9:30 from his Senate office. Along with Senator Henry "Scoop" Jackson of Washington, he passed a bill rolling back the price of imported oil. President Nixon vetoed it. When a constituent in Columbus complained he could not get through on the telephone to the National Park Service's campsite reservation system, Metzenbaum's staff investigated. It seemed the system rejected most calls from would-be campers. By the time Metzenbaum was through, the reservation system contractor had been fired and the park service director, a friend of the concessionaire, resigned.

After Senate majority leader Mike Mansfield named him as a delegate to the World Food Conference in Rome, Metzenbaum paid his own way and then sharply criticized the head of the U.S. delegation, agriculture secretary Earl Butz, for being insensitive to world hunger. He successfully managed a bill designating a greenbelt between Cleveland and Akron—the Cuyahoga Valley National Recreation Area—Ohio's first national park. The idea of an urban national park was ridiculed by some, but congressmen John Seiberling of Akron and Ralph Regula of the Canton area pushed hard for it in the House. Metzenbaum got the job done in the Senate and then personally called President Gerald Ford, on vacation in Vail, Colorado, to make sure he would sign the bill. The new park prospered.

Metzenbaum averaged four news releases a week and two news conferences a month, and he compiled a 98 percent voting record following the May primary. In his maiden speech in the Senate, less than a month before the primary, he complained about the "leisurely" pace on Capitol Hill. "The part of me that remains a back-home citizen looking in fails to detect a sense of purpose, a sense of urgency in our deliberations over major national issues. . . . We have become an elephantine government that moves clumsily to set policy by reacting to crises."

It was an insightful speech that could easily have been given twenty-five years in the future during the days of gridlock that slowed down both the George H. W. Bush and Bill Clinton administrations. "The people pay a terrible price," Metzenbaum continued. "While we discuss what to do, the citizen wastes hours in line waiting for gas that is too expensive; he must pay exorbitant prices for basic foods he needs to keep his family from going hungry; he must walk the streets looking for work."[42]

Metzenbaum went on to propose the Economic Preparedness Act. It was the first of his many attempts to "redistribute the tax burden" by closing loopholes used by corporations and wealthy individuals and creating new tax breaks for the poor and middle class. Metzenbaum introduced two other major bills: one requiring more disclosure from foreign investors in U.S. business concerns, and the second calling for the release of money from a conservation fund to help pay for new national parks, like Cuyahoga Valley. Neither passed.

The Senate was burdened that summer with Watergate and the prospect of an impeachment trial. Metzenbaum called for the president's resignation but softened his rhetoric after the House Judiciary Committee opened impeachment hearings. "We are afflicted with a preoccupied president who is unable to offer the nation guidance on many urgent issues," he said, shortly before Nixon quit.[43]

Glenn, of course, wished the lame duck would waddle back to Cleveland and turn over his Senate seat. In those days, departing senators sometimes resigned early to give successors from the same party transition time and an advantage in seniority over other freshmen. Metzenbaum wanted Glenn to ask him personally. When that didn't happen, he clung to the seat until December 23, giving Glenn only a small edge.

Metzenbaum's campaign had ended on a sour note, with $130,000 in debt and a new set of enemies. "I stayed on after the campaign," Schiller said. "There was a significant debt, which he blamed me for. . . . He said, 'Damn it, I thought you told me we were on budget.'"[44] Then Metzenbaum backed off, sending an unusual letter to Schiller that was as close as Metzenbaum would come to an apology. After praising the political operative's commitment, he wrote, "You did it without irritating people and became the accepted leader. In a campaign effort, that is not always an easy thing to do. At times I may have used strong language to express my enthusiasm or lack of it, but I think you always understood that that's my nature. I hope that if at any time I was the least bit offensive you will make allowances for a candidate who at times was probably uptight."[45] Schiller framed the letter and hung it on the wall in his law office at the Arcade on Euclid Avenue.

Metzenbaum's stay in Washington lasted only 337 days, but he had fallen in love with the Senate and never doubted he would run again to reclaim what had been taken away. He knew he was good at being a senator, and he relished the respect that went with the title. John Glenn would not stand in his way the next time. "I never stopped campaigning," Metzenbaum said.[46]

"He was SENATOR Metzenbaum," the *Cleveland Press* wrote. "And he will be SENATOR Metzenbaum, no matter what the fortunes of politics will bring him in the coming years. The difference is that he wants the title to be official again."[47]

CHAPTER 6

The Senate Years I

Howard at the Bridge

"Howard had the ambition, the drive, the hunger."
Bob Dykes

By 1976, Howard Metzenbaum was twenty-eight years removed from his last victory in a general election. This would be his final try, his last chance. He was almost sixty years old. A defeat would make him a three-time loser and put him in danger of picking up the perennial-hopeful tag hung on his brother, Irwyn, twenty-five years earlier.

To this point, the 1970s had been years of struggle for a man accustomed to success and a fair amount of deference. A decade that had begun with so much promise—the stunning upset of Glenn—had ground down to defeat, rejection, and uncertainty. Although Metzenbaum had no financial worries—he was worth at least $3.6 million—he had not experienced such insecurity about his future since the 1940s.

Shortly after his loss to Glenn, the *Cleveland Press* speculated in a May 8, 1974, article that "this may be the end of the political road" for Metzenbaum. A year out from election, he trailed Senator Taft by twenty-eight points, according to the University of Cincinnati's Ohio Poll. Another survey put his negative impression at 35 percent of the electorate, a terrible place to start. Many of his friends told him not to run again, but nothing would stop him. "By that time, I had it in my bones," he said. He told his daughter Susan, "I am doing this. I will do this."[1] Harold Stern said his friend "thrived in that arena" and "truly felt he could contribute to improving the lives" of working people.[2] "It was a pivotal time," said Jim Friedman, the onetime top aide to Gilligan, who advised Metzenbaum. "He enjoyed some of his greatest victories and [suffered] some of his greatest defeats."[3]

Others in Metzenbaum's position—wealthy and with a successful law firm—might call it a day, said Cleveland political consultant Bob Dykes. But not Metzenbaum. "No," said Dykes, "Howard came back driving as hard as ever. Nineteen-seventy-six [could] have been the last gasp, but I will tell you that quite a few potential candidates would have fallen by the wayside before 1976, if they had had happen to them what happened to Howard."[4]

At least one thing boded well for a Metzenbaum Senate run. On April 14, 1975, Metzenbaum settled his case with the Internal Revenue Service. The government conceded that he and Bonda acquired the Rayne, Louisiana, ethane plant in a "bona fide transaction" and refunded 80 percent of the money Metzenbaum had deposited into escrow. Metzenbaum stipulated that a lower depreciation rate should be calculated for the unsuccessful plant, which produced a hydrocarbon gas of the methane series, often used as a refrigerant. In its 1969 audit, the IRS claimed Metzenbaum and Bonda had bought the $3.4 million plant for the express purpose of using it as a tax shelter. Once the government backed off, "the taxpayers conceded a minor subsidiary issue as to the amount of depreciation allowable and agreed to depreciate the property on the basis of 150 percent declining balance," Metzenbaum's lawyer, Stephen L. Kadish, said.[5] Metzenbaum blamed Nixon, claiming the only reason that he and Bonda were audited in the first place was because they showed up on the disgraced president's "enemies list." He had no proof that he had been targeted. What mattered was that he had been vindicated and cleared for takeoff in 1976. The settlement would have meant more had it come in 1974 when Glenn tormented him with the tax charge during their primary contest. "It was politically and personally embarrassing," said Metzenbaum.[6]

But the wild ride in and out of the Senate had not changed him. There was no regret—no "new Metzenbaum" for voters to check out. "The aggressive, sometimes abrasive style continued after the [1974] election," the *Dayton Journal-Herald* reported.[7]

Within days after the 1975 tax ruling, Howard Metzenbaum was sizing up the field. What were Governor Gilligan's intentions? Would the young lieutenant governor, Dick Celeste, consider the Senate? "Unless you have been through something like that, you can't understand the kind of determination and strength of character and singleness of purpose that takes," said Jim Friedman. "To take that pounding, to put yourself out in public and subject yourself to every fair and unfair criticism and then get beaten. To take a licking and keep on ticking, to have the fortitude to stay the course, to be called everything from a kike to a Communist, to a tax cheat. And he just went on."[8] But it wasn't stubbornness alone. The first presidential election in the wake of the Watergate scandal looked promising for Democrats. "It was not a good year to be a Republican," said Friedman. "It was a post-Watergate election. That was in the heyday of the Ohio Democratic Party. We were winning everything else in sight."

Taft, also fifty-nine, was not a dynamic presence in the Senate, and he had waffled during the House impeachment hearings. Gilligan, who lost to Taft in a 1966 congressional contest in Cincinnati, passed on a rematch. And Dick Celeste was eyeing the 1978 governor's race. But nothing would be given to Metzenbaum.

The Stanton Challenge

James V. Stanton, a popular Cleveland congressman with strong ties to the Irish-American community, jumped into the Democratic primary. Two other Clevelanders also filed petitions of candidacy: Richard B. Kay, a lawyer who ran under the flag of George Wallace's American Independent Party in 1970, and nursing home operator James Nolan, who nicked Gilligan in the Democratic gubernatorial primary in 1974.

Nolan and Kay were conservative nuisance candidates in a Democratic primary. But Stanton, then forty-four, was darkly handsome, unafraid of controversy, and a serious challenger. He was strongly supported by Ohio House Speaker Vern Riffe, U.S. House leader Thomas P. "Tip" O'Neill, and Glenn's loyalists. Steve Kovacik, Glenn's hardball coach, was in Stanton's corner and plotted strategy over lunch at the Pewter Mug, a watering hole in downtown Columbus.

While the brash Stanton fancied himself a Kennedyesque figure— down to the practiced speech inflection and arm gestures—he was not nearly as liberal as Metzenbaum. A firefighter's son, Stanton was closer to the God-and-country Democrats of Harry S. Truman's time than to the young liberals inspired by George McGovern's 1972 campaign. After he was elected to the U.S. House, Stanton confronted O'Neill, the powerful Massachusetts Democrat who had raised money for his opponent, Michael Feighan, the incumbent ousted by Stanton in a primary. "Are you O'Neill? What the heck are you doing holding all those fund-raisers for Mike Feighan?" he demanded.[9] In time, Stanton became one of the future Speaker's closest allies.

Former Cleveland mayor Carl Stokes, who feuded with Stanton when the latter was Cleveland City Council president, had this to say about Stanton.

> For a long time I was unable to understand how a West Side Irish kid could be as street-wise as Jim Stanton at such a young age. He was only 35 when he became council president [in 1964]. He had a sure political sense. He was shrewd and hard, and he knew how to count votes. . . . Stanton grew quickly into an effective and strong leader. He had the toughness that you need when you are trying to hold together a number of men, each with his own little fiefdom, and he quickly found the glue needed to hold the pieces together. He developed good relations with the media, both the editorial offices and the working press. He had the kind of bully-ing good humor and ebullience that appealed to reporters. . . . Stanton worked at politics. He spread his base.[10]

This from a political enemy, yet Stanton downplayed his scrappy street guy image. When he stumped outside of northeast Ohio, he told voters they didn't know much about him because he had been so busy doing good things in Washington during his six years in Congress.

The state party organization, wary of an intramural bloodbath in Cuyahoga County, did not endorse a candidate. But the *Plain Dealer,* which was delivered to the doorsteps of both the East Side Metzenbaum and West Side Stanton households, backed Stanton; the probusiness paper snubbed Metzenbaum without so much as a mention of his name in its editorial. Metzenbaum decided to ignore his rival, not even bothering to bait him as a closet conservative as he had with Glenn. Stanton returned the favor, making little of Metzenbaum's tax problems or left-wing connections until the final days of the campaign.

Neither wanted to alienate the other's supporters and divide the party going into the fall campaign.

Stanton paid little heed to his base in northeast Ohio and tried instead to build his name recognition in the rest of the state by pouring $200,000 into downstate television advertising. Maybe Ohio voters were still exhausted by the Glenn-Metzenbaum brawl, but the matchup attracted minimal interest. "Compared to 1974, this year's race for the Democratic nomination for the U.S. Senate almost seems like no race at all," Joe Rice wrote.[11] That collective yawn was to Metzenbaum's advantage as his three statewide campaigns gave him a head start over the others in name recognition. "I'm not unhappy about the situation," he said of the apparent voter apathy.[12] On the major issues, the differences between the candidates were few. Metzenbaum kept attacking the oil industry and Republican economic policies, which he said were stoking inflation and shrinking workers' paychecks.

"I'm more comfortable not pounding the table all the time. I now believe in myself with a total conviction," Metzenbaum said of his more laid-back campaign. "I am not a charismatic candidate, but I think people know I like talking to them."[13]

Tom Chema, a lawyer recruited by Metzenbaum to raise money, was puzzled by Stanton's strategy and wondered why he wasn't playing up his strengths. He thought Stanton was making a "terrible mistake" by concentrating his time and money downstate and taking for granted the huge Democratic constituency in Greater Cleveland. "In politics, you have to pay attention to your base," Chema said.[14] Steve Kovacik, who was squeezed out as the campaign stumbled along, could not understand why Stanton adopted the role of a statesman and ran away from his image as a savvy, nimble politician.

Maybe Stanton should have listened more to Kovacik, who helped Glenn beat Metzenbaum just two years earlier. On primary day, the congressman's downstate strategy failed and Metzenbaum won by 176,000 votes, or 53 percent, out of less than one million cast. Although Stanton won an 87 percent victory in his congressional district in 1974 and should have had stronger support at the grass roots than Metzenbaum, he narrowly lost Cuyahoga County. Metzenbaum scored heavily in black wards where some voters resented Stanton because of his clashes with Stokes. Despite his effort downstate, Stanton won only four of Ohio's eighty-eight counties. Even Wayne Hays's endorsement could not swing little Belmont County for Stanton in Ohio's coal mining country. He polled only 37 percent statewide. Kay and Nolan together accounted for another 10 percent of the vote.

Stanton was outspent by Metzenbaum but had stayed competitive financially, putting $415,000 into the race. His committee was left with $145,900 in debt—more than $100,000 of it owed to the candidate, who loaned his campaign chunks of his own money. "I knew it was a risk when I took it," Stanton said. "I've got no regrets; I was bored in the House."[15] After conceding on primary night, he immediately endorsed Metzenbaum in the upcoming campaign against Taft. As for himself, Stanton said he would walk away from politics—and he did, never running for public office again. He kept his Washington home but abandoned Cleveland for Buffalo in 1981. He moved to operate the Delaware North Cos, a huge sporting event concessionaire. A decade later, he became an even wealthier man as a Washington lawyer-lobbyist. "Howard Metzenbaum made a businessman out of me," he told his friends. At one point, Delaware North owned APCOA, Metzenbaum's old parking lot company.

In 1988, Stanton sought the chairmanship of the Democratic National Committee, but the job went to Ron Brown, later to become secretary of commerce under President William Jefferson Clinton. (Ron Brown died in a 1996 plane crash in Croatia.) Stanton gave Metzenbaum $1,000 for his 1982 reelection race, and another $1,000 in 1988. But he disliked his old rival and declined to publicly discuss the 1976 primary or the man who bested him. The most he would say was, "He doesn't have a very long lunch list, I'll tell you that."[16]

Most of the Democratic establishment rallied to Metzenbaum after the primary. Vern Riffe, a strong fund-raiser, came to his aid without hesitation, although the moderate southern Ohioan had little in common with the Clevelander. "You beat me fair and square," Riffe had told him. "I'm on your team now. I'll be there with you."[17] Senator Glenn was nowhere to be found. Refusing to mention Metzenbaum's name, he allowed only that he would vote for the Democratic Party's Senate nominee.

The thirty-year-old Chema ran the day-to-day campaign with help from Stern. But they had to compete for the candidate's time with Metzenbaum's son-in-law, Joel Z. Hyatt, a brash young lawyer married to the second daughter, Susan. Hyatt and Susan Metzenbaum had talked to several prospects before settling on him, Chema said. But Chema felt he got the job almost by default. "Heck, I was the campaign manager, frankly, because I think Howard could not find anyone else to do it," he said. "He had been a two-time loser at that point, and some of the people who were a lot more experienced declined to do it." Because Chema was not part of Metzenbaum's circle, he was surprised by the job offer. In fact, former Metzenbaum campaign manager Jim Schiller "was pretty negative about the whole thing" and warned Chema about the stress of working closely with the high-strung candidate. Metzenbaum reminded Chema of the *Peanuts* character Lucy, who stared up at the sky, musing, "I love mankind. It's people I can't stand." Chema thought about turning him down rather than playing the tortured Charlie Brown role but in the end decided to accept the challenge. He would hold the football and wait for the kicker, hoping not to be suckered.[18]

Hyatt had Metzenbaum's confidence and asserted himself as chief strategist. He pressed for a less traditional campaign that would pour resources into television advertising at the expense of a field operation and public events, such as rallies designed to attract free media coverage. "The toughest fights of that campaign were between Joel and Howard," said Chema. "They were just yelling at each other because Howard would not go to Los Angeles for another meet-the-stars party or something."[19] But Metzenbaum went and raised the money, often one-on-one with a donor he barely knew. And this time, Metzenbaum stayed on message, unlike his mercurial performance against Glenn in 1974.

"He looked senatorial," Schiller said, marveling at the evolution. "When I first met Howard he had a crew cut. But he let his hair grow . . . and he photographs well. I thought he was an attractive looking person—–and he looked like a senator. There was a certain, maybe crisp, dignity to him, a bearing. I think people like that in politicians."[20] With that crispness, Metzenbaum depicted himself as the successful up-from-the-bootstraps American businessman who would fight for the interests of consumers. Metzenbaum "came to understand," Bob Dykes said, "that his appeal to voters was a populist appeal. He genuinely cared about the consequences of government action on ordinary people."[21]

Taft, on the other hand, was a do-nothing senator who had not taken a strong stand on Watergate. That, at least, was Metzenbaum's message. "Taft ran on his father's name in 1970 and it was a good one," Metzenbaum said at the outset. "He has to run on his own record in 1976, and it's not a good one."[22] Voters were also concerned about

Taft's health; he suffered a heart attack the year before. Metzenbaum felt certain that he would run strong in northeast Ohio. The key was the swing vote downstate—Ohio's vast, Republican-leaning center—which had broken for Taft in 1970. That year, Metzenbaum was beaten badly in central Ohio, in Taft's base in the southwest, and in most of northwest Ohio outside of Toledo.

The *Blade* again endorsed Taft. Senator Taft had done "nothing spectacular," the newspaper editorialized, but Metzenbaum "proved disappointing, given more to headline-oriented flamboyance than to substantial achievement" in his 1974 Senate stint.[23] Bob Dykes, however, who wasn't involved in the campaign in 1978, found the Republican incumbent far from spectacular. "I would ascribe part of the reason for Howard's success as Taft's failure," he said. "It looked to me as if once Taft became a senator—once he won—that he had achieved his ambition. He wasn't so much interested in what he was going to do as a senator, as being a senator." Not even all Democrats would agree with the claim that Taft was not a serious senator, but Dykes had a point. Taft had been in public office for twenty out of twenty-two years, yet he left some Ohioans with the impression that he was disconnected and indecisive.

Dykes got irritated when he received constituent mail from Taft during the election year. "You know this is the first piece of mail I can remember receiving from this guy in six years. I thought to myself, gee, I wonder if the average voter feels this way too . . . It was basically the notion that he had not cared enough about the job, or the people, to stay in touch." Instead of having a "hunger," Dykes felt, Taft had a sense of entitlement stemming from his family name. "The thing that people look for in candidates, often above all else, is, do they have the fire in the belly? Do they have the hunger? Do they really want it? Howard had the ambition, the drive, the hunger."[24]

Metzenbaum's campaign relied heavily on paid television and avoided confrontations with his stately adversary. Senator Taft, a genuinely nice guy, came across warmer than Metzenbaum in personal encounters. Metzenbaum ran only four ads: one questioning Taft's effectiveness; one taking on big business fat cats; another with Metzenbaum talking about his proconsumer stands; and the clincher, the "Shirley ad," a wife humanizing her husband. "I never would have been a United States senator if Shirley hadn't cut a spot for me in my first election," Metzenbaum said years later. "Shirley won it for me. My wife was on twenty-seven seconds and that was the campaign. She just sat there and said she knew her husband would be a great senator."[25]

Shirley Metzenbaum was fifty-four, but looked younger, and she spoke to the camera from a kitchen setting in warm, reassuring tones about the man many thought of as stern and unsympathetic. There was evidence of this in the high negatives that pollsters consistently saw associated with his name. Instead of describing a meanie, his attractive wife of thirty-five years talked about a family man who loved his four girls and always looked for the best in others. If you had doubts about him, she seemed to be saying, you can trust her. "Howard, you're robbing the cradle," one reporter ribbed him after seeing the commercial featuring his comely wife.

Fritz, Grits, and Metz

Ohioans were also seeing a television ad blitz from each side of the presidential campaign, as both President Ford and Jimmy Carter considered Ohio a must-win state. Watching the developing national campaign, Metzenbaum was bewildered by Carter's success. He thought of the former Georgia governor as a not very progressive southern Democrat with few distinctions. "It is an amazing country where people of all stripes can rise up from nowhere. Jimmy Carter came out of nowhere and became the president of the United States. I remember being at a convention somewhere and a *Time Life* magazine fellow was saying to me, 'See this fellow Jimmy Carter down in Georgia. He is really a comer.' Nobody had ever heard of [Carter] at that point. To me, it is incredible."[26]

Metzenbaum liked the liberal credentials of Carter's running mate, Minnesota senator Walter F. "Fritz" Mondale of Minnesota, so he teamed up with the national ticket despite reservations about the nominee. He even made the pilgrimage to Georgia to meet with Carter. Rosalynn Carter served coffee and cookies, and Harold Stern captured the event with a camera he borrowed from one of his daughters. Soon bumper stickers in Ohio were carrying the banner "Fritz, Grits and Metz." Stern's photo of Metzenbaum and Carter was used on a campaign poster.

Democrats in Ohio and nationally sensed a big year was in the making, with Republicans reeling from scandal and Ford's pardon of Nixon. Metzenbaum, for his part, was a better candidate this time. He wasn't as impetuous as he had seemed two years earlier. Maybe Taft was an easier target, or more likely Metzenbaum had matured as a candidate at the age of fifty-nine. He took charge of his campaign and exuded a confidence that rubbed off on his lieutenants.

One Saturday in October, Metzenbaum returned late to Cleveland from a long day on the hustings and learned his campaign was nearly broke. Hyatt drove to Metzenbaum's home, screeching into the driveway around eleven PM in a near panic. He told the older man of his fears, how a round of crucial television commercials would have to be scrapped if money could not be found by the beginning of the week. "The whole campaign rode on keeping the commercials on the air," Hyatt later said. "I just didn't see how we were going to pay the bills." Metzenbaum was a picture of calm. "My whole life I have had challenges to face," he told Hyatt. "You go home and get a good night's sleep. We'll raise the money." Hyatt drove home reassured, though he was not sure why. By Monday, the needed $172,000 was pledged. "Howard Metzenbaum has never had any self-doubt," Hyatt concluded.[27]

Ohio voters still harbored doubts about the millionaire from Cleveland—the gruff liberal with the tax problem. So Metzenbaum, who generally avoided political gimmickry, went to lengths to appear more like a regular guy. Shirley Metzenbaum's ad about the fellow she called "Babe" was one thing. At a Lorain United Auto Workers' union hall one night, just before the primary, Metzenbaum was persuaded to behave as one of the boys. As a belly dancer gyrated before him, Metzenbaum reclined on a pillow with several union chieftains. He had been cajoled into donning a bejeweled headband and a purple sash for the occasion, a benefit for cancer research. For some reason, lost to memory, his pants legs were rolled up to his knees. A newspaper reporter, visualizing a hilarious picture in the next day's paper, tried in vain to line up a freelance photographer. When the embarrassed Metzenbaum realized what was going on, he exploded in anger and the fun was over. He threatened to abandon the reporter—dependent on the campaign for transportation—at the union hall. "You son of a bitch!" he bellowed. "I drive you around all day and that's how you repay me." It had not occurred to the newsman, George Condon Jr., that he owed the candidate anything for covering the race.[28]

Despite the lapses, Metzenbaum was more relaxed in this, his fifth statewide contest in seven years. Taft was often the aggressor in a lackluster campaign. He pushed Republican issues, such as reducing taxes and the size of government, but also portrayed himself as an independent thinker who did not always go along with the party line; for instance, he had supported amnesty for Vietnam War draft resisters, a minority position among Republicans. Metzenbaum hammered away at consumer prices, utility costs, and rising inflation that he blamed on Taft's presidents, "Nixon and Ford." Metzenbaum called for a $15 billion cut in military spending but quietly backed away from costly health care and job creation proposals.

At the customary City Club debate closing the campaign, Taft went on the offensive and tried to draw out his foe. But the disciplined Metzenbaum, prepped for the debate by aide Barry Direnfeld, stayed on message. He avoided the tit-for-tat and maintained a positive tone through most of the debate. Reporter Bill Carlson, who covered the debate for the *Plain Dealer*, recalled one exchange that began when Taft "really lambasted" his Democratic rival. Carlson described Metzenbaum's response: "He stood up and said, 'Bob, that just is not like you. I am just not going to say anything in reply.' Then, he sat back down. Suddenly, the tables were turned."[29] But it wasn't easy for Metzenbaum. "You could see him fighting all his demons," said Direnfeld, Metzenbaum's chief counsel at the time.[30] "In a lot of ways I think our opponent in 1976 lost the election rather than our winning it," Chema said. "We didn't make mistakes. Look at the record. Howard didn't make any faux pas. Howard didn't do in 1976 what he did in 1974. That was the key for us." Voters knew that Metzenbaum was a hard guy, Chema said, that "he may be all the bad things you've heard about him, but he's on your side."[31]

Taft's biggest mistake was his failure to convince everyday Ohioans that he had made a difference for them in Washington. He lost by three percentage points, or just over 117,000 votes, as Metzenbaum led the Democratic ticket on election night, out-polling the fading Carter. He prevailed by convincing Democratic voters and independents that he was the genuine article—a straight-talking man who could win and clean up the mess made by Republicans in Washington. "He was positioned in the election against Taft as a populist who'd stand up for the little guy," Friedman said. "That people in Ohio were not very liberal did not mean they did not respond to a populist stance."

In 1970, Metzenbaum had carried his home county, Cuyahoga, by 61,000 votes, not enough to offset the Republican advantage downstate. Six years later, Metzenbaum won Cuyahoga County by 125,000 votes and ran stronger in Republican-leaning Franklin County (Columbus), losing to Taft by just more than 17,000. Metzenbaum also increased his winning margins in Democratic strongholds like Akron, Dayton, Toledo, and Youngstown. In hilly southeastern Ohio, the least popu-lated region, Metzenbaum widened a 2,200-vote margin in 1970 to 16,500. Swing voters were heading his way. Glenn came around with a lukewarm, last-minute endorsement. And Metzenbaum was helped by a larger overall turnout than in his first match with Taft.

Taft knew Watergate had hurt him, but even so he never understood why he had lost in a state that had long embraced his family. "There was no reason why I should not have run ahead of Jerry Ford," he said in a postmortem, "but I did not."[32] When Taft died on December 7, 1993, Metzenbaum called him a "gentleman and a friend." "I felt there was a mutual respect between two men of differing political philosophies. He will be missed."[33]

In the Senate—Again

In January, Metzenbaum resumed his Senate career, acting as if he had never left. Democrats still controlled the body, but they had a new ma-jority leader, Robert Byrd of West Virginia, a tradition-bound lawmaker who played a mean bluegrass fiddle. And they had a would-be ally in the White House, President Jimmy Carter.

The newly elected senator quickly came up with a gimmick to get a conversation going with his constituents—and to attract attention from the media. At least three days a week, he resumed his practice of taking calls from constituents, sitting behind a desk for an hour in the morning in his Russell Building office on Capitol Hill. "Hello, Howard Metzenbaum speaking," he typically began conversations. A flattering article in the *Plain Dealer* told of Metzenbaum scolding secretaries who picked up the calls—"I'm perfectly capable of answering my own telephone."[34] This, from the man who had instructed a receptionist when placing calls for him in Cleveland to make certain the other party was waiting on the line before connecting him. A copy of the story in Metzenbaum's Senate file has the handwritten scrawl, "PR!" in the up-per left corner.

If taking calls from the home folks was a stunt designed to ingratiate him with average voters in Ohio, his disregard for Senate niceties was losing him what few friends he had in Washington. Metzenbaum wasn't a true freshman, having served the eleven-month appointment, and he certainly didn't act like one. Right out of the box, he leaked a story about his old friend Cincinnati financier Marvin Warner's nomination as ambassador to Switzerland. That enraged Glenn. The senior senator always went by the book and rarely passed information to reporters in advance of a public release. "I'm not going to throw stones," Glenn huffed. Then, acting as if national security were at stake, he added, "but I was given the information in close confidence and asked to treat it confidentially."[35]

On the floor, Metzenbaum borrowed a tactic associated with segregationist senators from the South—exploiting the Senate tradition of unlimited debate through the filibuster. In a Senate controlled 62–38 by his party, Metzenbaum used the filibuster threat to stop legislation he regarded as anticonsumer. "I never saw a man come in here and become an ace filibusterer so fast," Senator Russell Long of Louisiana said.[36]

Metzenbaum was assigned to the Armed Services Committee in 1977 as a placeholder as the session opened. "I'd like you to stay on the committee," the chairman, Mississippian John Stennis, said to him. But Metzenbaum declined, even though he liked the idea of connecting with one of the most conservative Democrats in the Senate. He knew it wasn't a good fit. "I didn't believe in that," he said of the committee's record of boosting military spending. Later on, he blocked Stennis's project, the proposed Tombigbee Dam in Tennessee. "I'm not going to let it pass." But Stennis argued passionately for the dam one night into the wee hours, flailing away with his arms and imploring as the hour reached three AM. Metzenbaum feared the old gentleman would have a heart attack and backed off. "I'd be seen as the man who killed John Stennis. I let it go."[37]

Instead of military matters, Metzenbaum focused on energy issues and the utility industry. And he picked a complex subject on which to make his first stand: the deregulation of the natural gas industry. Taking government controls off of natural gas would encourage exploration and allow the cost of fuel to ebb and flow with market forces. That was a prospect he vehemently opposed, believing it would be a great cost to the public.

"Master of Obstruction"

Metzenbaum and his partner in obstruction, James Abourezk, an Arab-American from South Dakota, called their struggle "the first filibuster in the history of the Senate on behalf of consumers." The September talkfest was the first one in thirteen years to run round the clock, with cots set up in the adjoining Senate cloakroom during the final three days and nights.

Instead of talking bills to death by reading from the U.S. Code or a phone book, Abourezk and Metzenbaum stalled the amendment of Senators Lloyd Bentsen of Texas and James Pearson of Kansas by offering 508 amendments of their own. A three-fifths majority eventually achieved cloture, limiting extended debate to one hour for each of the 100 senators. But there was a loophole and Metzenbaum was among the first to exploit it. Thanks to him, senators had to dispose of hundreds of time-consuming amendments that had been introduced by the filibusterers prior to the cloture vote. Time spent on reading the amendments and roll calls disposing of them would not be counted against the hundred hours of debate.

"The postcloture filibusters . . . were extremely unsettling to most senators: the assumption had always been that invoking cloture would bring the Senate to a final vote. Exploiting the rules via postcloture debate was really an invention and innovation of the late 1970s," said Sarah Binder of the Brookings Institution, who has written on the impact of filibusters.[38] Before this one was over, the Senate had endured one all-night session, considered 400 amendments, and waded through 600 roll calls. Metzenbaum knew he could not kill the Bentsen amendment in an up-or-down vote, but he thought he could at least call attention to the peril he saw in the natural gas plan—namely, higher prices for consumers. "By one maneuver or another, we were able to keep the show going to the point where we actually got the Senate to a situation where it actually couldn't move forward with the natural gas deregulation bill," he said, with satisfaction.

On it went. In a chamber where wearing a sport coat and slacks could be seen as overly casual, Barry Goldwater showed up one night in his stocking feet. Fritz Hollings came to the floor in a yellow jogging suit. The exasperated minority leader, Howard Baker of Tennessee, said rules should be changed to bar the new-style filibuster, which relied not on languorous speeches but rather on hundreds of amendments and quorum calls. Often, the text of amendments was read verbatim. It was dull, time-consuming stuff.

"The filibuster has few of the trappings of a Hollywood filibuster, except for the cots last night, off the Senate chamber. There is no James

Stewart setting a sandwich down on his desk to signal his determination," wrote Adam Clymer of the *New York Times*.[39] And no protracted monologues, without so much as a bathroom break, as Strom Thurmond managed to avoid in 1957, when he held the floor for twenty-four hours and eighteen minutes to filibuster a civil rights bill.[40]

The Abourezk and Metzenbaum filibuster was a tactical one. The only option for foes of the death-by-amendment maneuver was to simply suspend the Senate rules. Such a break with precedent and tradition seemed highly unlikely, or so Abourezk and Metzenbaum thought. Although they were on the same wavelength with the Carter administration on gas deregulation, the blabbing senators got ambushed by Vice President Mondale, a man they regarded as a comrade in arms. When he heard that Mondale was likely to aid those trying to shut down the filibuster, Metzenbaum was stunned. He had miscalculated. "I couldn't believe that would occur, and I discussed the subject with Jim Abourezk, who said to me, 'It just couldn't be.' I actually asked him to talk with Mondale about it, but he was so certain that it couldn't be that he wasn't inclined to do so. I then spoke with Ted Kennedy and asked him if he would speak with Mondale. Kennedy was also incredulous and shook his head in wonderment."[41] The filibuster against natural gas deregulation rolled along for thirteen days, but on fourteenth day, with Mondale presiding over the Senate, Majority Leader Byrd ruthlessly choked it off.

Metzenbaum didn't get his audience with Mondale, so he approached him on the Senate floor, sensing that the fix was in. Et tu, Brute? Metzenbaum said as much to the vice president of the United States: "I told him that if he was up there to participate in a parliamentary procedure, I would think the administration was speaking out of both sides of its mouth. He took umbrage at that but then cooled. He said to me, 'We had the votes [to stop the filibuster].' Those might be considered famous last words, because, as a matter of fact, they never did have the votes."[42]

Despite sympathy for the two senators' goals, the filibuster was delaying passage of the Carter-Mondale energy policy—the centerpiece of the new administration's legislative agenda. With Byrd making rapid-fire motions, Mondale began ruling amendment after amendment out of order. Vice presidents typically assume their role as president of the Senate in anticipation of a close vote since they have the power to cast the tiebreaker. This was different—Mondale was taking sides in a far more proactive way. The usually good-natured Abourezk and other panicked filibuster supporters shouted for recognition. "Steamroller, steamroller!" they yelled. But Mondale ignored them. "I was dumbstruck and tried to get [recognition on] the floor," Metzenbaum said. "The Senate was hot and steaming."[43]

When senators, other than Byrd, finally were allowed to speak, they condemned the bum's rush and accused Byrd of unilaterally changing the Senate's rules. Byrd rose, full of indignation, his twangy mountain voice cracking. "I've not abused leadership. I'm trying to keep senators from abusing the Senate. I'm trying to put a stop to this filibuster. That's why the vice president is here today. He's trying to get the ox out of the ditch."[44] Metzenbaum and Abourezk surrendered to the inevitable.

Mary McGrory, writing in the *Washington Star,* cast it as a plot against Senate liberals orchestrated by the conservative Byrd. "The friends of the October recess, that is, the impatient Senate leaders of both parties, met secretly over that weekend, recruited the vice president to lead the surprise attack, and without a word of advance warning, cut the throats of liberals, who had been talking themselves hoarse for the president's stated goal. The brutal suppression of the filibuster left blood all over the Senate floor. The president was accused of lying by a member of his own party, and the vice president of being a dictator."[45]

Metzenbaum lost, yet he recovered quickly. The media spelled his name right, after all. "Metzenbaum keeps Senate up all night," headlined the *Cleveland Press.*[46] "No longer 'Ohio's other senator,'" the *Plain Dealer* declared.[47] Metzenbaum cataloged the coverage, critiquing the newspaper stories and complaining that the Ohio press did not give his provocative legislative style the attention it deserved. "I think I added to my stature during the entire debate and have had many favorable comments from members of the Senate, as well as a large number of members of the House," Metzenbaum said in a self-centered analysis of the session. "The comments from back home have been extremely good, in spite of the fact that the local media, with the exception of Scripps-Howard, never did give the filibuster the kind of coverage the national media did."

Plain Dealer Washington bureau chief Bob Snyder said Metzenbaum had established himself as a player—a serious senator—even if it did earn him enemies. Besides, Snyder wrote, "He loves publicity and he has never got this much—ever. When his wife Shirley stopped by the chamber Wednesday afternoon, she showed him his picture on page one of the *Washington Star*. He beamed."[48]

Yes indeed, Metzenbaum was now a presence, a fellow who didn't mind infuriating colleagues even when the issue at hand was a lost cause. Metzenbaum realized he could not win the debate in the short run, as natural gas shortages, real or manipulated, were a major element in the energy crisis of the mid-1970s. But by raising awareness of the difficult issue, he thought he could alert the public to the likelihood of the higher prices that deregulation would bring. Perhaps he could win the argument in the future. "I never got tired because the adrenaline kept moving. I think others tired far more rapidly than I. Some of the senators became somewhat peeved and even irritated, but in retrospect I don't believe any of them will carry any malice or antipathy after the fact."[49]

Not all of the reviews were flattering. "In legislative terms, Senator Howard Metzenbaum's 13-day filibuster won him nothing. . . . Some of his important colleagues are sore as hell at him. . . . He won over only one or two senators during the long fight," Jim Herzog wrote in the *Cleveland Press*.[50] *Congressional Quarterly* had a similar take. "The incident generated hard feelings all around—particularly toward Metzenbaum—who lacked Abourezk's jovial sense of humor."[51] Price controls eventually came off and the quick skyrocketing of prices that Metzenbaum feared didn't occur. One thing was certain: he had expanded the scope of the filibuster and made it an acceptable tool for liberals as well as conservatives. The ends now justified the means in the Senate across the political spectrum. The so-called good government types would go to the same obstructionist lengths as mossback conservatives to get their way. If the Senate got shut down in the process, so be it. *Congressional Quarterly*, a bible for students of Capitol Hill, dubbed Metzenbaum the "liberal master of obstruction."[52]

The Metzenbaum-Abourezk filibuster had a lasting impact. Rules were altered in 1979 so that time taken voting on amendments and other procedural matters *would* count against a maximum of 100 hours of debate once cloture was invoked. In 1986, the allowable 100 hours—after a three-fifths majority voted (cloture) to limit debate—was scrunched to thirty hours. "They only changed the rules when Howard Metzenbuam and I filibustered on behalf of the consumer!" a bitter Abourezk wrote years later. "I thought that was very interesting about the U.S. Senate."[53] "We were here when Jim Abourezk and Howard Metzenbaum . . . closed down the Senate day in and day out because of their concerns on the deregulation of natural gas," Senator Kennedy said in a 2000 Senate speech that put a softer edge on the historic filibuster. "People respected this. And at the end of three days and three nights, members of the Senate were going out and embracing and shaking hands because they respected the fact that people had strong views and that this institution responded to them."[54]

Metzenbaum had his niche. He was the stopper, the uncompromising individual willing to operate, if need be, as if he didn't care whether his colleagues liked him or not. One need not confuse respect with affection. In his Senate office, he ran the show with the same hardheaded determination. He had difficulty keeping staff early on because he drove people so relentlessly. At his worst moments, he treated aides like servants. "It's not exactly a walk in the park when he is constantly moving, constantly demanding," said Barry Direnfeld, who worked for Metzenbaum as a mail clerk in 1974 and rose to the position of chief counsel.[55] The boss was appreciative and easy to get along with, he said—as long as you did your job perfectly.

An internal memo to his staff near the close of his first term gives a glimpse of his demanding nature: "Time after time I am given material for a speech that I have to make just a few hours before I'm to leave the office. And each time it occurs I lose my temper. So that there's no misunderstanding on the part of any of you, the next time it occurs I'm going to ask you to take a week's vacation at your expense."[56] Because of his poor eyesight, his speeches were always typed in boldface with all capital letters. "He demanded total commitment and quality of work and when you produced that quality he would take it and get something done," Direnfeld said. "He could carry those facts out in battle and go to extremes that other senators would not go to." Metzenbaum wanted his staff to perform with the precision of a well-drilled football squad paying attention to every detail. "It's like jumping offside," Direnfeld said of the expectations. "Every person should be able to go off with the snap. We were all pretty tough. It was a hyper place."[57]

When one senior staffer, Mary Jane Due, quit, Metzenbaum sniffed, "She does not like to rock the boat, whereas I do."[58] He was fiendish about punctuality. The office opened at 8:30 AM and he would wander the suite and peek into cubicles to make sure his employees were not tardy. One October, he blew his top when he phoned into his office from home between 8:30 and 9:00 AM and no one was there. When he finally reached a top aide, still at his apartment, he was told, "Uh, Senator, it's only eight AM. You must have forgotten to set your clock back to adjust for the end of Daylight Savings Time."

He kept track of most everything else. The first-term senator chronicled his early months—highs and lows. One day was dull, another, "not a particularly exciting day." After a meeting with Carter at the White House in 1977, he gushed, "It's tremendous to sit across the table from the president of the United States. No person in his right mind, or who has any sense of ego, would fail to feel a certain sense of excitement about being a participant. It makes one feel that there is a sense of history about that which he is doing. And if one doesn't let it go to his head too much, it is probably all right. But since I have no ego, it's no special problem for me."[59]

In a body filled with big egos, Metzenbaum was probably right. It was "no special problem" for him. But even after attaining the success he longed for, he could be extraordinarily petty and impatient. In early 1980, he wrote a scolding letter to George M. White, a fellow Clevelander who was then architect of the Capitol. Metzenbaum was fed up with having to wait for slow-moving elevators in the northwest corner of the Dirksen Building. "You are my friend. I love you, but I am not willing to wait more than two minutes for an elevator," he told White. "If you cannot get them fixed, turn it over to me and I will. If they aren't fixed promptly, I am going to take the subject up with the Rules Committee. I don't mean that as a threat, but I mean it as an indication of my frustration. . . . I am sorry to keep bugging you, but when a Senator is in a hurry to get to a meeting and stands around twiddling his thumbs."[60] Fifteen years later, after his departure from the Senate, the elevators were still a problem in the musty old building.

Metzenbaum gravitated toward Ted Kennedy, who was emerging as the Senate's liberal voice at a time when pundits thought Carter would pull the Democratic Party back to the center of the political spectrum. "I see a possible close-working relationship developing here, and I think Kennedy might need it. He seems to be somewhat left out of the mainstream, although he has pretty much become the main liberal spokesman on the floor of the Senate."[61]

But Metzenbaum kept a line open to his party's conservative faction. He met with majority leader Byrd, a stickler for rules, to complain about the frequent junkets his fellow senators took at the cost of negative publicity. "I think I made a ten-strike in discussing the subject with him, and I felt I had probably accomplished something."[62] When Byrd later invited him to attend a conference of parliamentarians in Mexico City, Metzenbaum insisted on paying his own way, just to make the point. He couldn't please everyone in the lordly U.S. Senate, so why even try? "When he got there he had something to prove," said aide Joel Johnson, who worked for Metzenbaum nearly fifteen years. "Clearly, when he came to the Senate, he was hell-bent on making his mark."[63]

Ups and Downs

Metzenbaum's aggressiveness and intuition for hot-button issues won him the media attention he craved but also reinforced the notion that he was a publicity hound who would do almost anything to get on the front page. Reporters nicknamed him "Headline Howard." In 1977 when he dropped a bill to break up the big gas-pipeline companies, he was giddy because "the *Cleveland Press* gave it a blaring headline in all editions." An aide told him he "had never seen a bigger headline and could only assume similar size type would be used if the Martians landed. I told him that when the *Press* reported Metzenbaum's net worth was $3.9 million and that he had paid no taxes in 1969, the headline was equally bold."[64]

But all was not well. His feud with Glenn was ongoing, although Metzenbaum wanted a thaw for appearance's sake, if nothing else. After the filibuster, he made a note to himself that Glenn was among the "most critical" in judging "my actions." Glenn had said "that 'the filibuster was wasteful' and that 'the Senate should get on with its business.' No further comment need be made on this subject."[65] Glenn was among those senators turned off by the futility of the stalling tactic. He voted against Metzenbaum's position ninety-two times. "We've got a lot of filibusters besides his around here. I don't like that. I think it delays the whole setup," Glenn said.[66] The news media, loving a good fight, tried to draw out the two senators on their hard feelings, the continuing civil war of Ohio politics. Metzenbaum brooded about the relationship, fearing it could affect their ability to work together even on routine matters important to the state.

Sure enough, shortly after Metzenbaum's election, he and Glenn were stalemated on a recommendation for United States attorney for the Northern District in Cleveland. "Suffice it to say that, as of this moment, it appears to be somewhat of a donnybrook with Glenn, [Cleveland City Council president George] Forbes and Stanton on one side and [Congressman Louis] Stokes and I on the other. . . . I think I'm going to win, because the Stokes crowd has really gone to work on the subject."[67]

But there were no winners. The Carter administration ran out of patience with both men and insisted that they jointly recommend a third candidate. The hostility was cause for amusing and awkward moments, as two senators from the same state could not avoid each other all the time. Disasters, plant closings, ribbon cuttings, and other events forced them together. Shortly after taking office in 1977, Metzenbaum found himself cooped up in a car with Glenn and a driver, heading down Route 23 in southern Ohio for a visit to a uranium enrichment plant—a Cold War–era bomb factory—near Portsmouth. The Piketon facility, a big employer in Appalachian Ohio, was struggling to avoid a shutdown. "While we were on our way to Portsmouth John Glenn got sick to his stomach and threw up in the car," Metzenbaum noted in a memo to himself. "I tried to be as gracious and helpful as I could. The retching came about by reason of some medicine he had apparently taken to try to knock out a sore throat."[68] No notation is made of who cleaned up after the launch.

In Washington, both men denied there was any feud. They just didn't like each other. "The press really has blown this thing bigger than it is," Glenn said. But then in a burst of candor, he added: "I don't want to comment about holding grudges, or not holding grudges. We've had things on both sides, I'm sure, that were aggravating in the past, that didn't sit very well with either one of us and probably never will. I think, in all likelihood, Howard and I will never be extremely close, but that doesn't mean we don't cooperate on things for Ohio."[69]

Yet they didn't always cooperate. As with the U.S. attorney post, the White House looked to the senators to make joint recommendations for nominations of U.S. district court judges and other high-level appointments. "I can't get him [Glenn] to sit down and meet with me and

I just sent him a second letter on the subject," Metzenbaum complained. "I think he is far more uptight about who the judges are and whether he's been out-maneuvered than I am."[70]

Metzenbaum and Glenn had so much trouble agreeing on their choices that Attorney General Griffin Bell eventually met with each man separately to insist on compromise. "You couldn't find two men who are culturally, socially, philosophically more divergent," a top Glenn aide explained. "While Howard Metzenbaum and Ted Bonda were wheeling and dealing to park cars at Hopkins Airport, John Glenn was puffing on a pipe and studying the stars—literally. While Howard Metzenbuam was reclining in his seat in the Ohio legislature, John Glenn was doing a hundred-and-some odd [air combat] missions."[71]

When the *Plain Dealer* tried to arrange a photo shoot for a story about the chill between the two men, they refused to pose for the innocuous grip-and-grin picture, much less any lighter takes, such as standing back to back. Finally, Glenn's press secretary, Steve Avakian, sensing an embarrassing anti-Kodak moment coming on, suggested the senators stand next to each other while shuffling through some papers. "Glenn obligingly took out a folder that served as a prop for one of those stiff, can't-wait-to-get-out-of-here photos politicians are used to posing for."[72] The subsequent front-page story began this way:

Q. How would you describe the personal relationship between Sens. John H. Glenn and Howard M. Metzenbaum?
a. They hate each other.
b. They despise each other.
c. They loathe each other.
d. They can't stand each other.
e. All of the above.

The answer was *e,* as the unsparing newspaper account reported how the animosity between the two men had reached the point that the annual summer softball game between their staffs was called off in 1981. Glenn wouldn't even say whether he would endorse his fellow Democrat for reelection in 1982. The story, quoting mostly unidentified sources, traced the mutual rancor to the personal attacks in the previously documented 1970 and 1974 Democratic primaries. "I think if we have difficulties, they go back to personal things," Glenn said.

"It doesn't have much to do with philosophy, or Democratic national or state politics. . . . I'd be the last to deny, as I have said before, that Howard and I are ever going to be visiting and traveling buddies. Lots of past things didn't sit well with either one of us on both sides."[73]

"Certainly, we're not close," Metzenbaum admitted. "I think we both come from very different backgrounds. Our upbringing is totally different."[74] An unnamed Ohio House member described how the distrust between them could affect business important to the state. "You have to decide which one can help you the most because once you approach one, you lose the support of the other. If you call Howard's office, they'll say, 'Did you call Glenn on this?' And visa versa." When Glenn does not like someone, said one of his political advisors, "It's set in concrete. You can forget it."

The advisor was dismayed by the senselessness of the feud—it didn't add up politically. Glenn could help Metzenbaum in his reelection bid the next year, but more importantly, Metzenbaum could help Glenn with fund-raising if he ran for president, as expected, in 1984. "John does not have the political acumen to even think about it, and he won't listen to anybody on it. There's no percentage in being an enemy of Howard Metzenbaum's at this point. If you can't have the support of the Democratic colleague from your state, how the hell are you going to win the Democratic nomination?"[75]

The two senators went their separate ways. Glenn was the plodder, relishing modest victories and enduring small defeats. Metzenbaum, who didn't regard caution as a virtue, delighted in the killing of a bad bill almost as much as he did in the passing of a good one. In 1979, he jumped at the chance to join a third major committee—Human Resources, which handled social programs—adding to his work on the Budget and Judiciary panels. He also assumed the chairmanship of the Judiciary antitrust subcommittee, where he knew he would take a back seat to Kennedy.

The serious, disciplined Metzenbaum wasn't at Kennedy's side during Teddy's forays to the District's finer watering holes. While Metzenbaum enjoyed an occasional scotch, he was nobody's drinking buddy. He didn't have time for that sort of thing and preferred to spend free hours with Shirley. But that didn't mean Metzenbaum could not work closely with Kennedy within the confines of the Senate.

It will mean my sharing with him some of the media attention, but frankly, as I have said to my staff, I can well afford to operate in his shadow, because he is such a high profile individual at the present time. It is an accepted fact that were he to run in the Democratic primary in 1980, he would swamp Jimmy Carter. Wherever he turns crowds gather these days. If I were to be speaking out on antitrust issues on my own, I would get far less attention and the issues would not be of as major a moment. . . . He's not difficult to work with, although there isn't much question about the fact that he always is and will continue to be number one in that kind of relationship. Being number two to a Kennedy these days is not that bad.[76]

Metzenbaum always thought that the administration—whether run by a Democrat or a Republican—did not enforce antitrust laws with enough vigor. This mindset contributed to his antibusiness reputation. In his new role, he wanted to work against mergers and fend off the looming deregulation of the airline and trucking industries. He was a capitalist, to be sure, but not a laissez-faire one. He believed antitrust laws existed to rein in the free market. "You knew what Howard was going to do politically. He was predictable," said his former law partner and political confidant, Byron Krantz. "You knew the one thing he would do was support people over corporations and institutions, which he always did."[77] But he was wily. Maybe friends and colleagues knew where he would end up, but they were never sure how he would get there. "He had an intuitive feel for leverage. He really understood when his leverage was the greatest and when it was waning," said his legislative director, Joel Johnson. "And when it waned, he'd reach out, or change his position, give a little something."[78]

In a bill regulating strip mining, Metzenbaum succeeded in narrowing a loophole that would have exempted mines producing less than 200,000 tons of coal for the first year and a half after the law took effect. That was 93 percent of all mines, Metzenbaum calculated. "I proposed an amendment to return the bill to the condition it was in when it left the House, which provided no exemption, knowing full well that I was prepared to compromise at a hundred thousand tons."[79] And that's what he got.

Even though he routinely aggravated his colleagues, he was sensitive to the desire for a collegial atmosphere. In 1979, when the Senate agreed quietly to push forward the date when limits would be clamped on honoraria for speeches and appearances, Metzenbaum threatened to make an issue of the extension. Then he backed down, just as he had in the tiff with Stennis, not wishing to become "persona non grata with many members of the Senate . . . I must confess that I didn't show the greatest courage in not insisting on a roll call [to highlight what was going on] but at least I raised the issue."[80]

He also lost his nerve in a dispute concerning budget overruns for a new Senate office building named after deceased colleague Phil Hart. Metzenbaum first voted to stop work on the unfinished building, and then he agreed to reconsider that vote. On the next roll call, he again said "nay" to a $57.4 million supplemental outlay for it but finally agreed to let construction proceed when it appeared his vote could kill the whole project. "I decided it would be irresponsible of me to stop the building for a year or two," he explained to the *Plain Dealer,* though the newspaper offered another explanation for his flip. "Cynical observers offered the theory that Metzenbaum, who had voted for the Hart building in the past, might have taken a politically expedient route by voting against the unpopular project this time, figuring it would pass without him. His scheme was undone, so the theory goes, when the count was so close his vote would save or doom the building."[81] When the nine-story Hart Office Building was completed, one of its first tenants was John Glenn, who often could be seen strolling through its spacious atrium. Metzenbaum kept his suite in the old Russell Building.

Metzenbaum became more surefooted with each battle—and how he delighted in the battle. "You can be involved in a battle, win it or lose it, and not lose your ability to work with your fellow senators, provided that you don't get into any personal involvement," he said during an effort to force out Carter's abrasive energy secretary, James Schlesinger.[82] Strongly opposed to Schlesinger's call for decontrol of oil prices, Metzenbaum came up with his own mandatory energy conservation plan, including one of the first attempts to discourage "gas guzzler" automobiles. He was thrilled with the coverage of his plan, saying the *Plain Dealer* gave him the "greatest banner headline that I've had since I've been in office."[83]

In the Minority

As inflation rose and Schlesinger and Carter struggled with their energy plan, Metzenbaum watched the president's political decline and looked forward to the national campaign in 1980. "At this point, the enthusiasm for Ted Kennedy continues to grow and the lack of enthusiasm for Carter continues to grow," he wrote. "I've stayed on the sidelines and indicated that it was premature, but there isn't much doubt in too many people's minds that if Kennedy got into it, I'd probably get into it on his side."[84] He didn't have to. Kennedy folded his tent before the Ohio primary in 1980, so Metzenbaum had no need to choose sides among Democrats. But his ambivalence over the 1980 presidential campaign persisted. He was dismayed by Carter's politics and governing style and still harbored a grudge against Mondale for his role in breaking the 1977 filibuster. "I've never quite forgiven him," he admitted.[85]

Metzenbaum was intrigued by the growing popularity of Congressman John Anderson of Illinois, a maverick Republican. Anderson was issue oriented and more liberal than some Senate Democrats. "I saw in Anderson a personally acceptable alternative to Carter," he said. When Anderson bolted the Republican Party and opened a serious independent campaign, rumors abounded as to his choice for a vice presidential running mate. Metzenbaum's name made the "Great Mentioner's" list, and—although it was not reported at the time—the lifelong Democrat seriously considered it. Since his own reelection was two years away, he could run from cover and join Anderson's ticket without risking his Senate seat. "Would you take it?" his startled press secretary, Roy Meyers, asked him in 1980. "I think so," Metzenbaum replied.[86] Instead, the bid went to the former governor of Wisconsin, Pat Lucey, one of the least remembered of all vice presidential candidates. Metzenbaum supported Carter, and Anderson faded, winning less than 7 percent in November.

Reagan's landslide victory and the Democrats' loss of the Senate majority shattered Metzenbaum. He didn't want to believe that the country was in a conservative cycle. But the Democrats' seventeen-seat advantage was wiped out, and Republicans, led by Howard Baker of Tennessee, took charge in the Senate for the first time since 1954, holding a seven-vote majority. Metzenbaum insisted he was "comfortable" with the new president, a man he called a well-intentioned moderate conservative. After meeting with Reagan's secretary of state designee, Alexander Haig, Metzenbaum said he recognized the need for the United States to reassert itself as the preeminent world power "throughout the world," adding, "I am a realist enough to recognize that our conventional forces are not up to snuff."[87] He even gave the steely General Haig a box of nails as a humorous peace offering before voting to confirm him.

This talk of being a "realist" and having a comfort level with Reagan made Metzenbaum watchers wonder if he was edging to the center with his own reelection campaign just two years away. Not at all, the old tiger said. "That is a price I'm not willing to pay . . . to change my stripes."[88] "The fact that I even got elected to the United States Senate sort of blows my mind—because I was always a liberal," Metzenbaum said in a rare bit of introspection years later. "I came from poor parents. My name is Metzenbaum."[89]

Privately, Metzenbaum fretted. His Senate colleagues Gary Hart and Paul Tsongas talked about *new* Democratic politics, "But when we try to dissect what they are saying it comes out as, 'We can't rely on the old philosophy and programs, but we don't have the new programs and the answers.'"[90] He was already thinking what Mondale would articulate three years later in a debate with Hart: "Where's the beef?" A memo to Metzenbaum's close political aides written by a staff member noted the conservative mood of the electorate and urged that Metzenbaum avoid wearing his liberalism on his sleeve in the 1982 reelection campaign. "Howard's liberalism is too specific a part of his image for him to try to out-conservative Reagan, but he can seek to neutralize the issue by refusing to address it. He can simply be for the people, and let his detractors claim that means he is liberal. He can then turn around and ask whether that means that conservatives are not for the people."[91] If only politics were that simple.

When Americans for Democratic Action rated Metzenbaum the most liberal member of the Senate, the *Plain Dealer*'s Bob Snyder wrote a column saying that Metzenbaum's political aides were worried. "One Metzenbaum advisor said of the publicized ADA rating, 'I think that's a liability . . . I think it's a terrible liability." Metzenbaum told Snyder he wasn't bothered and considered the term liberal "outmoded."[92]

Harold Stern figured his old friend could pull it off, without breaking a sweat. "He was a liberal on social issues and a conservative on fiscal issues. He railed against government waste and became known as the watchdog of Senate spending," Stern said. "He was thought of more as a populist rather than a liberal senator," and though "more liberal than most Ohio voters, he still attracted a lot of support from independents and even conservatives."[93]

In the Senate, Metzenbaum soldiered on, learning how to be effective as a minority senator. He was gaining prominence, if not popularity, as the Senate watchdog. In a 1980 letter to Senate majority leader Byrd, Metzenbaum formalized a process that would be standard operating procedure in the Senate until the day Metzenbaum retired—all bills and amendments would have to be checked off with "Senator No" of Ohio. "It is in the closing hours of the session that I become concerned that amendments that could not pass on their own merits come to life and get enacted into law," he wrote. "I believe that we have worked out a procedure with the [Byrd] staff so that I may protect my position without actually sitting on the floor on such measures. . . . I would appreciate being notified in advance in connection with any unanimous consent request pertaining to a measure to be held at the desk so that I may come to the floor to protect my position."[94]

In the stuffy language of the Senate, that meant legislation of consequence would be run by Metzenbaum before going to a vote. That gave him a chance to exercise the prerogative of any senator to temporarily "hold" a bill or amendment, no matter how important or, conversely, how insignificant. Eventually, senators would circulate a small form so Metzenbaum could sign off on a given bill or mark that he had an objection. Better to check with him beforehand than to see business come to a standstill on the Senate floor due to his maddening delay tactics, Senate leaders decided.

Without a process, bills believed to be noncontroversial could slip through by "unanimous consent"—that is, without a roll call vote since no one present objected. Metzenbaum demanded to be notified ahead of time when such "UC" consent motions were likely so he could go to the floor and protest, breaking the supposed unanimity. Now, his power was institutionalized.

Metzenbaum was on guard until the early morning hours when mischief often slipped into legislation with only one or two senators in the chamber. He always kept one staffer there as a lonely lookout for stealth legislation. In his first term, he stopped or altered a bailout for timber companies, a railroad giveaway to the state of Alaska, and royalty-free leasing of federal land with valuable oil shale deposits. Senator Ted Stevens, a legendary pork-barrel baron, called the Ohio senator a "pain in the ass," a rare public rebuke. Metzenbaum took it as a compliment and eventually talked the cranky Alaskan into playing tennis with him on mornings before Senate sessions.

Metzenbaum referred to minor special-interest bills as "cats and dogs," but he was prepared to stay late into the night to catch them. He succeeded because he was willing—though not eager—to make enemies, and because he was willing to linger on the Senate floor when others wished to recess for a fund-raiser or social occasion. He exerted maximum leverage at the close of a session, when the attention span of some senators is on the wane and special interest items are tucked into bills. One Friday—without a warning to antsy colleagues about what was coming—Metzenbaum launched a filibuster against a water reclamation bill meant to help large farms with irrigation needs. Metzenbaum "exasperated almost everyone in the chamber," *Congressional Quarterly* reported, yet he managed to modify the legislation, limiting the types of farms eligible for cheap water from federal reclamation projects.[95] He had few allies in the mid-year fight, losing one vote 75–7. Even so, Metzenbaum succeeded in reducing the size of the farms qualifying for the subsidized water from 2,080 acres to 1,280 acres. "I'll bet Will Rogers never met him," joked his friend Ron Cohen, a Cleveland accountant who worked for Metzenbaum.[96]

In 1981, as oil patch senators attempted to win a multibillion-dollar reduction in the windfall profits tax on producers, Metzenbaum filibustered and cut the tax break in half. In the fall of 1982, Metzenbaum blocked more than a dozen bills for weeks by merely threatening to filibuster or by weighing them down with a flood of amendments. Among the items was raising the threshold for declaring bankruptcy; protecting beer wholesalers and international shippers from antitrust laws; giving the National Football League antitrust immunity so franchises could be blocked from switching cities; and allowing timber companies to cancel government contracts with no penalty. When E. J. Hess, then vice president of Exxon, scoffed, "That was another lengthy speech," after Metzenbaum griped during a hearing on price manipulation by oil companies, the senator fired back petulantly, "I don't intend to apologize to you for my concern. I'll make as many lengthy speeches as I want to."[97] And so he did. Metzenbaum also fought against Reagan's supply-side economics and budget cuts in programs that he cared about, such as job training. He told the president's flamboyant budget director, David Stockman, "I think you've been brilliant. I also think you have been cruel" in trimming programs for the poor.[98] Some of his colleagues accused Metzenbaum of playing to the galleries in the dustup with Stockman.

But it didn't faze him. "I'll tell you the secret to success in the Senate," Metzenbaum once said to Senator Richard Durbin, an Illinois Democrat who succeeded Metzenbaum's friend Paul Simon. "Don't be afraid to make a few people mad once in a while."[99] He told Joel Johnson that "I am just not happy unless I can fight with somebody." His aide later said, "Metzenbaum was probably the most restless person I ever worked for. There was never a vacuum."[100]

Metzenbaum was restless, but he also exhibited skill, guile, and pure endurance, which enabled him to work effectively in a body run by Republicans. "Senators in the minority have used this tolerance of unlimited amendments and debate to good effect. Democratic Senator Howard Metzenbaum (Ohio) and former Republican Senator Lowell Weicker (Connecticut) were acknowledged masters of the 'endless amendments' ploy to block legislation. Senators can also try to talk a bill to death through a filibuster," authors Edward Greenberg and Benjamin Page wrote in *The Struggle for Democracy*.[101]

Congressional Quarterly, taken by Metzenbaum's style, said he broke the rules, often mounting sneak attacks by not warning others when he intended to block a bill. "Metzenbaum refused to go along with the informal agreements and understandings that senators use to help one another and their constituents," the publication reported. "Any senator who wants to pass a bill adding a particular company or home-state interests—the sort of thing that often goes through without much opposition—must figure out a way to get around Metzenbaum," who had an "unyielding temperament and a thick skin that hostility never seems to penetrate."[102]

Alaska's Stevens said Metzenbaum "violated one of the basic rules of the Senate, which is to be a gentleman."[103] The ornery Stevens was in such a lather over Metzenbaum's block of his Alaskan railroad bill that he threatened to go to Ohio in the fall of 1982 to campaign against him. Metzenbaum flippantly offered to send him an airplane ticket. Stevens, a self-described "mean, miserable SOB," never did go to Ohio, at least not to campaign against Metzenbaum.[104] "Howard does not want to be a pariah," insisted aide Barry Direnfeld. "He goes out of his way to be nice to people, when he can be nice to them. But it is not going to keep him up at night."[105]

Others were less generous. "It fit naturally with Howard's role in life to be the mean dog in the manger—kicking his colleagues around in their individual appropriations—because he knew that sold well with the public," said a political rival who had felt Metzenbaum's sting. "But one man's pork is another man's building project. Most people are sensitive to what their colleagues think of them. Howard had no sensitivity."[106]

In 1980, Metzenbaum's staff calculated that he had saved the taxpayers $5 billion by derailing tax breaks and other goodies during the sprint to *sine die* adjournment that fall. "You could be a downright curmudgeon," Congresswoman Marcy Kaptur of Toledo told him years later. "[But] you made a difference for all of us."[107]

His growing notoriety could not allay his uneasiness when he looked toward reelection in 1982. He felt stale and somewhat intimidated by Reagan's popularity. He was a good blocking back, but how could he move the ball forward in conservative times? His legislative assistant, Peter Harris, promoted kitchen-table issues with an eye toward answering the question, What have you done in the last six years? "The answers do not have to boil down to the traditional liberal theme of throwing money at a problem," Harris advised Metzenbaum midway through his term. "Many of these allow us to help a group of constituents, at the same time that we take a special interest to task. The projects come together into some natural themes: helping Ohio cities, working for better health care, improving the energy situation, job security and job safety for Ohio workers."[108]

Maybe the challenge from the right was getting to him. In 1982, he voted the same way as Jesse Helms on one-third of the roll calls, according to a *Chicago Sun-Times* analysis. "It just goes to show that even Jesse Helms can be right some of the time," said Metzenbaum's press secretary, Roy Meyers.[109]

In a confidential memo from "HMM" to his innermost circle, written just after the 1981 off-year election—a year out from his own bid for another term—Metzenbaum wrote that he was out of ideas and worried that the "new politics" of the decade was passing him by. "Last night I spoke at the Democratic Leadership Circle and it wasn't my greatest achievement. Shirley rightfully pointed out that I was talking about some of the old Democratic programs," he wrote. "There was no new thrust. She said it sounded like 'old politics' and she was right."[110]

—— ⫴ ——

CHAPTER 7

The Senate Years II

"Thank God for Metzenbaum."
Washington Post, *December 12, 1982*

Howard Metzenbaum was racked with doubt as he approached his Senate reelection campaign in 1982. He was a minority senator, short on new ideas. He was puzzled by the conservative resurgence and wary of the indomitable James A. Rhodes, Ohio governor and looming rival. This campaign would be a proving ground, validating his iconoclasm or sending him packing as a one-term wonder. To be a serious player, a senator wanted the security and seniority of a second term.

Metzenbaum needed another run of good luck. He had gotten the Senate seat in the first place because of Bill Saxbe's surprise departure in the turmoil of Watergate. He defeated Taft in 1976, a year that swept in the "Watergate babies," as the newly elected Democrats were called. Despite his angst, the political climate favored Metzenbaum again in 1982. His comfortable position was one of the ironies of the staggered six-year Senate term. Had Metzenbaum succeeded in winning reelection in 1974, he would have faced drowning in the Reagan tide of 1980. But by 1982 the decline of the automobile and steel industries had severely affected Ohio, creating a favorable forum for Metzenbaum's feisty brand of economic populism.[1] According to a regional governors' report, between 1977 and 1982, Great Lakes states lost 15 percent of their manufacturing jobs. In some north-central states, including Ohio, unemployment doubled during the recession of the early 1980s. The Bureau of Labor Statistics reported that jobless rates climbed above 12 percent in Ohio, Michigan, and Indiana in the opening months of 1982.

Going into the election year of 1982, Metzenbaum was still suffering aftershocks from the triumph of Ronald Reagan and his fellow conservatives. In 1981, the right-wing journal *Human Events* urged conservatives to make defeating Metzenbaum a national cause. The magazine tapped Congressman John Ashbrook, not Rhodes, as the GOP frontrunner: "This sets the stage for what would clearly be the nation's top ideological confrontation in 1982, if Ashbrook faces Metzenbaum."[2]

Rhodes, then seventy-two, nearing the end of his fourth term as governor, and barred by law from running again in 1982, was still in the picture. It had been more than a decade since his narrow loss to Taft in a Senate Republican primary, yet when asked whether he would campaign for one more office, his friend Cuyahoga County Republican chairman Bob Hughes said confidently, "If he's breathing, he's running."[3]

Human Events reported that both Rhodes and Ashbrook believed Metzenbaum "would be very vulnerable in 1982, because he's an unrepentant leftist-liberal who has built a bad reputation for his anti-business and pro-big government activities. Metzenbaum has shown great ability to attract publicity by being constantly on the attack, but has been rated as a lightweight by many of his Senate colleagues, who tire quickly of his headline-grabbing antics."

The conservative movement preferred Ashbrook but recognized Rhodes as a fact of life. He was a formidable political force, invigorated by Ronald Reagan's success in demolishing the "age issue." Age aside, Reagan was a relatively fresh face whose entire political résumé amounted to eight years as California governor. But Rhodes's political journey began in 1939. "He is clearly a candidate subject to the age and length-of-service time bombs," noted *Human Events*.[4]

The energy industry was also eager to see its nemesis, Metzenbaum, booted out of Washington. "Two of the worst enemies of the oil industry remaining in the Senate are Howard Metzenbaum and Ted Kennedy. Sen. Metzenbaum is up for re-election in 1982."[5] Metzenbaum was no lightweight, but a Cambridge Survey Research poll taken for Ohio attorney general William J. "Billy Joe" Brown found 30 percent of Ohioans rated his job performance only fair or poor. And a Market Opinion Research poll conducted in January 1982 had Rhodes running slightly stronger than Ashbrook in hypothetical matchups against Metzenbaum.

The incumbent, however, held a comfortable margin over either Republican, according to MOR's Robert Teeter, polling for the Republican National Committee. What's more, 41 percent of the 800 Ohioans surveyed by the Michigan firm regarded Metzenbaum as a conservative. "What we're going to have to do is pick out some specific issues and show he is a liberal," a Republican strategist told the *Plain Dealer.*[6]

Metzenbaum's staff and family soon responded to his demands for new ideas to take into battle. In fact, a year earlier, an unsigned staff memo titled "Getting Howard Metzenbaum Re-elected" advised, "Broaden perception of constituents: folks know Howard fights for blacks, the poor, the elderly. Expand image to include fighting for the middle people—the family of four making $25,000 per year." Metzenbaum should stress his kitchen-table issues with middle-income folks, the electorate's biggest voting bloc. "Focus on consumer protection/pocketbook issues," the memo concluded.[7]

Metzenbaum's former administrative assistant, Rick Sloan, amplified the "fighter" theme in July with advice for the campaign organization: "The issues of abortion, busing, gun control and capital punishment will be used like a meat cleaver to cut into HMM's natural constituency" (Taft never used them in 1976). Let's try this, Sloan urged: "Ohio's Metzenbaum . . . a Friend, a fighter, an Effective Senator" and "HMM fighting for the little guy and against Big Oil and the Special Interests." In December, Sloan wrote again to key advisors and staff, using language that came right out of Jim Rhodes's playbook. The December 12, 1981, memo from Sloan, a onetime labor lobbyist, argued, "The BIG issue in Ohio today is jobs, jobs and more jobs . . . Let's give HMM something positive to talk about. It is an issue that should be ours: let's grab it and run with it."[8]

Besides, if the polls were correct and some Ohioans mistook Metzenbaum for a conservative, why disabuse them of the notion? Why harp on issues like gun control and the death penalty? Indeed, Metzenbaum often referred to himself as a businessman and fiscal conservative. "They didn't know he was Jewish—they didn't know he was liberal," aide Dick Woodruff said of Ohio voters in 1982.[9]

On Our Side

A campaign battle plan was coming together as a result of brainstorming involving the senator, his family, and top aides. Artificiality—calculated shifts from previous issue stands—would not work. "What should we do—move to the right? The hell with it: be yourself and let the chips fall where they may," was the way legislative assistant Barry Direnfeld characterized the growing consensus.[10] A statement, drafted for the 1982 race, gave an idea of where the campaign was headed: "When I ran for the Senate in 1976, I made two promises to voters of Ohio: that they would always know where I stand on the tough issues; and that I would stand up and fight for what I believe is right for Ohio and the country."[11]

But fighting for what he believed in didn't mean Metzenbaum had to wear liberal orthodoxy on his sleeve. Undated talking points directed to his inner circle prior to the election spelled it out: "Since his arrival in the Senate, Howard Metzenbaum has placed one mission above all others: to fight for the average Ohioan and the average American." A series of examples of Metzenbaum's battles against "powerful corporate lobbyists" was listed for use in a campaign brochure—unassailable issues such as working to preserve the child-care tax credit, repairing a vital bridge in Cleveland, and forcing Ohio utilities to buy more Ohio-mined coal. On top of the unsigned memo, someone had handwritten, "he's on our side."[12]

In January, Rhodes, having consulted with Bob Hughes, former Ohio Republican chairman Kent McGough, and other advisors, decided Washington was not for him. He had spent a political lifetime bashing Capitol Hill—"Congress giveth, Congress taketh away," etc.—so the decision came as no great surprise. When asked by Hamilton County Republican chairman Earl T. Barnes why he would even think of going to the Capitol, he answered, "Burning Tree, Earl, Burning Tree"—an allusion not to forestry policy but to an elite male-only golf club in the Maryland suburbs. By 1982, Rhodes said, he'd lost the urge to travel down the "glory road" and would stay in the Columbus area, comfortable in his Upper Arlington home not far from the campus of his beloved Ohio State University and its two golf courses, the Scarlet and Gray.[13]

Metzenbaum, an occasional golfer who favored the faster pace of tennis, still had a fire burning inside. Rushing around the Capitol, he often addressed people by their last names, using a mock guttural growl. He scolded those he thought were complacent to "get off your butts!"

His conversation was peppered with shopworn one-liners such as "I kid you not" from the Jack Paar era, "I'm frank to say" (often prefacing a mundane utterance), and "I make no bones about it" as a way of conveying sincerity. Though his thick blond hair had gone mostly white, his faced was lined, and his was voice raspy, he was still up for another fight at age sixty-five. One obstacle to his reelection—Rhodes—had been removed, but one remained. He braced for a classic ideological matchup with Ashbrook. Voters would have a choice between an urban liberal who believed the federal government should be an active force in the lives of individuals and a small-town conservative who wanted to rein in Washington at every turn.

The Harvard-educated Ashbrook was a gentle man but a combative conservative with some libertarian leanings. The year before his Senate campaign, he said, "If men were angels, there would be no need for government," and "if government has any legitimate functions, they are quick and heavy sentencing of felons, the prevention of terrorist threats to the public safety, and the halting of Communist imperialism." Certainly, those were federal functions that would come into play in the years ahead.

Ashbrook was the son of Congressman William Ashbrook, a conservative Democrat nicknamed "Pennypinching Bill" for his reluctance to spend taxpayer dollars. After a two-year hitch in the navy, John Ashbrook graduated with honors from Harvard, where he had driven a bakery truck to earn pocket money. He went on to the Ohio State University College of Law, Metzenbaum's alma mater, and became chairman of the Young Republicans national organization. He didn't practice law for a living. A voracious newspaper reader, he took over as publisher of the *Johnstown Independent,* a weekly paper founded by his family in 1884. He was elected to the Ohio legislature in 1956 while still in his twenties and jumped into a vacant congressional seat in 1960, the year John F. Kennedy was elected president.

"I would probably be more conservative as a congressman than as a state senator," he predicted during his years in Columbus. "I believe there are probably a lot of things the states should do, but the U.S.

government should not." He was true to his word. He was the only congressman north of the Mason-Dixon Line to vote against the 1964 Civil Rights Act.

At dinner one night, while serving in Congress, he told then state representative William Batchelder that those on the right "must be the Vietcong of the conservative movement, sneaking up on the established at night, and throwing bombs over their walls." This was more than idle dinner table chatter. Ashbrook acted on his principles and had challenged Richard Nixon in the 1972 Republican presidential primary because he thought Nixon strayed too far from conservative principles. The president had endorsed wage and price controls at home and détente abroad with the Soviet Union. During a historic trip to China in early 1972, Nixon embraced the Communist People's Republic in Beijing as the "one China" and threw old ally Taiwan overboard. Nixon was too pragmatic for Ashbrook's tastes. Mainstream Republicans were furious with the upstart from Ohio. But Ashbrook said he was "an American first, a conservative second, a Republican third."[14]

Ashbrook campaigned actively in three states—New Hampshire, California, and Florida—pulling only 10 percent of the vote and capturing not a single delegate. Lacking money and name recognition, his conservative protest was crushed. But Ashbrook's admirers credited him with keeping the pulse beating for an ideologically pure movement and also for prompting Nixon to veto liberal legislation that year. "He was willing to risk everything for an idea, even undertaking what he surely knew was a hopeless presidential campaign," said Ashbrook fan Jack Kemp, a congressman and Republican vice presidential candidate in 1996.[15] Ashbrook's was an unyielding brand of conservatism—the notion that the power of an idea, left undiluted, will eventually prevail. Ashbrook had stepped up when the right wanted a champion.

"Goldwater started a conservative counter-revolution with his stubborn, splendid presidential candidacy. Ashbrook kept the counter-revolution alive, with few workers and little money, when many conservatives were content to go along with a president, who, far from being 'conservative enough,' had turned into an agreeable Keynesian and an avid détentist," said conservative author Lee Edwards.[16]

In contrast, Ashbrook stayed true to his vision of limited central government, states' rights, anticommunism, and "what are now called family values," Batchelder said. "He was remarkable for his strict, consistent adherence to those ideals, regardless of political cost."[17] Ashbrook and Metzenbaum could agree on one thing. Metzenbaum did not view his fellow men as angels—far from it. Metzenbaum thought big guys were forever trampling on little guys and often said he preferred the company of children to adults. He just thought government had a responsibility to provide more than the bare necessities to the butchers and bakers, the tramps and the thieves, whether they liked it or not.

And so it started in the winter of 1982, the right taking on the left in a campaign where no one could claim voters did not have a choice. Metzenbaum put together a strategy that would serve him well in a state that had little patience with ideologues. Some credit his daughter, Susan Hyatt, with first coining a phrase that transcended ideology. "He's an SOB," she said, quoting what she suggested might be the view of some voters, "but he's an SOB on my side." Susan said she was amused by the remark because, "Howard was a tough guy." But someone else at a morning campaign staff meeting—she didn't remember who—first came up with the phrase. You don't have to love him, in other words, but you have to respect that he is fighting to make a difference.

Metzenbaum raised money in prodigious amounts. He was fearless—some would say shameless—in his pursuit of campaign cash. "I think we knew each other years ago when you did some business in Cleveland—or I could be in error on which Arnow it was," he wrote to wealthy New Yorkers Robert and Joan Arnow on July 1. Just in case they didn't remember, he advised the couple that he was the "ranking Jewish member" of the Senate. "At any rate, I need your help and take this means of asking you whether it will be possible for the Arnow family to contribute a total of $10,000 toward my campaign. As you well know, there is a maximum of $1,000 per person and I am not sure just how many are in your family. I do know what I need."[18] A month later, the Arnow family joined Metzenbaum's list of donors, although the gifts were less than what he had hoped for. In an earlier letter that April, he asked New York lawyer Myer Feldman to intervene on his behalf and solicit Jackie Kennedy Onassis's close friend Maurice Tempelsman. "Would you be in a position to ask him for $2,000, which is the maximum he could contribute, unless he marries Jackie, then they could contribute $4,000. If you would prefer not to do so, be good enough to call me and give me his telephone number and I will go to him directly."[19] Tempelsman eventually gave $1,000.

To his old friend, Ted Bonda, Metzenbaum wrote, "Just a reminder that you and Gabe [Cleveland Indians general manager Gabe Paul] were going to try to get some of the baseball owners to set up some fund-raisers. Would you please follow up on it?"[20] Metzenbaum would also make cold phone calls to well-off types he barely knew, telling them, "I think you should be supporting me." Former Austrian ambassador Milt Wolf, a longtime acquaintance of Metzenbaum, recalled a conversation he had with actor Tony Randall. "About a week ago, I got a call from a guy named Howard Metzenbaum," Wolf quoted Randall, describing a solicitation. "I had never met him in my life before. I knew he was a liberal." The celebrity money poured in. Harry Belafonte, Leonard Bernstein, Goldie Hawn, Paul Newman, Alan King, Marvin Hamlisch, Isaac Stern, and Danny Thomas were all supporters. So were folk singers Peter, Paul, and Mary. Wolf said Metzenbaum "remembers the names of everyone who ever gave money to him, and he remembers the names of those who turned him down too."[21] Steve Kovacik, Glenn's political guru and no friend of Metzenbaum, hedged his bets this time, chipping in $500.

On the campaign front, Metzenbaum's minions were digging up dirt on their opponent's fund-raising activities. Ashbrook was also active, planning to expose the Democrat as an ultraleft liberal out of touch with heartland values. But it was over almost before it began. Ashbrook collapsed while appearing in Mansfield that March. He seemed to re-cover within a few days and continued campaigning. But on April 24, at fifty-three, he died of a heart attack in his office in Johnstown.[22] His untimely death was a profound shock to Metzenbaum. The two men got along all right on Capitol Hill and "used to kid around."[23] Metzenbaum told his aides that he wanted to win, but not this way. He immediately canceled his campaign schedule and suspended all activity. He tried to call Ashbrook's wife, Jean, but could not get through. "I liked John," he said years later. "He was not flaky. You knew what he was. That was what made the race so interesting."[24]

The race was essentially over. Metzenbaum wouldn't characterize it as such—fate had stepped in with another man's death—but he had lucked out again. State senator Paul Pfeifer of Bucyrus, Ohio's bratwurst capital, moved into the breach. Pfeifer, a moderate, ran a vigorous campaign, borrowing from Ashbrook's game plan. He painted Metzenbaum as a mean-spirited liberal far to the left of most of his constituents. Metzenbaum's voting record on the liberal Americans for Democratic Action (ADA) scorecard in 1982 was 100 percent. His grade with the probusiness U.S. Chamber of Commerce was 7 percent. But another Market Opinion Research poll done for the Ohio Republican Party found that 32 percent of those surveyed thought Metzenbaum was a conservative, 7 percent said he was moderate, and 22 percent didn't know his political philosophy. Only 39 percent described him as liberal.

The December 1981 poll indicated where a majority of Ohioans stood: 53 percent said they regarded themselves as conservative. There was Pfeifer's challenge. "The thrust of the Pfeifer campaign," a GOP fund-raising memo said, "will be to let Ohio voters know the truth—there is a big difference between Howard Metzenbaum and Senator Paul Pfeifer. Howard Metzenbaum is a free-spending liberal!" The survey findings were included in a five-page GOP mailer that warned ominously, "Metzenbaum has successfully obscured his liberal philosophy in Ohio . . . Metzenbaum is, if nothing else, a consumate [*sic*] politician. Though his liberal voting record is second to none, he has the uncanny ability to tell the not-so-liberal Ohioans exactly what they want to hear. He has even convinced many that he is a conservative."[25] Surprisingly, the Republican campaign did not emphasize his wealth—the seeming contradiction picked up by others who regarded him as a limousine liberal. For all of his antibusiness stands in the Senate, Metzenbaum had made millions as a hardnosed businessman who profited, in part, from nonunion labor.

In critiquing his record, the strategists said he voted against a 1977 bill that banned the interstate sale of material showing children under sixteen in sexual acts, even if the images were not judged obscene. The Justice Department said the bill was probably unconstitutional, and Metzenbaum agreed. Pfeifer road-tested the issue. "With child pornography reaching epidemic proportions, Metzenbaum voted against strengthening a kiddie porn law," he said in a mid-summer news release.[26] The charge didn't stick and faded from the conversation. But the notion that Metzenbaum was soft on child pornography would be used against him in a future campaign.

Pfeifer never had a chance. The aforementioned GOP fund-raising memo turned up in Metzenbaum's collection of Senate papers, suggesting his office obtained it during the campaign. The Reagan White House, smelling defeat, stayed away from Ohio. And with the economy in the tank, the president wouldn't have been of much help anyway in 1982.

Metzenbaum raised $3.7 million for the race but spent only $2.7 million of it, cruising to a 525,000-vote victory, a 56 percent margin. He won in every region of the state, carrying fifty-one of Ohio's eighty-eight counties. He had captured only twenty-seven counties against Taft four years earlier but eked out victory by piling up huge margins in northeast Ohio and making inroads in the Appalachian region. In 1982, Metzenbaum prevailed in Republican-leaning Franklin County and Taft's home turf of Hamilton County, both of which had gone Republican in 1976.

On election night, claiming victory at his Cleveland headquarters, Metzenbaum said the outcome "convinced me the people of Ohio will support a senator who has the courage of his convictions and who will stand up for them."[27] Metzenbaum had not come up with any grand new vision, but he honed his message and now had his mandate. His battle cry resonated with the great political center. Simple as it sounded, this focus on "fighting" for issues important to ordinary Ohioans was how a "blue" senator prospered for nineteen years in a state that leaned "red." "Metzenbaum had a tremendous knack for being right about issues people care about—job security, safeguarding pensions, workplace safety, healthcare, keeping banks honest," said John Green, director of the Bliss Institute of Applied Politics at the University of Akron. "We had a joke at the institute, and I do not mean this in a disparaging way. 'Oh, there goes Howard Metzenbaum, friend of the working man.' He was able to identify with a large cross-section of voters in Ohio."[28]

In this election at least, the Republican strategy of painting the Democratic candidate as a free-spending, anything-goes liberal had failed. Voters simply did not make a connection between Metzenbaum's service in Washington and unpopular social policies. (In succeeding decades, GOP strategists like Newt Gingrich and Karl Rove would find new, more successful ways of tainting their opponents as dangerous liberals.) Metzenbaum's old friend Dave Skylar had it right in his analysis of the Ohio electorate. Most voters were not worried about Metzenbaum's ideology. They had decided he was "on our side."

"See, I don't think Howard's legacy is an ideological one among the voters of Ohio," Joel Hyatt said. "I think there is much, much more to his attributes as a senator. He probably never had majority positions in Ohio. But he was honest and a fighter who stands up for what he believes in. It is a legacy of leadership."[29]

Pfeifer raised a respectable $1.02 million and came out of the contest with his head high. He went on to a long career on the Ohio Supreme Court as a maverick Republican, often siding with Democrats. Rhodes finished his term at the statehouse, reopened James A. Rhodes and Associates, a development firm, and plotted another campaign for governor.[30]

The Abominable No-Man

Metzenbaum was emboldened by his success at the polls. He decided to demonstrate the "courage of his convictions" at the postelection lame duck session of Congress, which President Reagan called for in December to finish overdue work on 1983 spending bills, according to the *Washington Post*. In a little more than three weeks at the close of the Senate session in 1982, Metzenbaum blocked or amended twenty-six bills, saving $10 billion that otherwise would have been doled out to special interests. Metzenbaum shut down or modified a Colorado irrigation project, drug patent extensions, a proposed ban on fetal research, and a tax break for luxury cruise ship patrons. He and Senator Bob Dole even stopped a tax deduction for a budding computer firm called Apple. It seems the young entrepreneurs at Apple wanted a write-off for donating some computers to schools.

Metzenbaum seldom went after spending on what he called "people programs." But when it came to corporations or large institutions, he was a capitalist with a strong libertarian streak; that is, he despised corporate welfare in the form of handouts or bailouts. So that December, he stopped legislation forgiving timber companies $2 billion in obligations on government contracts; he blocked another bill writing off $38 million that a Colorado water irrigation district owed the government, and he refused to waive a $300,000 income tax liability for wealthy California winemakers. He said "nay" to antitrust immunity for the National Football League and for some beer wholesalers, arguing that a "Six-pack bill" would raise retail beer prices at carryouts. And Metzenbaum knew Joe Six-pack wouldn't be seen very often aboard Caribbean luxury liners, so with the help of other senators, he capped a tax deduction for expenses at $2,000 while attending conventions aboard cruise ships. His rich friends—and he had quite a few—could afford to pay their own way. In the same session, he finally agreed to Senator Stevens's rail transfer, but only after Alaska agreed to pay more than $22 million, the fair market value for the railroad and its 38,000 acres of land.

"I wound up being a policeman on the floor," Metzenbaum said with satisfaction. "Nothing—literally nothing—passed without its being brought to my attention for an okay . . . I could have gotten myself in a real snit and could have caused a lot of resentment. However, it didn't come out that way, and I wound up in this instance on my feet. I had a tremendous amount of national publicity crediting me with stopping any number of special interest rip-off bills . . . I myself am somewhat surprised that I was able to get by without venom or bitterness, except in a few instances."[31]

In December, the *Washington Post* confirmed that the newly reelected senator from Ohio had arrived as a serious player on Capitol Hill. "Thank God for Metzenbaum" was the headline of a story by Ward Sinclair about the senator's "war against the raid on the treasury." The story in an influential national publication marked total victory for Metzenbaum in the aftermath of a campaign that he had once feared, worrying he was out of step with conservative times.

In a glowing piece on his antiboondoggle tactics, the *Post* dubbed Metzenbaum the "abominable no-man" and declared, "he's about the most important man on Capitol Hill these days. Nothing moves through the Senate without his say-so." Metzenbaum acknowledged, "It may be arrogant to say I am not going to let a bill pass. You're damned right there is an arrogance, but I'm too old to go along for the ride . . . The Senate would be a better place if the leadership didn't let all these special interest bills see the light of day." Few of his colleagues were "willing to run the same gauntlet-of-scorn," leaving Metzenbaum as the "righteous gadfly."

"There's a big irony here," the newspaper noted. "Metzenbaum, as a result of his sallies against special deals for American business, is often labeled an enemy of the venerated free enterprise system. Fact is, the free enterprise system helped him become an immensely wealthy lawyer-businessman back in Cleveland."[32] It was an irony that smacked of hypocrisy from the perspective of Metzenbaum's enemies. But Republican candidate Pfeifer did not exploit it in the campaign that ended the month before.

In the Senate, Ted Stevens may have considered Metzenbaum an ungentlemanly pain in the posterior. But Metzenbaum believed he got through the stormy three-and-a-half-week lame duck session without making any new enemies. He liked the *Post* story so much that his staff put out a news release bragging about it and detailing the legislation he stymied. In his diary, Metzenbaum also noted the formalization of a process that would continue throughout his Senate career. He was one of the "good guys" in his way of thinking and his niche had been institutionalized. "On every bill," he wrote, minority leader Robert "Byrd's aide would get a sign-off from the ranking minority [Democrat] member of the committee, or anyone else particularly affected, and in each instance bring it to me for my okay . . . These were good days for me . . . quite often I would have to say no to people with whom I worked regularly. The fact that I was able to get by without embittering them pleased me much."[33] Metzenbaum's positive take on reaction to his combative tactics didn't surprise his wife, Shirley. Her husband was a natural optimist, she always said. "He sees the glass as half full. I see it as half empty. I'm the worrier in the family, no doubt about it."[34]

Metzenbaum was sworn in for a second full term in January with his party still in the minority and pitted against a Republican president. Reagan was even more popular after surviving a would-be assassin's bullet with courage and grace. But Metzenbaum was full of confidence after his strong showing in 1982. "I'm not worried about my reputation as a gentleman in opposing legislation of this kind [a water rights bill]. If I'm not the most popular guy in the Senate, well, I can live with that," he said after successfully altering the 1982 bill giving farmers subsidies to irrigate their land.[35]

As for his standing in a club where everyone is addressed as "my friend," saying he was "not the most popular guy" was overly generous in terms of how he was perceived. "'Obstructionist' is one of the nicer names thrown at Metzenbaum in the past couple of years," *Congressional Quarterly* said in its profile. "'Breach of etiquette' is one of the milder descriptions of his legislative style."[36] Metzenbaum "plays hardball with the kind of detachment you don't often see," said the Bliss Institute's John Green.[37]

Metzenbaum started his second term by welcoming back his colleagues with a good scolding. In an op-ed piece published in the *Washington Post,* he said the Senate had "become increasingly paralyzed by our own rules and traditions," rules that Senator Metzenbaum had used to full advantage just two months earlier. "In the lame duck session, I helped prevent passage of 26 separate measures," he wrote. "But that does not mean I approve the procedures that allowed me to succeed."

His audacity came easier since his party did not have a majority and did not control the calendar in the Senate. The filibusters, irrelevant amendments, and "holds" were the Republicans' problem, not his. And one more thing, he lectured in print, "Let's stop playing games with the schedule and establish procedures to bring bills to the floor promptly and provide ample time for their consideration."[38] Of course, the very reforms he advocated for a more orderly process would have made him a less effective senator. But little was done.

Metzenbaum was still a terror in his office suite, bawling out aides for slipups in the presence of other staffers and sticking his nose in cubicles in the mornings to check for tardiness. Starting time was 8:30 AM, not 8:31 AM, and the workday could extend beyond midnight for some if he suspected other senators were up to mischief on the Senate floor. "He was demanding and impatient," said Joel Johnson, a top aide during Metzenbaum's third and fourth terms. "He wanted to accomplish a lot."[39]

Juanita Powe, an African American hired by Metzenbaum as his personal secretary at the law firm in 1964, witnessed many such outbursts after going to Washington with him in 1974. For years, he addressed her only as Powe (pronounced Poe). She understood her boss was a perfectionist, but she upbraided him for his rudeness and rough language. "I would tell him, 'You have to stop that. I think it is inappropriate.' He apologized a lot. He was not a good listener, wasn't interested in the other side of the story."[40] Nancy Coffey, his last press secretary, said Metzenbaum once reduced a young receptionist to tears by chewing her out for mistakenly cutting off an important phone call. Powe and other senior staffers confronted him, and the boss marched out to the front desk and apologized profusely to his unfortunate aide. "You could call the man on his bad behavior and he would apologize," Coffey said.[41]

Even with the boss's blowups, the first-floor Senate office was a special place. On good days, there was a sense of electricity—a group of committed public servants on a mission to change the country, if not the world. As a backdrop for this human energy, Howard and Shirley Metzenbaum transformed the office suite at 140 Russell into a virtual art gallery. Instead of grip-and-grin shots of the senator mugging with dignitaries, Metzenbaum's walls were lined with quirky modern art from the likes of Robert Rauschenberg, Red Grooms, Frank Gallo, and others. His office furnishings included whimsical sculptures and antiques. "Enter Senator Howard M. Metzenbaum's office and suddenly you are in the midst of a small art gallery of revolving sculptures and paper cutouts, silk screens and serigraphs," wrote Martin Tolchin of the *New York Times*. "There are African and East Indian pieces, a portable desk used by a general in the Revolutionary War and an English jockey's weighing seat."[42] "You get weighed in stones," Metzenbaum explained as he showed another reporter the rider's scale. "I like to kid when women come into the office. I say, 'you wanna' get weighed?'"

After watching Shirley and Howard dance together at a party, Red Grooms gave the couple "Fred and Ginger"—a yellow and black depiction of the famous tandem of Fred Astaire and Ginger Rogers. Metzenbaum, who loved dancing and popular music, would never be mistaken for a leading man. He took singing lessons and also classes in French, but the instructions didn't take. "He can't sing," Shirley Metzenbaum said, "and he can't talk French."[43] Nor could he tell a joke. Over the years, Metzenbaum invited artists and performers to his office for informal get-togethers with friends and fortunate reporters. At one of these, composer Marvin Hamlisch asked guests to throw out one-liners so he could improvise a new song on the spot. When Metzenbaum suggested "The Senate is a Barrel of Laughs," Hamlisch winced slightly and asked for another entry.

Tom Brazaitis, the *Plain Dealer*'s respected Washington bureau chief, got a tour of the office gallery on a hectic day in 1987. He shadowed Metzenbaum in his office and also in the halls of Congress. With phones ringing nonstop and buzzers going off signaling stacked votes on the Senate floor, Metzenbaum informed a nervous legislative aide, "I'm going to kill the bill if they don't take it my way. You can tell that to anybody that wants to know." Metzenbaum refused to agree to a time limit for debate on the bill in question, and when the staff member left, he explained his reasoning to Brazaitis: "I can tie up this bill and drag it out as long as I want, which becomes an obstacle to the leadership. They don't want to get tied up in this kind of horseshit bill. That isn't one of their priorities. That's the tactical game I play. You've got to be prepared to be a son of a bitch. You've got to be prepared to stand up and fight and be willing to commit your time and effort."[44]

He told Brazaitis that being elected to a second term had boosted his confidence. "Maybe it was after the last election. I saw I was able to win. I felt confident of winning, even against John Ashbrook, but you have that kind of apprehension. It's the first time out, people are judging you, and you're just not quite sure."

Minutes later, outside the Senate chamber, Metzenbaum huddled with speechwriter Dan Grady and Peter Harris, who succeeded Sloan as chief of staff, and. The subject was a contentious tobacco subsidy bill. "Tell them I'm not going to go along with that. Tell them the senator's gone as far as he's willing to go. You're taking advantage of the situation. We'll take our chances on the floor." Harris told Metzenbaum, "Howard, in my bones I think the time to have compromised was yesterday. Let's get the deal now before it all falls through." Metzenbaum listened respectfully to Harris, scrunched his brow a little, but didn't budge. "No. Don't worry. Relax." Recalling the confrontation, Harris shook his head. "The next day, they'll [Metzenbaum's opposition] come up with something better . . . He just hangs in there, hangs in there, hangs in there, and makes them come to him."[45]

"I would just cringe at the pressure he's under and at how uncomfortable the situation is," Harris told Brazaitis, "but he'll just be leaning back at the desk, honestly just truly relaxed, and he'll say, 'No, the answer is no. That's not good enough.'" *Congressional Quarterly* observed, "Making deals with Metzenbaum is not always easy because of his uncanny ability to read his opponents and extract maximum concessions."[46]

By the mid-1980s, he had become a master of the filibuster, the threatened filibuster, the de facto filibuster by amendment, and the "hold"—a broad courtesy afforded senators of both parties. Putting an anonymous hold on an item allowed senators to freeze legislation while negotiating for concessions. According to the Brookings Institution, senators varied widely in the frequency with which they requested holds; for some, holds were a central feature of their legislative activity. Party leaders were skilled at estimating which senators meant business when they placed a hold and which senators' bluff could be called.

"Liberal Democrat Howard Metzenbaum is one senator who means business and has developed an extraordinary role in the Senate with his use of holds and threatened filibusters," wrote Steven S. Smith of the Brookings Institution. "Nearly all legislation is scrutinized by

Metzenbaum as a young boy, lower right, with his brother Irwyn, lower left, and father Charles, top right. Juanita Powe

Metzenbaum with his brother Irwyn and parents Anna and Charles after graduation from Ohio State University, 1939. Metzenbaum Family

RE-ELECT

HOWARD M. METZENBAUM

State Representative

DEMOCRATIC TICKET 78 **REDUCE THE SALES TAX**

Election Tuesday, November 7th, 1944

VOTE THE STRAIGHT DEMOCRATIC TICKET

Early Metzenbaum campaign fliers. Metzenbaum Family

Howard Metzenbaum campaigning in Cleveland with former president Truman, 1958, with candidate Stephen M. Young at Truman's right and Metzenbaum partner Harold Stern behind. Metzenbaum Family

Howard Metzenbaum with Robert F. Kennedy and Ethel Kennedy, 1968. Metzenbaum Family

Howard Metzenbaum with John Gilligan and Senator Edmund Muskie, 1970.
Metzenbaum Family

Howard Metzenbaum with Cleveland mayor Carl Stokes, spring 1970.
Juanita Powe

Metzenbaum with
Senator George
McGovern,
Cleveland, 1972.
Metzenbaum
Family

Senator-Elect at last. Metzenbaum claiming victory over Senator Taft at the
Sheraton Cleveland Hotel. His wife, Shirley, star of an effective television campaign spot, is at his side. *Plain Dealer*, Nov. 3, 1976

Senator James Abourezk, Senator Metzenbaum, and President Carter in the Oval
Office, 1977. Metzenbaum Family

Old rivals on the same side. Senator John Glenn speaks on Metzenbaum's behalf
in Cleveland at Burke Lakefront Airport rally in 1988 campaign against George
Voinovich. Metzenbaum is holding his two-year-old grandson, Michael Sherwood,
daughter Barbara's child. *Plain Dealer,* March 7, 1988

Metzenbaum and family celebrate his 1982 victory over state senator Paul Pfeifer at the Bond Court Hotel in Cleveland. The banner behind him carries the slogan that became his battle cry: "He's On Our Side!" *Plain Dealer,* Nov. 2, 1982

Rush Hour. Metzenbaum in his last term talks to commuters aboard "The Rapid," Cleveland's subway. Metzenbaum, considering the Regional Transit Authority's request for more federal mass transit money, asked the passengers if they valued the Rapid Service. *Plain Dealer,* March 11, 1991

Metzenbaum's staff, with the possibility of a hold always in mind." Metzenbaum's obstructionism became so widely anticipated, yet unpredictable, that even Republican majority leaders of the early 1980s regularly screened measures coming to the floor with him in advance, rather than depending on the Democratic floor leader to serve as an intermediary. In the Ninety-ninth Congress, Democratic leaders took official recognition of Metzenbaum's role on a form used for clearing measures for floor action: the form had check-off boxes for the floor leader, ranking committee member, and Howard Metzenbaum. Arkansas senator David Pryor noted, "When you prepare an amendment or a bill, subconsciously you're thinking about Howard Metzenbaum. Will it pass the Metzenbaum test?"[47]

Writing for Scripps-Howard, Adam "Jerry" Condo confirmed that Metzenbaum "has been playing watchdog for so long now that the bureaucracy has accommodated him, to an extent. The cover sheet on every bill up for consideration used to carry the typed names of the majority leader, the minority leader, and committee heads. They would initial the cover sheets indicating the legislation was cleared for action. Now, that same cover sheet carries Metzenbaum's name as well. His initials are a sort of good housekeeping seal of approval."[48] Senator Bob Dole of Kansas nicknamed Metzenbaum "the Commissioner," as in, clear that bill with the commissioner before you bring it to the floor.

To his friend from Illinois, Paul Simon, Metzenbaum was "the Tiger from Ohio." Metzenbaum's mastery of the parliamentary rules gave him "the ability to tie up the Senate, and he is feared and respected for that ability," Senator Simon wrote in his weekly newspaper column.[49]

As Metzenbaum's reputation grew, he flailed away at familiar demons. He questioned the tax-exempt status of the Daughters of the American Revolution, argued that J. Edgar Hoover's name should be torn off the nameplate of the FBI Building, and criticized the Pentagon's spending on military bands, which totaled $100 million in 1983. Throughout his public life, Metzenbaum griped about the money going to army, navy and Marine bands. He was unimpressed with their traditions of inspiring troops going into battle. And perhaps he was unaware of the pleasure they brought proud veterans and the general public. The Marine Band, for one, is so revered that it is known as "The President's Own," so named by Thomas Jefferson. It remains the nation's oldest continuously active musical group, numbering John Philip Sousa among its alumni. John Glenn and his wife, Annie, often attended the band's weekly summer concerts at the Capitol. It is doubtful they ever ran into Howard and Shirley there.

Metzenbaum, in a terse letter to Secretary of the Army John Marsh Jr. on June 6, 1983, demanded dates and locations of all band functions, names of sponsors, and costs of the appearances, including travel, lodging, and per diem expenses. Those kinds of detailed records were not kept, the senator was told in a polite letter dated June 28. But "military bands offer a unique service to all Americans," Major David J. Matthews III wrote to Metzenbaum. "Whether fostering patriotism or instilling esprit, they represent a proud lineage of service and sacrifice that extends back over the entire history of our great nation."[50]

A $250,000 Phone Connection: "What I did was very little"

Metzenbaum's own esprit was about to be deflated with release of the 1983 financial disclosure reports, giving data on senators' personal holdings and income on top of their annual $69,800 salaries. Metzenbaum revealed that he collected a $250,000 finder's fee for putting the owners of an elegant Washington hotel, the Hay Adams, in touch with a prospective buyer from California. When his secretary, Juanita Powe, asked him where the money came from as she prepared the disclosure form, he answered without concern, "It doesn't matter." For his earnings, Metzenbaum made at most a few phone calls linking Cleveland developer Jeffrey I. Friedman and hotel co-owner George F. Mosse with Los Angeles developer David H. Murdock. He used an intermediary, whom he wouldn't identify, to help convince Murdock that the owners were interested in talking.

Metzenbaum knew what he was doing. He became skilled at making deals during the late 1960s and early 1970s before beginning his Senate career. He believed he would have been fabulously wealthy had he pursued his deal-making career and not entered politics. "I make no bones about it," he once said in a conversation at the University Club in Washington. "I think if I had not gone into political life, I would have been extremely wealthy—extremely wealthy."[51] "He loves making deals—he loves bargaining," said Joel Johnson. "He used to love playing poker."[52]

Metzenbaum would lose this hand. When critics in the media and conservative circles questioned the propriety of the payments to a public servant, Metzenbaum reluctantly gave the money back, plus $24,524 interest. The incident came at a time when Judiciary Committee member Metzenbaum was aggressively probing attorney general nominee Edwin Meese's financial dealings. Metzenbaum had initially asked Friedman to give the $250,000 to a charitable trust he controlled at the Jewish Community Federation of Cleveland, he said. "There was no legislative matter involved. Of all the bad shots I have had in my life, I thought this was the most unfair."

He never admitted a mistake, or the appearance of a conflict. Friedman and his wife, Susan, had given $4,000, the maximum allowed, to Metzenbaum's 1982 campaign. "It was one of those stories that irritates me more than any other. What I did was very little. But in the business world what you often do is very little, but you get paid very well."[53] Friedman said that when Metzenbaum first approached him about a potential buyer, he told the senator the hotel was not for sale. "The amount of money I would want, nobody is going to pay me," he warned Metzenbaum. "Don't be so sure," Metzenbaum shot back.[54]

The stately hotel, across the street from Lafayette Park and one block from the White House, was a favorite lunch spot of Nancy Reagan and others in the Washington social scene. Two old friends, retired navy doctor Bill Narva and his wife, Rose, alerted Metzenbaum to its value. During the ensuing negotiations, Friedman said he got a phone call from former Nixon chief of staff H. R. "Bob" Haldeman, then in private life and acting as a go-between for Murdock. "I understand we may have something to talk about," Haldeman told him.

Metzenbaum denied flatly that Bob Haldeman—a man who once viewed his name on a White House enemies list—had anything to do with the deal. In any event, the transaction went through with the Hay Adams selling for about $30 million. Metzenbaum called soon after the closing, inquiring about his fee. By then, Friedman was having second thoughts about the arrangement. He said he was uncomfortable making a check out to the charity in Metzenbaum's name and preferred to pay him directly. "He said, 'fine.'"[55]

After the story broke almost a year later, Metzenbaum insisted he had done nothing wrong. He seemed to miss the point of the arguably disproportionate fee. For placing as few as three phone calls, he made more than most of his constituents would earn in five or six years. His hard-charging staff was demoralized by the episode, fearing it would hurt his effectiveness. "That was a sad time," said Powe. "He tried so hard to be [scrupulously] honest."[56]

"I can't touch anything in the business world," he moaned. "I got all that bad publicity for doing something that was legal and ethical."[57] The District of Columbia Real Estate Commission eventually determined that Metzenbaum had not acted as a "broker" under D.C. law and did not violate any "rules or regulations." He felt righteous enough in the aftermath of the flap to ask Friedman to make a $50,000 soft-money contribution to the Democratic Party. When Friedman said he thought the sum was a little steep, Metzenbaum told him not to bother giving a lesser amount. "He and I did not remain close after that," Friedman said. Yet Friedman was sympathetic to the plight of Metzenbaum and other well-off lawmakers who took pay cuts when they came into office—and then faced constant scrutiny. Metzenbaum "never agreed to stop being a businessman when he took the oath of office," Friedman said.[58]

The Hay Adams incident would haunt Metzenbaum into retirement. He questioned whether the *Plain Dealer* reporter who pursued the story was anti-Semitic. Informed that newsman Amos Kermisch was born in Israel, Metzenbaum asserted that Jewish reporters were hard on him to avoid any hint of favoritism. "This may surprise you, but I feel it is always the reporters of my own faith who are the toughest on me."[59] When the old federal courthouse in Cleveland was renamed for Metzenbaum four years after he retired, commentator Dick Feagler, who hosted the event, wisecracked, "They were going to name the Hay Adams after him too, but that fell through." Metzenbaum managed a weak smile.[60]

The pounding didn't slow him down in the Senate. He browbeat the aspirin industry into putting labels on pillboxes to warn of a possible link between the product and Reye's syndrome, a children's disease. He and others successfully blocked the sale of Conrail, the government-owned freight rail carrier, to Norfolk Southern. Metzenbaum said it was a bad deal for taxpayers and would weaken competition among railroads. "Any deal would be a raw deal if it costs railroad worker their jobs or cripples rail service to the Midwest. We should not and I will not allow us to pass legislation in haste," Metzenbaum said.[61] It didn't pass. And Conrail stayed in government hands.

Aides marveled at Metzenbaum's intellect and his attention to detail. Nothing, it seemed, got past him. Don Sweitzer, a political advisor who served briefly on his staff and married his scheduler, Sherry Clapp, recalled sitting in on a private meeting between the boss and L. Stanley Crane, the head of Conrail. "They were negotiating these complex finance issues dealing with railroads. Nobody but the two of them knew what they were talking about. It was rapid fire, back and forth— numbers crunching, depreciation allowances, and so on. At one point, Metzenbaum leaned back in his chair and gazed in thought, running numbers in head. He looked upward at the chandelier in his office. Then he picked up the phone right in the middle of the negotiations. 'Sherry, has anyone dusted this chandelier lately?'"[62] Sweitzer practically spit up his coffee. Crane and the other railroad men glanced at each other, bemused.

Metzenbaum also maintained a keen interest in energy issues. He led a separate fight that succeeded in defunding the U.S. Synthetic Fuels Corporation. The faltering effort to extract oil from coal, or methane from plant cellulose, cost taxpayers $7.4 billion by the time the Senate pulled the plug. And when the 1986 tax reform act—cutting taxes for some and eliminating breaks enjoyed by others—proposed billions of dollars worth of "transition rules," he declared war on what he called "greed rules." The idea was to hold harmless those groups already engaged in an activity or transactions based on the old tax law. But Metzenbaum said the so-called transition rules "have one common thread, each one is custom-tailored to provide a single taxpayer or a very small group with special tax benefits not available to anyone else."[63] He and his staff read the legislation line by line and rooted out $1.6 billion in tax forgiveness that Metzenbaum deemed unjustified. He managed ultimately to stop $1.26 billion in transition aid, stripping it from the bill. Yet he left himself vulnerable as he quietly let pass half a dozen transition rules protecting Ohio interests, including tax advantages for a proposed domed sports stadium in Cleveland—a fantasyland never built.

Despite his self-professed fiscal conservatism, he was cool to the proposals of the Grace Commission, appointed by Reagan in 1982, which said $424 billion could be trimmed from the federal budget over three years, much of it from welfare and other domestic programs. At Reagan's request, business mogul J. Peter Grace recruited 160 top executives who urged the government to impose standard business practices on its spending habits. By 1984, Grace's group produced 2,478 cost-cutting recommendations in a report called "Burning Money: The Waste of Your Tax Dollars." Among the commission's ideas were a call for less government support for legal services to the poor, shorter vacations for federal workers, and a scaling back of the bureaucracy at the U.S. Energy Department.

Grace, a vigorous, chippy fellow, blamed Congress, not Reagan, for out-of-control spending in Washington. At a Senate hearing, Metzenbaum fought back, challenging Grace's priorities. "Howard Metzenbaum was very mean when I testified before his committee," Grace said later in a Cleveland speech. "He seemed to be trying to downgrade my commission's work. He's very smart, but he can be very tough."[64]

Grace wasn't the only Reagan appointee to face Metzenbaum's wrath. Metzenbaum lectured William Bradford Reynolds, the administration's assistant attorney general for civil rights, on lax enforcement of the very laws he was sworn to carry out. "All white-maned indignation, Metzenbaum's bony face reddened as he pressed for an explanation of what he called Reynolds' 'obscene' and 'shameful' decision to allow a Selma, Alabama, polling place to be switched from a black neighborhood to a white one," syndicated columnist Mary McGrory wrote.[65] Once, battling over confirmation of an Occupational Safety and Health Administration board member in the Judiciary Committee, Metzenbaum infuriated Republican chairman Orrin Hatch, who began shouting at him. "I get tired of these inquisitions . . . Every Reagan nominee goes through this, and it's crazy." Metzenbaum airily replied, "Calm down . . . take a sedative."[66]

On the Senate floor, Metzenbaum strengthened a 1980 law meant to assure the safety of infant formula. His bill forced formula makers to meet certain health standards that would include tests of each batch of formula to assure required nutrients were present. While not heavily publicized, this was one of his proudest achievements and was seen as a huge victory in his inner circle. He also passed and saw enacted legislation requiring the government to print photos of missing children on government mail. He got the Congress to authorize $5 million for research on Alzheimer's disease, and he created financial incentives for makers of "orphan drugs," scarce medicine for rare diseases. He cosponsored the 1986 Age Discrimination and Employment Act, outlawing forced retirements on the basis of age.[67]

In his own search for government waste, Metzenbaum didn't need help from the Peter Graces of the world. In 1985, he stalled a $3.5 billion effort to divert Colorado River water to central and southern Arizona with the help of what he saw as an overly generous 3.3 percent interest rate to the state. Metzenbaum "looks at those figures and cringes. This hard-nosed bean counter, who has a reputation for sniffing out pork barrel give-aways and using parliamentary maneuvers to stop them, says he's not anti-West, anti-water, or anti-Arizona—just anti-handout,"[68] reported the *Dayton Daily News.*

The point of the bill was to send cheap water to farmers in the southwest. But Metzenbaum thought the growers already had a good deal since they had a fifty-year window, interest free, to pay their share for water-producing projects. He went on to suggest that western conservatives supporting the Colorado River plan were hypocrites. Members of the so-called Sagebrush Rebellion demanded balanced budgets while at the same time seeking subsidies for water, irrigation, and dam projects, Metzenbaum argued.

"Helms . . . set the record for the five congresses examined with eighty-four floor amendments in 1979–80. That is a rate of more than one amendment for every four days the Senate was in session," said Steven Smith of the Brookings Institution. "Metzenbaum nearly reached that level in 1985–86, when he sponsored seventy-two floor amendments, also nearly one amendment for every four session days. These hyperactive senators, including Morse and Proxmire, had relatively extreme policy views. Indeed, very conservative and very liberal senators are over-represented in the group of senators with more than twenty floor amendments."[69]

Metzenbaum's reputation was growing nationally. But another embarrassing distraction loomed. He prided himself on quiet but resolute backing of the state of Israel. Although he was not deeply religious, he felt a strong affinity for the cultural aspects of "my faith," as he called his Jewishness. He had played a behind-the-scenes role in Operation Moses—the airlifting of the Falasha (Ethiopian Jews) from Africa to Israel. He had become alarmed by the eccentric behavior of Libyan strongman Muammar Gadhafi, a sworn enemy of Israel and a ruler widely suspected of state-sponsored terrorism. President Reagan said he had evidence that Libya trained gunmen who were responsible for killing eighteen people in attacks at the Rome and Vienna airports in 1985. (Others blamed Palestinian terrorists.)

Metzenbaum, a lifelong opponent of the death penalty and a critic of cowboyish covert activity by the Central Intelligence Agency, had heard enough. On Dick Feagler's WKYC television show in Cleveland in early 1986, Metzenbaum said the United States should consider eliminating Colonel Gadhafi with a "single action," assassination by any other name. "I have difficulty in distinguishing between a warplane dropping a bomb on the headquarters of [Gadhafi] and perhaps taking the lives of dozens or hundreds of people, or a singular kind of attack," he said.[70] Reaction to his clumsy comments ran from bemusement to ridicule—and no such action was attempted by the CIA. "Rambo" Metzenbaum appeared inconsistent and out of his depth on a complex foreign policy matter. "I thought he should have shut up—that was one point where he should have held his tongue," said his wife, Shirley.[71]

Reagan almost certainly wasn't listening to Metzenbaum's counsel. But that spring, the president, blaming Gadhafi for a lethal terror attack on a German disco, ordered air strikes on the Libyan cities of Tripoli and Benghazi. Gadhafi's headquarters were hit, and his two-year-old adopted daughter was among those killed. The dictator escaped with his life, and by the turn of the century appeared to have turned away from support of terrorism. In 2004, President George W. Bush normalized U.S. relations with Libya.

On the home front, diplomacy was going better for Metzenbaum. In fact, he finally achieved a state of normalcy in his relationship with Glenn. The cold war between the two Ohio Democrats was thawing. "La Guerre est fini," the *Plain Dealer* wrote of the détente between the adversaries. Key aides to the two men, most notably Metzenbaum's press secretary Roy Meyers and Glenn spokesman Dale Butland, worked quietly for several years to end the feud. When Metzenbaum was red-baited as an "unrepentant Stalinist" and taken to task again for the Hay Adams deal in the conservative *Washington Times*, Glenn sprang to his defense. He denounced the op-ed piece by media critic Reed Irvine on the floor of the Senate and called the article tawdry in a letter to the editor of the newspaper. "Though we have had our differences over the years, we have always shared a common commitment to the American values of freedom, opportunity and social justice. Howard Metzenbaum is a patriotic American who time and again has been willing to fight for those values regardless of the odds or the opposition," Glenn wrote.[72] Metzenbaum reciprocated by cosponsoring a fund-raiser to help retire Glenn's debt from his 1984 presidential campaign.

The real breakthrough came almost unnoticed in late 1983 when Metzenbaum—doing what he did best—deliberately delayed a roll call vote in the Senate to accommodate Glenn, who was mired in presidential campaign business in downtown Washington. Glenn missed the vote anyway, but the gesture was noticed and the warming trend started. When Glenn ran for reelection to the Senate in 1986, Metzenbaum served as his campaign cochairman. A humorous news release after the renewed summer softball game between the "Amazing Metz" and "The Right Staff" celebrated the partnership. "Glenn took the mound wearing a tee-shirt that said 'Glenn '86' on the front and 'Metzenbaum '88' on the back."[73]

The implications of the new cordiality "for the Democratic Party and the people of Ohio are considerable," the *Plain Dealer* said.[74] Glenn won reelection easily in 1986 and the relationship was cemented as the two men returned to Capitol Hill the following year to take key committee assignments for a new Democratic majority. After six years, Republican rule in the Senate was over. Working cooperatively, Glenn and Metzenbaum were in position to bring more benefits to their state.

The political pressure was all on Metzenbaum. The old obstructionist had at least two years to prove that he could pass bills, as well as stop them. His enemies would watch his every move—every head-fake, every offside call, every turnover—determined to slam him down when he faced reelection to a third full term in 1988. Metzenbaum had "burst the myth of the Senate as a club, and epitomized its modern-day evolution as a place where mavericks and individualists can thrive," *Congressional Quarterly* reported. "Being Peck's bad boy was one thing when Republicans held the Senate. But now Metzenbaum's party has the majority, and the responsibility to govern. The test is whether Metzenbaum can succeed in that contest, or whether he will find himself one Democrat who prefers life in the minority."[75]

Metzenbaum rebounded from his odd foray into foreign policy by capturing a seat on the Senate Select Committee on Intelligence, giving him firsthand scrutiny of the secret CIA budgets he had long questioned. "I welcome the opportunity to oversee the intelligence activities of our government, particularly at this time when there is so much public concern about the private conduct of our foreign policy," he said in reference to the arms-for-hostages Iran-Contra affair, not his own comments on Libya.[76] But, sure enough, he would pay a price for not being the most popular guy in the club. He failed to land the chairmanship of a full committee, unlike Glenn, who was picked by the Senate leadership to head the dull but important Governmental Affairs panel. "Metzenbaum was there a long time and never got that committee chairmanship," said his legislative director, Joel Johnson. Johnson blamed the seniority system that put Ted Kennedy and Joseph Biden of Delaware—two senators interested in the same issues as Metzenbaum—ahead of him in line.[77]

Undeterred, Metzenbaum instead chaired three subcommittees from the Judiciary, Energy and Natural Resources, and Labor and Human Resources committees. In the first weeks of the 1987 session, he set an ambitious, prolabor, proconsumer agenda, an action plan for a politician in the majority and facing reelection in less than two years. Harris began bringing aboard new legislative aides in 1985—hard chargers "who can get headlines, and also get things done." New hires were told to come up with "accomplishable" legislative goals "that you can pass." "We would focus very much on enhancing our legislative record," Harris said.[78] Metzenbaum wasn't much on brainstorming or touchy-feely staff retreats. His assistants were supposed to be self-starters. "You were under tremendous pressure to produce. You needed to be bringing him issues," said Johnson, who became legislative director in the mid-1980s. "It was just understood that the general order of business was to make things happen and get things done."[79]

Red-Bait Redux

Even with his improving legislative record, Metzenbaum had been fretting about the 1988 election. On paper, he had good cause to worry. An internal poll showed Cleveland mayor George Voinovich running almost even with him in Cuyahoga County, home turf for both men. Voinovich looked more formidable as a Senate candidate than Ashbrook. He was Metzenbaum's nightmare opponent—a moderate Republican, Catholic, and ethnic with a strong base in Cleveland. Voinovich had run statewide, getting elected as Rhodes's lieutenant governor in 1978. "The textbook way to defeat a Democrat in Ohio is to run a moderate Republican from the Cleveland area to cut into the Democratic base and simultaneously hold onto the normally Republican central and downstate region," the respected *Cook Political Report* said.[80]

Nearing seventy, Metzenbaum even toyed with the idea of not running for a third term. "He didn't want to lose to Voinovich," Harris said.[81] Metzenbaum decided to work all the harder in the Senate, advocating for "unassailable issues" and continuing to walk his beat as the Senate's "policeman" on the floor.[82] As a wave of factories shut down in northern Ohio, he introduced a plant-closing-notification bill and also called for restrictions on companies hiring scabs to permanently replace striking employees. He submitted the Brady Bill—a waiting period for handgun sales, named after the fallen White House press secretary James S. Brady, who was nearly killed and left severely disabled in the assassination attempt aimed at Reagan. Metzenbaum also introduced a second bill banning sales of certain semiautomatic assault weapons.

Metzenbaum had grown close to the Brady family, especially Brady's wife, Sarah. The Bradys formed Handgun Control Incorporated, which became the nation's leading gun control advocacy organization. The idea of the Brady Bill was simply to enforce laws already on the books. The waiting period gave authorities time to check a prospective buyer's record to make certain he or she did not have a felony conviction, bench warrant, or mental health issue. Yet the National Rifle Association opposed it vehemently from day one, arguing that the wait was an intrusion on the Second Amendment. In the NRA interpretation, the Bill of Rights guaranteed an unfettered right for law-abiding citizens to own firearms with these words: "A well regulated Militia, being necessary to the security of a free State, the right of the people to keep and bears Arms, shall not be infringed." Metzenbaum knew passing even a modified version of the handgun legislation would probably take years. So he pressed ahead with less controversial, more doable issues, including his perennials.

As chairman of an antitrust subcommittee, he pushed Reagan to increase staff at the Justice Department's antitrust division. He fought for additional incentives for firms to produce "orphan drugs." He offered new labeling legislation that forced food and drug producers to list what was in their products so consumers could determine their nutritional value. His interest in healthy eating was genuine. "He hasn't got much patience for heavy people; he thinks people should take care of themselves," said Juanita Powe. "Juanita," he once said to his slender secretary, "do you know nine out of ten African American women are overweight?"[83] Despite his love of desserts, Metzenbaum kept in fighting form. He avoided heavy foods and often opted for a salad at lunch.

He didn't win on the nutrition-labeling bill in the One Hundredth Congress and had little luck convincing Reagan to turn loose trust-busting bureaucrats on businesses. But he was victorious on the plant-closing bill and a companion worker-retraining bill. He also guided to enactment other measures: further aiding in Alzheimer's research, protecting retiree benefits, and extending the statute of limitations for age discrimination claims. And although the Brady Bill failed, Metzen-baum even got a crumb on gun control by coauthoring legislation in 1986 that outlawed powerful armor-piercing bullets, sometimes called cop-killers. With law enforcement supporting the ban, the National Rife Association backed down and it became law.

In 1988, Metzenbaum won again by attaching a rider to a bill un-related to gun control. His amendment barred manufacture, sale, or possession of plastic guns and other lethal weapons capable of slipping through metal detectors. His cosponsor for the plastic gun ban was South Carolina conservative Strom Thurmond, an ally of the NRA, which decided not to fight the amendment. "It is aimed at keeping terrorists from getting powerful undetectable firearms which could be smuggled past security devices at airports, courtrooms, and even the White House," Metzenbaum said.[84] Mississippi Republican Thad Cochran, a political adversary, took note. "There's a new willingness" on Metzenbaum's part "to reach out and develop bipartisan consensus where possible, rather than just charging off without regard to whom he may hurt or aggravate."[85]

That "new willingness to reach out" began paying off for him. After LTV, the big Cleveland-based steel company, declared Chapter 11 bank-ruptcy and threatened to cut off benefits to retirees, Metzenbaum won passage of the Retiree Benefit and Bankruptcy Act. It barred unilateral termination of health and life insurance retiree benefits in bankruptcy and created a negotiation process for the imperiled plans. "On most pension issues, he would be considered 'Senator Yes,' among ordinary working people and organized labor," an influential pension newsletter said.[86] Metzenbaum also managed to beef up SEC investigations of hostile takeovers. It was far from a total breakthrough. He tried again and failed again to significantly strengthen antitrust laws. But as election year approached, he was satisfied he had built a positive legislative record, which he would emphasize over his skills as an obstructionist.

You know me, he would tell voters. I'm the guy who will warn workers if a factory is about to go belly up and then help them get retraining for a new job after the plant gates close. I will assure that infant formula is healthful and assist parents of sick kids in getting the hard-to-find drugs they need. And older Ohioans must know they have a friend in Howard Metzenbaum, who's fighting age discrimination and pushing to get more money for Alzheimer's research. "We worked on accomplishing things that would make voters want to not fire the guy," Harris said.[87]

Metzenbaum also cooled his anti-Reagan rhetoric and shocked longtime supporters by voting for a narrowly drawn death penalty clause in a popular anticrime bill. He was a lifelong foe of the death penalty, but he went along with a plan making gang leaders subject to capital punishment if convicted of murderous, narcotics-related activity in a federal case. "Their victims," Metzenbaum said, "can be found on our street corners, at our school yards, and in our city morgues." He had never opposed the death penalty as an ethical question, he said, but only because it was imposed disproportionately on minorities and because of the possibility that innocents could be put to death. "In all of my years of public service, I have never voted to make the death penalty available to a prosecutor. But, in this case, my conscience dictates that it is appropriate."[88]

He was deeply resentful of suggestions that his switch had anything to do with the 1988 election, where his Republican opponent was certain to be pro–death penalty in line with a majority of the Ohio electorate. In another time, in another forum, he conceded some uneasiness with his motives during the emotional 1988 debate over the antidrug bill. In retrospect, he said, "I am not sure whether there was some rationalization [about that decision] or not," admitting that it was "not impossible" that his vote for the death penalty was colored by "political aspects."[89]

His legislative successes and his new resolve to execute drug lords and Libyan dictators did not relieve his worries about the impending campaign. He had $2.2 million in cash for the race, several times as much as Voinovich or Congressman Bob McEwen, and second only to Lloyd Bentsen among all senators facing reelection. A Market Opinion Research poll taken for Voinovich in January gave Metzenbaum a nine-point advantage—49 percent to 40 percent—with 11 percent undecided or having no opinion. Washington analyst Charlie Cook, who handicapped congressional races, said the Ohio Senate seat leaned Democratic but was too close to call.

Then, an unexpected gift arrived at Metzenbaum's Cleveland office in the summer of 1987. A friend of one of his aides came across a packet of information carelessly left behind in the lobby of a Howard Johnson's hotel. Just thought you might be interested in this little bit of serendipity, said the messenger, who the Metzenbaum camp never identified. Inside the envelope was a seventy-two-page master plan for a take-no-prisoners negative campaign that would at last destroy Metzenbaum and deny him a third term. It included red-baiting from his fling with the Far Left in the 1940s, a notation that he voted against the 1977 bill restricting transport of child pornography, and a redredging of his old battle over taxes with the IRS. It brought up the Hay Adams finder's fee and noted that Metzenbaum had intervened with the Internal Revenue Service in a failed attempt to save the government job of nephew Terry Metzenbaum, Irwyn's son. It urged attacks on Metzenbaum's character and integrity.

Red-baiting was nothing new for the Far Right. The critic Irvine had called Metzenbaum a "Stalinist" and the newsletter *Conservative Digest* reported in March on Metzenbaum's "Red roots." But this latest plan of attack did not come from the fringe. This was put together by the campaign committee of and for Senate Republicans. It was headed by a colleague, who happened to be Jewish, Rudy Boschwitz of Minnesota. Yet the first reaction of Metzenbaum's political advisers was not shock but delight at the forewarning. Now they knew what to expect. On reflection, they decided to make the document public, thinking it was so extreme that it would backfire and work to the benefit of the incumbent senator. "Caution should be observed to avoid having the attack look 'McCarthyistic,'" the memo advised would-be challengers. "Opponents should try to use the negative connotations that the Ted Kennedy liberalism has in Ohio to taint Howard Metzenbaum: Guilt by association."[90] Voinovich had briefly attended a private meeting in Cleveland where the document, drafted by the National Republican Senatorial Committee, was discussed. There was no hint he endorsed it.

Harris and other Metzenbaum strategists gambled that outrage over the heavy-handed memo would trump any harm done by another round of Communist-sympathizer charges. They would exploit the Republicans' dirty little plan. The GOP committee's report was leaked to the *Plain Dealer* in Cleveland, which spread it across the front page of the state's largest newspaper. In the article, Metzenbaum called the material "one of the most unbelievable attempted smears I have ever seen." He denied any Communist connections and said he voted against the pornography amendment because of constitutional problems in other parts of a broader bill. "That is so vile and evil that, as a grandparent of five adorable children of four daughters . . . that's a level to which I wouldn't descend to try to defend myself."[91]

This time, the gamble paid off. The *New York Times,* in an editorial, called the opposition research "campaign sleaze." Most Republicans quickly distanced themselves. Senate minority leader Bob Dole and Senator Boschwitz of Minnesota apologized to Metzenbaum on the Senate floor. C. James Conrad, Voinovich's campaign manager, denounced it as junk. Congressman Bob McEwen, another potential Metzenbaum rival, reportedly said, "If ever there was a document that should be shredded, this one is." John Glenn was on the floor the day the story broke. "This is character assassination of the lowest kind, a campaign of poisonous innuendo masquerading as a campaign of issue," he said. "I have always regarded holding political office as one of this nation's highest callings, so I shudder when I see my profession being dragged through the gutter. This personal attack on Senator Metzenbaum is scurrilous, tawdry, and dangerously irresponsible. It smacks of McCarthyism."[92]

The Metzenbaum camp, seeing an opportunity, immediately put out an "urgent" fund-raising appeal. "I am outraged over an attack so scathing and sordid and demeaning to the American political process . . . To survive this slander and win reelection, I need your immediate help . . . The stakes are so high and we cannot afford to lose. Your check for $25 or even $15 will make all the difference," Metzenbaum was quoted as saying in the mailing.[93] The conservatives fought back, and in fairness, some of the charges in their plan of attack were accurate. The *New York Post* headlined, "METZENBAUM STORM; BUT IT'S ALL

TRUE." Columnist Eric Breihdel conceded the attack document was a "bit rough" and called the Communist sympathizer charge "dumb stuff." But he said the groups Metzenbaum associated with in the 1940s were legitimately identified as "Communist fronts" and Metzenbaum "never even explained" his involvement.[94] That tack didn't move the Republican mainstream.

Metzenbaum had been affiliated in the early 1940s with groups that had Communist leanings. His friend Milt Wolf said Metzenbaum's flirtation with the far left started during his college years and was rooted in idealism, not Stalinism as his critics claimed. It was, Wolf said, "the feeling that around the corner was a better life. They would huddle together in rooming houses, plotting romantic revolution and eating boiled potatoes."[95]

The Republicans go-negative-early strategy had backfired, and round one of the 1988 campaign went to Metzenbaum. If there was ever any serious doubt that he would seek reelection, it was over. His ambitious son-in-law, Joel Hyatt, was not coy about his own desire to run and waited impatiently in the wings. Hyatt would have to wait six more years. Senator No would again be the Democratic nominee. At age seventy, he would run hard for a third full term.

___ ⫙ ___

CHAPTER 8

The Final Campaign

Six More Years

H oward Metzenbaum recognized that George Voinovich was the most formidable obstacle to his remaining in the Senate since John Glenn halted his eleven-month run in 1974. Metzenbaum was anxious, just as he had been six years earlier as he searched for a message he could sell to an electorate leaning more conservative. But this time his approach would be different. He *knew* where he was headed in this campaign: he would run on his record as a consumer advocate, a defender of working people and their children, and a fighter for his state.

George Voinovich, the popular Republican mayor of Cleveland—the guy who rescued the city from the brink of bankruptcy—presented challenges Metzenbaum had never faced. Like Metzenbaum, Voinovich was a household name in Cuyahoga County and would compete vigorously for the huge Democratic vote in northeast Ohio. If Voinovich could hold Metzenbaum to a 100,000-vote margin in Cuyahoga and beat him soundly in Columbus, Cincinnati, and rural Ohio, he would win the election. That had always been the calculus for a Republican victory.

"Metzenbaum looked ripe for the plucking to Republican strategists and political analysts looking forward to the 1988 senatorial race," Ohio State University political scientist Sam Patterson said. "Early in 1988, the Metzenbaum-Voinovich race was judged toe to toe. National Republican senatorial committee chairman Rudy Boschwitz [R-Minn.] said he thought the Republicans could regain control of the Senate by targeting a few vulnerable incumbent Democrats, including Metzenbaum."[1]

Voinovich, like Metzenbaum, was an East Sider. He grew up in Collinwood, a middle-class neighborhood of Eastern Europeans, Irish, and African Americans. To the north of Collinwood was Lake Erie and to the east was the sprawling Collinwood Yard, a gravelly maze of tracks, repair shops, roundhouses, switches, and spurs built originally by the old New York Central system and passed along to successor railroads. The influence of the trainmen was so great that Voinovich's secondary school, Collinwood High, was nicknamed the Railroaders after the big freight carriers.

Voinovich graduated from the Ohio State University College of Law, Metzenbaum's alma mater, and practiced from a neighborhood office in his early years. But he was really a career politician, beginning in the state legislature in the late 1960s when he was still in his twenties. Voinovich always said he was a "biological Democrat," since both of his parents were Democrats, as well as most of his neighbors. He was Serbo-Croatian from his father, George, and Slovenian from his mother, Josephine. George Sr., an architect, was a Lausche Democrat—a backer of Frank Lausche, a Slovenian American and stalwart in Cleveland politics. Young George, the aspiring politician, knew that Lausche did not support Metzenbaum politically. Metzenbaum had endorsed Jack Gilligan instead of Senator Lausche in the 1968 Senate Democratic primary, won by Gilligan.

Voinovich began inching away from the Democratic Party during undergraduate days at Ohio University, where he served in student government and was a member of Phi Kappa Tau fraternity. He was no right-winger, but he came to believe that the Republican philosophy of limited government and a strong military was closer to his thinking and more in line with the views of average Ohioans. At OU, he wrote a paper disparaging Democrats for not doing enough to assist the "captive nations"—usually identified as Estonia, Latvia, Lithuania, and Slovenia—then in the grip of the Soviet Union. He was also interested in what made government tick and thought he could get it to work better with a Republican approach to problem solving. His switch troubled family members, but they rallied to his side when he ran for the Ohio General Assembly in 1967. "Kid, are you sure you want to be a Republican?" his father had asked him. "With your name and your religion [Catholic], I don't believe there is a future for you in the Republican Party."[2] But Voinovich was sure. He and his wife, the former Janet Allan, campaigned around the Collinwood district, often wearing casual clothes and riding bicycles. Voinovich spoke forcefully, had a big smile, and laughed easily.

It seems unlikely that his Republican conversion bothered his neighbors in Collinwood or friends in other ethnic communities. The Democrats' hold on voters of Eastern European heritage had gradually loosened in Cleveland over the decades, just as it had in other urban centers. In part, this was due to the party's aggressive support for civil rights laws and desegregation of housing and schools. But many voters of Polish, Hungarian, and Slovenian ancestry also identified more closely with the conservative social stands of the Republican Party and with its unrelenting hostility toward Communism. The same was often true of Italians and Irish. Voinovich understood this sooner than most. He upset the incumbent Democrat and headed down I-71 for Columbus, where James A. Rhodes held sway as governor.

Voinovich was a restless politician. After two terms in Columbus, where he cosponsored the bill creating Ohio's Environmental Protection Agency, he went home to run for mayor of Cleveland in 1971, opposing Cuyahoga County auditor Ralph Perk in the Republican primary. He lost but earned the older man's respect. When Perk was elected mayor in the fall, the audacious Voinovich succeeded him as auditor.

In 1978 Voinovich, by then a county commissioner, got his big break when Ohio changed from an independently elected governor and lieutenant governor to a tandem system. For the first time, the offices would be paired on the respective Republican and Democratic ballots. Governor Rhodes was facing a campaign against Democratic lieutenant governor Richard F. Celeste, who was from the Cleveland suburb of Lakewood. To help neutralize Celeste's advantage in northeast Ohio, Rhodes tapped Voinovich to be his running mate. It was a masterstroke. Rhodes sent Voinovich on a get-acquainted tour across Ohio, from the hoots and hollers of the southeastern hills, to conservative, white-collar Cincinnati, to Republican heartland in the flatlands of the northwest. Rhodes knew Voinovich would be an asset in factory towns like Toledo and Akron. But he wanted to convince religious conservatives and also the country-club set that a guy named Voinovich—Rhodes mouthed it Vawn-a-vich—was really one of them, notwithstanding his hard-to-pronounce ethnic name. It worked. With the help of a strong anti-abortion vote, Rhodes and Voinovich overcame the Celeste challenge and prevailed on election day by about 50,000 votes out of 3 million cast. The Republican ticket lost Cuyahoga County by 55,732 votes, an improvement of more than 31,000 votes from Rhodes's losing margin in the Cleveland area four years earlier against Gilligan.

Rhodes and Voinovich settled into separate corner office suites about 100 feet from one another on the first floor of the statehouse. But Rhodes did not need, or wish for, a cogovernor, and Voinovich soon grew bored. Although he was given some duties—most notably heading a new local government liaison agency—he didn't have enough on his desk to stay busy. He decided not to move his family to Columbus and began spending a couple days a week in his Cleveland law office. It was perfectly legal but a sign that he viewed the lieutenant governor's post as a part-time job. When populist Democrat Dennis Kucinich foundered as mayor of Cleveland—unable to prevent the city from defaulting on its bank notes—Voinovich saw an opportunity. He abandoned Columbus after less than a year to run for mayor.

In Cleveland's "battle of the 'iches," Voinovich easily defeated the one-term Kucinich. Maybe Voinovich had an easy act to follow, but he faced a huge challenge: putting down-and-out Cleveland back on its feet. He wanted to rid the city of its "mistake on the lake" moniker. He worked harmoniously with the risk-averse business leaders whom Kucinich had alienated, and he cooperated with an all-Democratic city council. Voinovich stood up to Ronald Reagan when federal aid to cities was cut. He raised taxes and picked up additional help from state government. Soon, a small building boom perked up in downtown Cleveland.

"Voinovich has walked through a minefield—advocating higher taxes and utility rates, while vowing austerity—without igniting a minefield," the *Plain Dealer* observed in a report typical of the favorable press Voinovich was getting.[3] Serving ten years, winning reelection by wide margins, Voinovich helped Cleveland regain its respectability, if not prosperity. Then it was time to move on, and he set his sights on the U.S. Senate in late 1986. Congressman Bob McEwen, a southern Ohio conservative and heir to the Ashbrook tradition, considered challenging Voinovich for the GOP nomination but couldn't get any traction. The party wanted Voinovich as its candidate—and Ohio Republicans hated contested primaries.

Turning seventy-one that year, Metzenbaum stood slightly stooped, wore a hearing aid, and had a nagging cough. Trouble with his balance forced him to stop drinking coffee and soft drinks, and he cut back on his beloved chocolate. He was still hardy, arriving at the Russell Office Building an hour before his staff's 8:30 AM starting time. He stood at his desk as he worked the phones, studied briefing papers, and ordered aides around. And he routinely swam fifty laps in the Senate pool and played tennis. But he was badly shaken when his wife, Shirley, fell off of a bicycle in the fall of 1986 and was knocked unconscious. She was hospitalized with a severe concussion. "It frightened him," said aide Peter Harris.[4] Shirley eventually recovered after suffering some hearing impairment, short-term memory loss, and double vision.

In late January of the election year, the *Plain Dealer Sunday Magazine* headlined the looming battle between the two Clevelanders as the final campaign for Metzenbaum. In a lengthy piece, Washington bureau chief Tom Brazaitis summarized Metzenbaum's career and analyzed his strengths and weaknesses without handicapping the upcoming race. In the Senate, "Metzenbaum is working to reshape his image from that of an obstructionist into someone who can leave a more positive imprint on history," Brazaitis reported. In an extraordinary display of self-consciousness, the story quoted Metzenbaum speaking of himself in the third person: "Suddenly Mr. Feisty has the responsibility of getting legislation through. You don't do that by kicking people in the shins." But a few paragraphs down "Mr. Feisty" seemed to revert and contradict any notion of a new Metzenbaum. "I'm not here just to vote. I'm bound to alienate some people." Even Shirley Metzenbaum chimed in: "Howard has a lot of vinegar. If he doesn't like something, he talks out." Shirley described herself to Brazaitis as "sort of the leavening agent in our relationship," adding that while Metzenbaum was "tough," he was "also one of the warmest men I've ever met. It's most interesting that a lot of people have felt that he's a good friend when they have a problem. Some of the people who have found it difficult to accept some of his philosophy will turn to him when they have a problem."

Brazaitis noted that Metzenbaum had one of the Senate's most liberal voting records, "Yet polls show as many as a third of Ohio voters think his views are conservative," a testament to his populist stands against big oil and big business and to his reputation for being "hard as nails, not a quality normally associated with liberals." Ohioans do not view Metzenbaum as a "dewy-eyed whale saver," the reporter concluded.

That was the good. But the state's largest newspaper also found a lot not to like. "He's a knee-jerk liberal, with an emphasis on 'jerk,'" an unnamed Capitol Hill veteran was quoted as saying. And another slap from a former aide, also not identified: "I've seen senators come to him on the floor, and he'll say, 'not now, I'm busy,' the way you would a child. Senators don't like to be talked to that way."[5]

The *Wall Street Journal,* which excoriated Metzenbaum on its editorial page, weighed in with a news story. It stressed Metzenbaum's effectiveness but also portrayed him as an "abrasive" figure resented even by some Democrats. The story, by political reporter John Yang, was headlined, "Senator No: Metzenbaum Amasses Power in the Senate by Blocking Action . . . No Plan to Be a 'May Queen.'" Yang reported, "The Ohio Democrat sees himself as a silver-haired Horatius at the bridge, poised to repel special interest—read, 'big business'—giveaways. But his hardball tactics and sometimes self-righteous manner raise hackles on both sides of the aisle."

The newspaper credited Metzenbaum with forcing Congress to demand a fair market–value return for the government on Stevens's Alaska railroad grab, delaying decontrol of natural gas and helping to "badger" the synthetic fuels program "to death." It reported that he once discovered, and blocked, a bid to repeal a 2 percent tax on betting-parlor wagers, hidden inside a bill exempting a Connecticut church from paying duties on an imported pipe organ. "He hasn't actually mounted a filibuster since 1986," Yang wrote, and "his reputation is such that the mere suggestion that he dislikes a piece of legislation brings its sponsor scurrying to compromise rather than face a floor fight."[6]

Metzenbaum had invented the modern filibuster, the implied filibuster. Yet he paid a price. Republican Orrin Hatch said, "It's a very easy thing" to play Metzenbaum's role, "if you don't care what your colleagues think." Most senators would take offense at such a comment, but Metzenbaum merely said, "I never thought I was going to be the May queen."[7]

Busy as he was in the Senate, he always left time in his schedule for fund-raising. And in these instances, his nerviness paid off, as evidenced in earlier campaigns. "You never hesitated to tell me exactly how much I was supposed to contribute to a particular campaign. I accepted that," said Cleveland attorney George Aronoff in a video roast of Metzenbaum.[8] Aronoff was a friend. But Metzenbaum often made calls from his Capitol Hill office to wealthy potential donors that he barely knew. "I picked up the telephone and called Dinah Shore. I said, 'Dinah, I don't know if you know me; I'm Howard Metzenbaum.' She said, 'I know you.' I said, 'Come to Cleveland and do a fund-raiser for me.' I could almost name on the fingers of my hand the people that have turned me down."[9]

Money flowed to both campaigns at an astonishing pace. By midsummer, Metzenbaum was closing in on $6 million in contributions, while Voinovich raked in almost $4.7 million.[10] Only Senator Lloyd Bentsen of Texas had spent more on his race at that point than Voinovich, who had poured $3.8 million into the effort to unseat Metzenbaum leading into the fall campaign. Metzenbaum counted contributions from Walter Matthau, novelist Judith Krantz, singer Don Henley, and Harvard law professor Lawrence Tribe. He had some $5 million in the bank as the campaign headed toward the fall stretch. "Metzenbaum says he's on Ohio's side, but he's got money coming in from sea to shining sea," scoffed Voinovich's press secretary, Joe Wagner.[11] Voinovich spent more in the spring and early summer than his foe. He drew money from defense contractors like Lockheed and Northrop, energy companies such as Texaco, Mobil, and Phillips Petroleum, and accounting firms like Touche Ross and Arthur Andersen.

His campaign treasury was healthy, but Voinovich still struggled to make up ground. He blamed the incumbent for not doing enough to combat the drought that parched the midlands that year, and he tried to revive the issue of Metzenbaum's personal wealth and tax returns. "Even John Glenn, who today serves as his campaign manager, questioned Howard Metzenbaum's finances, saying during their primary election campaign in 1974 that it is unfair for anyone to make a sizable income and not pay taxes," Voinovich said. He dared Metzenbaum to reveal his financial holdings.

Voinovich's own tax returns indicated the fifty-two-year-old was not a rich man. He reported income of $56,098 for 1987, although that sum didn't include $15,031 he diverted to tax-deferred savings programs. His salary as mayor was $65,137 and his total assets were $323,289.[12] Metzenbaum subsequently released his tax returns, showing income of $5.2 million in the five-year period between 1982 and 1987. He had paid $1.8 million in federal income taxes. The rest of his wealth was tucked away in a blind trust, a common practice meant to shield politicians from conflicts of interest. A financial manager handled the trust and made investments without Metzenbaum's explicit knowledge.

Aide Peter Harris said he hoped the book was now closed on "this obsession the mayor has with taxes." But it wasn't. Voinovich's spokesman huffed that the Metzenbaum release was "hardly a full disclosure."[13] It would have to do. Metzenbaum wasn't interested in a mud fight, not this time. He chose not to engage his opponent. In fact, he refused to debate Voinovich at all, even shunning the traditional week-before-the-election City Club debate in Cleveland, the site of his drubbing by Glenn fourteen years earlier. "Voinovich was so frustrated by his opponent's unwillingness to debate that he took out newspaper ads charging that the Democrat was 'hiding in a TV studio,'" the *Plain Dealer* reported on October 10, 1998. "That campaign was like trying to hit the stealth bomber," Voinovich later said.[14] But there was nothing unusual about a front-runner's reluctance to mix it up with a challenger. "If you're far enough ahead, why risk going into a debate where the worst might happen," said University of Akron political scientist Stephen Brooks. "You really have no incentive to do that."[15]

Metzenbaum wasn't hiding. He had a battle plan and, for the most part, he stuck to it. "My basic feeling was that anything that didn't contribute to getting you reelected was a waste of time," Harris once told him. When "Metzenbaum wanted to visit farm workers in northwestern Ohio, I said, 'Nobody cares about migrant workers. What are you going there for?' [Metzenbaum] said, 'I care about migrant workers.'"[16]

Disciplined and on message, Metzenbaum talked up his record of accomplishment in the Senate and hit Republicans for not agreeing to his plant-closing bill, which was featured in a campaign commercial as an example of his struggle to save jobs. Reagan had vetoed the bill, but it was revived and pending in the Senate that summer. Privately, his aides were glad the legislation had not become law just yet, since it kept the issue alive in a state hit hard by factory shutdowns. "We called it the gift that keeps on giving," said Harris, smiling.[17] Once, needling

Senator Dan Quayle, Metzenbaum asked directly on the Senate floor if he supported the bill. "I don't know what it is. It's a moving target. I went downstairs and had a salad, and when I came back I found that you had changed it once again," he quoted Quayle as saying. "I did indeed change it. I picked up two more votes," Metzenbaum told the Indiana Republican.[18] Eventually, Voinovich offered lukewarm support for the concept of notifying workers before a plant closed.

Voinovich's attempt to identify with Glenn, a senator he viewed as more mainstream and personable than Metzenbaum, backfired. "Mr. Voinovich made the mistake of suggesting he was more like the popular Glenn than Mr. Metzenbaum would ever be. Mr. Glenn was furious at being used by Mr. Voinovich in a cheap political stunt. He cut a TV commercial for the Metzenbaum campaign in which he filleted Mr. Voinovich like a rainbow trout," the *Cincinnati Enquirer* said.[19]

The Republican right in Ohio resurrected the red-baiting and other charges detailed in the maligned National Republican Senate Committee battle plan. A group calling itself the "Goodbye Metzenbaum Club" hired a professional fund-raiser and sought to energize conservative Democrats and Republicans by exposing Metzenbaum's liberalism. A mass mailing included a "fact sheet" summarizing the negative material put out by the Republican committee earlier in the year.[20] In a "Dear Fellow Conservative" letter, State Representative Dale Van Vyven of Sharonville identified Metzenbaum as nothing less than "the leading voice of the liberal movement in America."

"Nothing would hurt the left more than to see him defeated at the polls," the letter stated. "Metzenbaum is a slick and slippery campaigner. He has a lot of people (conservatives included) believing that he shares Ronald Reagan's goals of lower taxes, less federal spending and a strong national defense." Consequently, Van Vyven wrote, Metzenbaum and Voinovich are running "neck and neck" in the polls among self-identified conservatives.[21] Voinovich's campaign disclaimed any knowledge of Van Vyven's "club." And Metzenbaum's past ties to the Old Left were not a major issue in the fall campaign.

With election day two months away, Voinovich was stalled. In early September, remarkably early in the campaign, the *Dayton Daily News* endorsed Metzenbaum—no surprise coming from a newspaper with a long-standing Democratic editorial bent. But it was another sign that Ohio's "junior" senator had become a commanding presence in Ohio and in Washington. Voinovich's press secretary, former newspaper reporter Joe Wagner, recalled a trip Senator John McCain made to Ohio to campaign for the Republican challenger that year. "I am going to get it from Howard," Wagner said McCain told him. "He saw me on the plane [coming to Cleveland] and said, 'What are you doing here?' Then he got it, and walked away." Wagner thought, "Here is a guy who survived in Vietnam, a prisoner of war, and he is afraid of Howard."[22]

Voinovich wasn't intimidated. But he was trailing in the polls and needed a turnaround in a hurry. Despite his time in statewide office, he was not well known downstate. His name recognition in Cincinnati, an area critical to a GOP victory, was 14 percent. So he tried dropping an H-bomb. Shortly after Labor Day, he aired television commercials charging Metzenbaum wasn't concerned about child pornography, because the senator had voted against a "kiddie porn" bill that he thought was unconstitutional, but he wasn't actively backing a new bill that was languishing in the Judiciary Committee. The ads specifically criticized Metzenbaum for his vote in 1977 against the interstate sale bill and also condemned him for failing to cosponsor, or aggressively push for, the 1988 Child Protection and Obscenity Act. Metzenbaum's aides denounced the commercials as "slimy" and "disgusting." And the candidate said he would not dignify the charges with a response. But press secretary Nancy Coffey said he was not blocking the child protection bill in committee and had only questioned a section of the legislation that didn't deal with child pornography. She produced a letter from cosponsor Dennis DeConcini, Democrat of Arizona, crediting Metzenbaum and his staff with help in "negotiating a strong bill." Voinovich had his own letter from another cosponsor, Republican Gordon Humphrey of New Hampshire, saying he was unaware of Metzenbaum playing any part in efforts to "accelerate committee passage."[23]

Failing to cosponsor one bill, and voting on constitutional grounds against another eleven years earlier, was thin gruel for a charge so serious. No one had touched it when the Republican National Senatorial Committee floated the idea in its attack document earlier in the year. In fact, Metzenbaum ultimately voted for final passage of the 1977 bill, despite reservations about outlawing material that might not meet the legal definition of pornography. He was a fierce civil libertarian, and he often used salty language, but he was no friend of pornography. If anything, he was somewhat puritanical in personal habits—not one for dirty jokes or crude comments about women.

Voinovich could have left it at that. But instead he took it on the road, using his own words to charge that Metzenbaum "puts the rights of people in the obscenity business over the rights of individuals who have been victimized by the kiddie porn industry."[24] His campaign produced two more commercials with the same theme. At a news conference in Dayton, he said a group called the National Coalition Against Pornography had accused Metzenbaum and Senator Ted Kennedy of bottling up the bill in committee. In the first few days after the first ad aired, Metzenbaum's political advisers, including media guru Robert Shrum, detected Voinovich gains in tracking polls. "We took an initial hit," said Harris, who left the Senate office to run the campaign. "It was day-to-day trench warfare."[25]

But the charges didn't fly with reporters covering the race, editorial writers, or those acquainted with Metzenbaum's activities in Congress. "A Voinovich commercial featured an actress playing the part of a decent, caring female American with good family values. . . . She turned toward the camera, furrowed her brow with concern, spat out a clothespin and said, 'I hear Howard Metzenbaum is soft on child pornography.' Now whatever they said about Howard Metzenbaum [and they said plenty] nobody had ever said that before. Or has since. Metzenbaum [and, in a way, Voinovich, too] were victims of campaign hit-men," commentator Dick Feagler said.[26]

Voinovich was indeed an unintended victim of his own advisers in this one. Metzenbaum may have been a raging liberal and a mean SOB, but few thought the father of four daughters and the grandfather of six was forgiving of pornography. Voinovich came to regret the ads. He blamed himself for not using common sense but also faulted shoddy staff research and bad strategic advice. "I had no credibility to begin with, and I start out taking a shot at Metzenbaum. And the research work was poor, to say the least. And it turned into being a boomerang and hurt my credibility in the entire campaign," Voinovich said.[27]

Metzenbaum was thick-skinned and had endured name-calling before, but the porn ads got to him. "I remember one time during the 1988 campaign—I was doing his press—I called him up in Cleveland and he seemed down," said campaign spokesman Dale Butland. "I said to him, 'What's the matter, Senator? You seem kind of down.' He said, 'I guess I am. You know, I am sitting here with my grandkids and one of those damned ads came on television. And it just makes you feel kind of bad.'"[28]

Soon John Glenn was on the case, thanks to a commercial produced by the campaign. Reading from a script written by Shrum, Glenn stared straight ahead at the camera, sternly intoning that the attacks said "much more about George Voinovich than they do about Howard Metzenbaum. Think about it." That closing line was Glenn's own. It was getting personal. Glenn's rejoinder infuriated Voinovich's wife, Janet.

The Metzenbaum-Voinovich contest would cost almost $17 million, a fund-raising record for a Senate campaign in Ohio that went unchallenged into the next century. Each man spent more than $8.3 million. Voinovich also had strong financial support from powerful interest groups like the Right to Life Committee and the National Rifle Association, which threw almost $45,000 into the effort to beat Metzenbaum. "Our biggest foe—Howard Metzenbaum—is up for reelection, but is not unbeatable," NRA president Wayne LaPierre said in an appeal for money. "As you read this letter, Senator Metzenbaum of Ohio is pushing his gun ban bill to another vote. . . . The strongest statement you and I can make for our gun rights is to defeat those who sell out to Metzenbaum, and to defeat Metzenbaum himself."[29]

It wasn't enough. Metzenbaum soon opened up a wider lead in the public opinion polls and Voinovich couldn't close the gap. The senator kept hammering away on his plant-closing bill, which became law in August without Reagan's signature. It was, he said, part of a record that showed he could enact good bills as well as block bad ones.

In a news story that ran the week before the November election, the *Dayton Daily News* said the "infamous Senator No" had been transformed to "Senator Can-Do." Reporter Tom Price explained how Metzenbaum conducted business from a narrow "hide-away" office, an auxiliary to his Russell Office Building suite, about seventy-five feet from the entrance to the Senate chamber. The newspaper listed bills Metzenbaum had passed, including plant-closing notification, new restrictions on lobbying by former congressmen and other government officials, and limits on adjustable-rate mortgage hikes. "The verdict now, even among Metzenbaum's enemies, is that he has passed the test" of being able to "pass his own bills," the article said.[30]

Metzenbaum capitalized on Voinovich's dwindling treasury during the last week of the campaign when his strapped opponent pulled down his television advertising. Voinovich had spent substantial amounts early in the campaign, in part to discourage McEwen from entering the GOP primary. That left Metzenbaum on the air, solo. As had been the case in his previous campaigns, he emphasized paid media over grassroots organizing. "I bought all of that available Voinovich time," Harris said. "In the seven days before the election, I was scared to death."[31]

Broke, Voinovich was staring at defeat as the race wound down. "I went dark [off of television] . . . and I ran out of money, and he didn't," he said of Metzenbaum. "He just beat the hell out of me the last two weeks."[32] But the only surprise on election day was the size of the Metzenbaum victory. Leading the ticket in a presidential year, he almost matched his margin against Pfeifer, grabbing 57 percent to Voinovich's 43 percent. George H. W. Bush took 55 percent of the Ohio vote in his contest against Massachusetts governor Mike Dukakis. In piling up a 607,322-vote margin, Metzenbaum had attracted 63,489 votes more than the vice president's 2.41 million. The conclusion was inescapable: thousands of Bush voters, Republicans and others, had cast ballots for the president-elect and for Metzenbaum. Forty-one Ohio counties, from Erie to Hamilton on the Ohio River, split tickets and gave majorities to both Metzenbaum and Bush. Maybe some of those voters really did think, as polls suggested, that the crusty Metzenbaum was a conservative.

Metzenbaum ran away from Voinovich in Cuyahoga County, carrying 66.5 percent, and edged him in Republican-leaning Hamilton and Franklin counties. Despite Voinovich's name recognition in northern Ohio and his ethnic identity, Metzenbaum increased his margin from 1982 in Lucas County, winning 68 percent in the Toledo area, up more than 8 percent. He made inroads in growing suburban "collar counties," such as Ottawa and Wood outside of Toledo, and Lake and Medina near Cleveland. He won all but Washington and Morgan counties in hilly Appalachian Ohio. Voinovich's only concentrated strength was in the GOP heartland of rural northwestern Ohio. A former lieutenant governor and mayor of a comeback city at the center of Ohio's largest media market, Voinovich had captured a mere thirty-four of eighty-eight counties. It was only his second election defeat.

An Ohio State University study determined that a "considerable number of Ohioans who did not like Metzenbaum very well voted for him anyway." And, to rub it in, "Quite a few Ohioans who liked Voinovich voted for Metzenbaum." There it was again. He may be an SOB, some of the voters were saying, but he is our SOB, and we just don't know enough about this other guy. OSU's Samuel Patterson and Thomas Kephart concluded Voinovich was a worthy candidate, who simply ran a god-awful race. "Voinovich was a quality challenger, but he conducted an ineffective, and in some ways an inept, campaign," according to Patterson and Kephart. "Metzenbaum was indeed properly considered a vulnerable incumbent in the early days of the campaign. But he conducted a very effective campaign for reelection. The campaign matters."[33]

Voinovich, humbled, said he had made a classic mistake in going on the attack before establishing his own credibility with voters statewide. In the heat of the campaign, he spent a small fortune trying to build up his name identification in Hamilton County. It was too late. A visit by President Reagan aimed at raising as much as $500,000 yielded only $20,000. Told years later that Metzenbaum was still aggrieved by the pornography charges, Voinovich apologized personally. "I found out from a mutual friend that he always felt bad that I never formally apologized to him, though I thought that I had because of the news media coverage. So I took it upon myself to communicate it . . . He accepted." His conscience salved, Voinovich said he felt better afterward.[34]

Ohio Republican chairman Robert T. Bennett said the party never nailed Metzenbaum in Ohio on his controversial voting record in Washington. "Howard would get by with votes here in Congress, and he never talked about them back home. That is what frustrated Republicans."[35]

"I don't worry about whether it is seemly"

Metzenbaum seldom spoke of voter mandates. But as the 101st Congress opened for business in January 1989, he seemed free of his demons. His lower-middle-class childhood, his scuffling early years, and the brushes with anti-Semitism were fading memories. He hadn't been an overnight success. His advances in politics had come grudgingly. But, nearing his seventy-second birthday, he was no longer "an unacceptable" person.

"Metzenbaum is involved as never before and pressing with unprecedented clout for the liberal causes he has championed since he joined the Ohio legislature in 1943, fresh out of Ohio State Law School," the *Plain Dealer* reported. "With a triumphal campaign behind him, and the power of the majority at his command, Metzenbaum is on offense." A keen Metzenbaum-watcher, Republican consultant John Morgan said, "Now he can be a liberal without being afraid of any reelection problems. Usually liberals hide. Howard, he has always pretty much been a liberal [openly]. Now, he has passed this last and final test. He is a crafty politician."[36]

In the first week of the session, Metzenbaum introduced seven bills, including the Ethics in Government Act and another attempt to repeal the insurance industry's antitrust immunity. The ethics bill promised to tighten lobbying restrictions on former members of Congress, their top aides, and former high-ranking executive branch officers. He also planned to reintroduce the Brady Bill to establish a waiting period for handgun sales. And he decided to press ahead with a relatively new issue in the gun control debate: a ban on so-called assault weapons, high-powered, semiautomatic firearms, such as the feared AK-47 and the Colt AR-15. Metzenbaum and California congressman Pete Stark unveiled the first assault weapons bills in Congress the previous year, but they didn't get a hearing in the Senate or House. Determined, Metzenbaum came back with a similar bill in February of the new session and taunted his old nemesis, the NRA, calling its leaders liars.

But having Metzenbaum's name on legislation was not the best way of attracting bipartisan support. Senator Dennis DeConcini, a moderate Democrat from Arizona, sponsored a similar bill set for debate. Metzenbaum signed on as a cosponsor and braced for a long battle. Although he was consciously building relationships and trying to turn old foes into friends, he kept up his combative ways. "Let me plead with the senator not to move to table the amendment," his friend Dale Bumpers beseeched him during debate on a whistleblower protection bill, shielding those who exposed government curruption. "Let us have an honest up-or-down vote. We have had a nice three-hour debate. Please do not move to table the amendment." Metzenbaum stood up, faced the Senate's presiding officer, and said, "Mr. President. I move to table the amendment." Metzenbaum said, "I remember one time a senator saying to me, 'Well, I don't know if I'd do that because it is not seemly.' [But] I don't worry about whether it is seemly."[37]

Now and then, Metzenbaum's willingness to make enemies haunted him—such as the time he refused at the last minute to go along with a pet proposal of Republican senator Alfonse D'Amato. The abrasive

New Yorker wanted to give tax breaks to real-estate investors facing losses when property values fell. Metzenbaum saw it as a windfall for wealthy speculators. D'Amato, furious, waited for a chance to strike back. When Metzenbaum sought "unanimous consent"—passage of a bill without a roll call vote—for his extension of tax credits going to makers of "orphan drugs," D'Amato was ready. Metzenbaum wanted the quick agreement to renew his 1983 law, giving 50 percent tax breaks to pharmaceutical companies for the costs of clinical research on drugs that treat rare diseases, such as Tourette's syndrome. "I object, I object!" D'Amato shouted when the Senate's presiding office sought consent for Metzenbaum's bill. The lone objection stopped the measure in its tracks, and due to the parliamentary situation, Metzenbaum did not get another chance to move it forward. "Occasionally, a senator will stab another in the back, and then there's hell to pay," a *New York Times* account of the 1993 incident said.[38]

D'Amato and Metzenbaum never did patch things up. But the partisan from Ohio managed to work on legislation with Republicans Bob Dole, Orrin Hatch, Charles Grassley, and even onetime Dixiecrat Strom Thurmond, a cosponsor of the ethics bill. The ethics law was enacted with bipartisan support in 1989. It phased out "honoraria," the speaking fees given to congressmen. It also barred lawmakers, top aides, and high-ranking executive-branch officers from lobbying former colleagues for one year after leaving government service. Metzenbaum, as a rule, didn't accept speaking fees. In 1988, he took $100 for one speech and accepted a gift of a crystal decanter. Significantly, the House of Representatives imposed new restrictions on its members' outside income. The House prohibited practicing law for compensation and also banned holding a position as a paid officer for a company or partnership. The Senate ignored this reform in its piece of the legislation. It placed no limits on senators' outside incomes beyond existing caps on legal and professional fees. Metzenbaum, apparently, could have still collected a finder's fee as he did initially in the Hay Adams Hotel deal.

Far thornier for Metzenbaum was an ethical and constitutional question that had nothing to do with personal finances. With patriotic fervor, the Senate in 1990 considered again the perceived problem of flag burning. Debate was prompted by Supreme Court decisions in 1989 and 1990 that overturned state laws criminalizing destruction of an American flag. Because the court ruled that flag burning was free expression covered by the First Amendment, many in Congress wanted to amend the Constitution to protect Old Glory. Metzenbaum, who never served in the military and had been accused of membership in Communist front groups, could have just stayed in the background on this one. But that was contrary to his nature and his commitment to civil liberties. Making an exception to freedom of speech to punish a few flag burners would be an attack on the core of the First Amendment, he argued.

Metzenbaum knew making a case against the flag amendment would open him up anew to enemies who questioned his patriotism and resented his sharp-tongued criticism of the military. This, after all, was a man who liked to pick on military bands playing patriotic music. "God, I was smeared all over. Communist legislator—there was actually literature saying that stuff," the senator said.[39] But he plowed ahead anyway. In a Senate speech he said he was "angry that once again we are going to turn the Bill of Rights into a political football. In 200 years, the Bill of Rights has never, never been curtailed. This country has gone through a Civil War, two world wars and a Great Depression—monumental events which tested our strength and unity. But in those moments, we resisted the temptation to cut back on individual freedom. Once you start fiddling with the Bill of Rights, outlaw offensive expression, where do you stop?"[40]

Suspected Confederate sympathizers held without charge under Lincoln, and Japanese Americans herded into U.S. camps during World War II, might have questioned Metzenbaum's history, if not his sentiment. The flag amendment stirred emotions in God-and-country Democrats as well as conservative Republicans. The American Civil Liberties Union led a lonely coalition opposing the efforts of veterans' organizations and patriotic groups promoting the amendment. Metzenbaum blamed its popularity on political operatives, manipulating public opinion. "Whatever merit there might be to the other side of this issue has been drowned out by the chorus of smears and threats directed at those of us who dare to oppose this amendment . . . the media advisors and campaign consultants here in Washington have poisoned the debate on this issue. They want Americans to believe that anyone who believes that it is wrong to jail unpopular protesters is unpatriotic."[41]

His distaste for flag wavers and concern that legitimate dissent would become a crime was in keeping with his utter disdain for the late J. Edgar Hoover. Near the end of his term, he reserved time on the Senate floor to mock the "squeaky clean, crime-fighting G-man" and reintroduce his bill to strip Hoover's name from the FBI Building on Pennsylvania Avenue. "It is time we remove that stain," was the way he put it. Metzenbaum was annoyed by a report that Hoover had attempted to label the late senator Quentin Burdick of North Dakota as a Communist sympathizer. "Hoover, we now know, thoroughly abused the powers of his office and completely trampled upon the individual rights of thousands of patriotic, law-abiding American citizens," Metzenbaum said. "As one who has himself been the target of these Communist sympathizer smears, I can tell you that it is offensive to have your patriotism questioned."[42]

Both sides claimed to be motivated by patriotism when the House of Representatives fell short of the two-thirds majority needed to put a flag amendment before the states. That should have been the end of it. The issue was dead for the 1989–90 Congress. But the Senate—to Metzenbaum's fury—went ahead and voted on flag protection anyway five days after its decisive defeat in the other body. Again, the proamendment side came up short, as John Glenn and others joined Metzenbaum in voting not to tinker with the Constitution.[43] "We do not need to pass a law to protect the flag from destruction by the citizens of this country. The flag is well protected by the affection and reverence felt by the millions of Americans who freely and voluntarily choose to fly the flag every single day," Metzenbaum argued.[44] The senator had kept faith with his convictions. He had voted no on the constitutional amendment, no on a flag statute, and no on a resolution condemning the Supreme Court flag decisions. Years later he confessed going against the flag amendment was his toughest vote in nineteen years in Congress. "I defended the constitutional right to burn the flag," he said, almost in disbelief.[45]

He had no such trepidation about his role in a dispute over another sensitive constitutional issue—the maddeningly ambiguous Second Amendment. Metzenbaum thought public opinion was on his side in the gun control debate. "I think they have overplayed their hand," he said of the National Rifle Association. "I've been told I was their number one target in 1988. I don't think they cost me many votes."[46] Although the gun control side usually won in public surveys, it most often lost the battles that counted on Capitol Hill. The firearms lobby was better organized and had more money than pro-gun control forces.

The Brady Bill, requiring a mandatory seven-day waiting period before the purchase of a handgun, was introduced on February 7, 1987, by Metzenbaum in the Senate and Congressman Edward Feighan of Cleveland in the House. The gun control marathon would extend to the final year of Metzenbaum's Senate career. Both he and Feighan were friends with Republican Jim Brady and his wife, Sarah Brady, whose personal stories gave emotional drive to the gun control movement. Jim Brady, who used a wheelchair and had difficulty speaking, was a victim of gunman John Hinckley in the assassination attempt on President Reagan on March 30, 1981. The week's wait was conceived as a "cooling off period," a time when a hothead might change his or her mind and decide to forego the gun. That judgmental rationale soon faded. Metzenbaum, Feighan, and Congressman Charles Schumer of New York instead maintained the waiting period was needed to give police time to check the records of would-be buyers so firearms weren't sold to felons or the mentally unstable. This was a powerful argument that drew support from law enforcement groups. How could the NRA oppose a measure that simply enforced existing law against selling a gun to a convicted criminal or a lunatic? With Feighan doing most of the heavy lifting, the House Judiciary Committee recommended passage of the bill in 1988. But it was beaten on the House floor at the insistence of the gun lobby, which asserted the wait infringed on Second Amendment rights.

Feighan and Metzenbaum reintroduced the bill at the outset of the 101st Congress with a twist: the waiting period would phase out once a nationwide instant check of criminal records was in place. The idea was to give the FBI technology that would make a records check as speedy as credit card verification at the sales counter. This time Feighan got it through the House on a 239–186 vote. Momentum had swung to the gun control advocates. Even President Reagan, Jim Brady's old boss, was for it. "This growing support, however, did not deter those opposed" to the Brady Bill, gun control lobbyist Richard Aborn said. "The anti-control proponents not only rallied supporters but also used effective lobbying to capitalize on congressional procedural rules," wrote Aborn. "The gun lobby clearly understood that the fight for the Brady Bill was anything but over."[47]

The rifle association knew it had a political advantage. For its hard-core members, opposition to gun control was a single issue trumping all others. The NRA was confident that, in some districts at least, it could target and defeat an enemy congressman. Gun control advocates tended not to be as threatening. "Politicians are not motivated by support for a particular issue in the polls, unless the polls overwhelmingly show that the topic is of 'single issue' importance to voters," conceded Aborn, who became president of the Bradys' organization, Handgun Control Incorporated, in 1992. "There are few such topics, and certainly gun control has never been one." NRA president Wayne LaPierre argued the Brady Bill not only curbed the rights of law-abiding gun enthusiasts but also simply would not work. What criminal would be so stupid, LaPierre wondered, as to buy a weapon in a retail store where his criminal past could be uncovered? The answer was obvious: more than a few criminals, perhaps ignorant of the law, perhaps not so clever, would still patronize gun stores. Handgun Control, the main gun control lobbying group, said 27 percent of guns used in criminal acts came from over-the-counter sales.[48]

"In the states that have waiting periods," Metzenbaum said of state laws, "thousands of illegal gun sales have been stopped."[49] In the Senate, the waiting period was added to an omnibus anticrime plan, making it more difficult for the NRA to knock it down. But the gun rights group had an ally in Senator Ted Stevens, Metzenbaum's grumpy adversary from Alaska. Stevens offered an amendment that ripped out the waiting period, leaving only the instant check. However, law enforcement officials were not prepared to implement such a system. Stevens's amendment lost 54–44 in the early morning hours of June 28, 1991. Majority leader George Mitchell of Maine and minority leader Bob Dole stepped into the breach and brokered a compromise. With Metzenbaum's agreement, the seven-day period was whittled to no more than five days. And the wait would cease altogether once technology was feasible for the instant check system, even if it was not in place everywhere.

In the heat of the give-and-take, Mitchell called Metzenbaum into his office in the hopes that a compromise could be reached. "George, I can't do this. I am not going to do it," Metzenbaum announced as he walked in the door. According to Joel Johnson, the exasperated Mitchell, a former federal judge, quietly instructed Metzenbaum on the importance of courteously hearing out the other side. As a jurist, Mitchell said he would patiently listen to opposing arguments even when his mind was made up. And "then I would tell them no." He asked as much from the senator from Ohio.[50] Metzenbaum eventually acquiesced to changes and the amended Brady Bill passed 67–32. But the NRA was not finished.

House negotiators agreed to the Senate version of the handgun bill and incorporated it in a reconciled crime bill conference report. (Conference agreements typically incorporate elements of House and Senate versions of legislation after negotiations among congressmen and senators on a joint panel.) But pro-NRA senators blocked final consideration of the agreement throughout the next year and the Brady Bill, so close to enactment, was buried as Congress adjourned.

Things changed the next year. A new president, sympathetic to the gun control cause, was in the White House. "If you'll pass the Brady Bill, I'll sure sign it," Bill Clinton said in his State of the Union speech. Metzenbaum introduced it, for a fourth time, in February. In the other chamber, Feighan had retired, choosing not to compete in a remapped district. So Schumer took the ball, with Metzenbaum urging him to move it quickly through the House of Representatives.

The bill again passed the Democratic-controlled House, but, to no one's surprise, there was another hitch. An NRA amendment mandated that the waiting period would end after five years, even if the instant check was not operational. Metzenbaum tried to yank out the amendment in the Senate but failed. The amended bill then passed 63–36 and gained final passage as part of a House-Senate conference agreement a few days before Thanksgiving. Only Mitchell's threat of a postholiday Senate session averted yet another stall.

Metzenbaum had his prize: a provocative anticrime bill had been enacted after years of grunt work by the senator, his staff, Feighan, and others. In 1992, the year before Brady passed, more than half of the nation's 22,540 murder victims were killed by handguns.[51] Metzenbaum was certain the Brady Law would help reduce that number by keeping some guns out of the hands of violent criminals. This would be part of his legislative legacy. He celebrated with Clinton and the Bradys at an emotional White House bill-signing ceremony the week after Thanksgiving, November 30, 1993.

On to Assault Weapons

With Brady at last on the books, Metzenbaum braced for an even tougher battle, where the lines were not so clearly drawn. He wasn't naïve or overconfident; he knew gun control would not stop crime, which was growing increasingly violent in the early 1990s. But he had little sympathy for or understanding of the sportsmen's culture and the notion that competitive marksmen enjoyed the fearsome appearance and rat-a-tat action of assault weapons. Since hunters did not generally use such firearms, Metzenbaum reasoned that they had no utility for anyone other than soldiers and criminals bent on mayhem. So he turned his attention to the proposed ban on semiautomatic rifles and pistols, even though they played a relatively small part in violent crime. The bureau of Alcohol, Tobacco, and Firearms (ATF) estimated that 1 to 1.5 million of the firearms in public hands shared "assault weapon" characteristics: rapid-fire action through a single pull on the trigger, large magazines, and such features as folding stocks and flash suppressors. That was about 1.5 percent of all legally available guns. Even so, the ATF said the weapons showed up in a disproportionately high number of crimes.

A handful of shooting sprees gave rise to the antiassault weapons cause. Most alarming was a shootout in a Stockton, California, schoolyard in 1989 when a madman wielding an AK-47 squeezed off 106 rounds, killing five children and wounding twenty-nine others. Metzenbaum pressed ahead. "This is an issue that cannot wait," he insisted. "Any delay means lives lost."[52] In practice, a gunman looking to knock off a convenience store or a gas station was unlikely to employ an AR-15 or an Uzi. A .38-caliber revolver was easier to conceal going in or out of a building and just as effective. Terrorists and drug gangs waging turf wars favored assault weapons. A growing majority of Americans decided these "weapons of war" had no place on the streets of their cities.

Metzenbaum got assault weapons bans through the Senate in 1990 (nine weapons were identified and outlawed) and in 1991, but both bills died in the House. In his 1993 bill, Metzenbaum named the weapons he wanted to ban—the AK-47, Colt AR-15, TEC-9, and the Uzi sidearm. He also proposed to stop sales of revolving cylinder shotguns—riot guns like the Street Sweeper and Striker 12. Many law-enforcement agencies supported the bill, but the NRA held out. The lobby argued that Metzenbaum's approach perpetuated a myth that there were good guns and bad guns. For practical purposes, the NRA said only cosmetic differences separated so-called assault weapons from other firearms. "The NRA has fought nearly every reasonable, common-sense piece of firearms legislation that has ever been proposed," Metzenbaum fired back. "But the NRA is out of touch with the American people, with gun owners, and, increasingly, with elected officials."[53]

Still, Metzenbaum was unable to move his bill. It was left to California Democrat Dianne Feinstein, a strong-willed in-fighter, to break the logjam. In November of 1993, she offered a compromise. Her bill banned manufacture or sale of nineteen assault weapons, copies of those guns, and ammunition magazines capable of holding more than ten rounds. This was similar to Metzenbaum's, which outlawed twenty weapons. But Feinstein also explicitly protected, by name, 650 rifles used by hunters, assuring that they would not be barred because they bore similarities to outlawed guns. Just as important, she did not include Metzenbaum's language giving the ATF authority down the road "to designate additional semi-automatic firearms as assault weapons." The broader anticrime bill also established mandatory sentences for three-time losers and promised to put an additional 100,000 cops on the street. Feinstein agreed that the gun law "would sunset in ten years"—that is, be taken off the books unless reenacted.[54]

Metzenbaum and DeConcini joined as cosponsors, but Feinstein was credited with the breakthrough. "Metzenbaum was the blocking back," said one congressional aide who followed the gun control debate closely. The senator was willing to step back because he knew others with more skill at building coalitions sometimes had to finish what he started. He knew he would still get his due, the aide said. "The person who gets into the issue first usually gets the credit."

NRA supporters mounted one last gasp to stop the assault weapons ban as they filibustered against the compromise House-Senate conference report in September of 1994, the twilight of Metzenbaum's long career. The tiger was aroused. How dare his foes, mostly Republicans, use the very tactic he had perfected during nearly nineteen years in the Senate? "It is shameful, literally shameful, to get forty-one members of the Senate to stand up and block passage of a bill to fight crime in America," he said to his colleagues on the other side of the aisle. "Have you no pride—have you no character? . . . You are going to deny the president of the United States a political victory, but you do not care what happens on the streets of America . . . Shame on you."[55] In another time, this tirade—questioning another man's character—would have stirred resentment in the courtly Senate. But after years of listening to similar rants, the reaction to Metzenbaum's over-the-top outburst was more along the lines of, "That's Howard." "Every time the senator from Ohio speaks, the NRA gets stronger," said Senator Larry Craig, an Idaho Republican who was close to the gun lobby.[56]

The filibuster was abandoned and the crime bill, complete with its gun ban, became law. But the NRA would live to fight another day, and the "political victory" that Metzenbaum envisioned for the president and his party did not materialize. Democrats lost majorities in the Senate and House that November. A chastened President Clinton credited the energized NRA with helping to defeat as many as twenty gun-control supporters.

On September 13, 2004, the assault weapons law went out of existence, a victim of its sunset clause. The Republican majorities in the House and Senate made no attempt to reauthorize it, even though President George W. Bush said he supported keeping the law. Critics said it didn't work that well while it was in effect. "We agree that the 1994 law is ineffective," said Kristen Rand, legislative director of the Violence Policy Center, a gun control group.[57]

"So what?"

The soccer moms and other swing voters may have supported Metzenbaum's stand on gun control, but he did not find wide sympathy among the public for another social crusade—this one to allow openly gay men and women in the military. Metzenbaum, who sat out World War II because of poor eyesight, had little to gain from the issue and stood to further antagonize the Pentagon, which resented his constant bird-dogging of defense spending.

But the navy's dismissal in June of 1991 of navigator-bombardier Tracy Thorne, who finished first in his flight training class, caught Metzenbaum's attention. Thorne, discharged after acknowledging his homosexuality, subsequently appeared with Metzenbaum at a Capitol Hill news conference. To Metzenbaum, it was "pure and simple—official government-sanctioned discrimination."[58]

At the time, men and women signing up for the all-volunteer armed forces had to state on their applications their sexual orientation. If they acknowledged homosexuality, they were excluded. If they said they were heterosexual and turned out to be gay, they could be kicked out for lying on their applications. Most senators were inclined to give the military the benefit of the doubt since enlisting was voluntary. Metzenbaum's June 12, 1992, speech on the floor was the first major challenge in the

Senate to the policy. "It is discrimination against a distinct group of individuals who repeatedly and throughout history have shown that they were every bit as capable, hardworking, brave, and patriotic as their heterosexual counterparts," he said. He blamed an inflexible military command and the administration of George Herbert Walker Bush. "Defense Secretary Cheney said the other day that 'a gay lifestyle is incompatible with military service.'[59] What is he talking about? There are tens of thousands of homosexuals in the military right now, excelling in their jobs every day," Metzenbaum said. "This administration is too afraid of the far right to change its anti-gay policies, even though it knows it is wrong."[60]

One might argue with his stereotyping of those with qualms about expanding gay rights—the Catholic Church and other mainstream religions among them. But Metzenbaum was undoubtedly correct about Bush not wishing to aggravate his conservative base. Besides, many average Americans found merit in the Defense Department's argument that gay soldiers and sailors could adversely affect the all-important unit cohesion in warfare. John Glenn, who saw combat in World War II and Korea, said, "You are trying to get people to do something irrational: advance in the face of enemy fire. When you are on that front line, it isn't the flag, or mom and apple pie, you are fighting for. It's your buddy, right there next to you."[61]

The unit cohesiveness argument didn't persuade Metzenbaum. On July 28, 1992, he introduced a bill to overturn the ban on gays in the four branches of the military. "I call it baseless prejudice founded on fears and ignorance," he said of the discharge of some 17,000 gays and lesbians during the 1980s.[62] Both sides had a case. The military had been used before as a social laboratory, as Metzenbaum pointed out. In 1948, President Truman integrated the army, and during the Persian Gulf and Iraq wars, women were used in virtually every role but front-line combat. Nonetheless, the military did not want social causes, however legitimate, to get in the way of its primary function: the fighting and winning of wars.

Metzenbaum's bill was not seriously considered, but he put it in again the next year and got a hearing before the Armed Services Committee on May 7. He wasn't pacified by President Clinton's "don't ask, don't tell" compromise. It promised tolerance if gays would keep their sexual preferences private while serving their country.

Metzenbaum told the committee he had heard the majority of uniformed personnel supported the continued ban on gays and asked, "So what? Did we take a vote of our armed personnel before we accepted women into the military, or before President Truman banned discrimination against African Americans in the military?"[63] His bill didn't come close to passing. The president's "don't ask, don't tell" policy would outlast the Clinton administration and Metzenbaum. Another windmill had withstood his tilting lance.

Metzenbaum's skepticism of the Defense Department was matched by his suspicion of the activities of the Central Intelligence Agency. His service on the Intelligence Committee beginning in 1987 gave him an opportunity to monitor the spy agency up close. Two days before the terrorist bombings of the World Trade Center parking garage in New York City in 1993, he wrote to Clinton urging him to open the classified National Foreign Intelligence Budget to public scrutiny. That April, he complained about published reports that the CIA's budget would be increased to $28 billion in 1994.

"The Cold War is over, yet the intelligence budget is more than double what it was in 1979," he said in a lengthy Senate speech. "Its growth was unbridled for a decade, and we have just begun in the last couple of years to pare down the fat. Does U.S. Intelligence need a budget increase today? No way!"[64] Prescient, he was not. Nowhere in the remarks did he mention terrorism, instability in the Middle East, or other emerging challenges facing American intelligence agencies in the post–Cold War era. Glenn, on the other hand, got it. He wanted to increase intelligence gathering, because "we have to cope with small, loosely knit and often religiously motivated terrorist organizations. . . . We're in a time period where we need more CIA, not less."[65]

The Senator and Saddam

Metzenbaum always considered himself an effective advocate for the state of Israel. He once said he was "at the table" when all of the important decisions on Israeli policy were made in Washington. While not religious, he felt strongly about his Jewish heritage and often looked to fellow Jews as top advisors and law partners. But he was no diplomat or foreign policy savant. When he tried to deal with Israel's enemies, such as Muammar Gadhafi, he embarrassed himself.

He was all over the map, literally, with Iraqi dictator Saddam Hussein. In May 1990, he joined Republican senators Bob Dole of Kansas, Alan Simpson of Wyoming, Frank Murkowski of Alaska, and James McClure of Idaho on a tour of the Middle East. Israel, Syria, Jordan, Egypt, and Iraq were on the itinerary. Metzenbaum was the only Democrat and, more importantly, the only Jewish senator.

He seldom complained loudly about anti-Semitism, but he had felt its sting. In late 1991, Senate sergeant at arms Martha Pope informed him of a death threat. She said the FBI had a letter, mailed to Ohio Wesleyan University, vowing, "Death to kikes and Sen. Metzenbaum." The FBI interviewed the letter writer, an old man, and determined that "he does not appear to pose a threat to you at this time," Pope said.[66] In the course of his journey a year earlier to the Middle East, Metzenbaum encountered the real thing up close and personal—a sworn enemy of Israel who was known to carry out his threats.

During the Cairo leg of the senators' trip, Egyptian president Hosni Mubarak set up a meeting for them with Saddam Hussein in Iraq. They flew to Baghdad on a U.S. military jet on April 12 and were met at the airport by Foreign Minister Tariq Aziz, a Christian with a good command of English. Saddam was elsewhere. After an unexplained delay in a VIP lounge, the senators were informed that an Iraqi plane would take them to the city of Mosul, where the Iraqi president awaited. It sounded a little cloak and daggerish. Senator Alan Simpson described what happened next.

> We didn't much care for the idea of leaving behind our military plane. Howard Metzenbaum—the only person of Jewish faith in our delegation—expressed some trepidation and not without reason; we were, after all, in a Muslim country which had recently vowed to turn Israel into a "fireball." I remember Howard saying with a great grin and a wink, "Just stick with me guys—I don't know where the hell that plane may set down." We told Howard that we were aware of the risks—political and physical—of his traveling in that part of the world, and that we appreciated his being there. I think we all had a surge of concern trudging up the ramp into that Iraqi Airlines Boeing 737.[67]

After an uneventful flight, the wary senators were driven in two cars on a circuitous route to a hotel on the banks of the Tigris River. After passing through heavy security and a maze of holding rooms, they came face to face with a dour Saddam, attired in a business suit. Dole handed the dictator a letter telling of the U.S. government's objections to Iraq's development of nuclear, chemical, and germ warfare capabilities. Then the Senate minority leader asked pointedly, "Are you developing this virus, these weapons?" Saddam responded, "Do the Americans possess biological weapons or not? Does Israel possess biological weapons or not?" Dole said, "Not in the U.S. Biological weapons have been banned in the U.S. since the Nixon administration."[68]

Saddam came back with a bombastic monologue. He bragged of his country's military might, denounced Israel, claimed the United States and Europe were waging an "all-out campaign" against him, and also protested that he wanted peace. At one point, he said the Americans should board one of his helicopters, disembark at a spot of their choosing, and question the citizens about their leaders. The senators demurred. Metzenbaum, in his turn, told Saddam he was Jewish and a staunch supporter of Israel. He had some uneasiness about coming along on the visit, he admitted. "I have been sitting here and listening to you for about an hour, and I am now aware that you are a strong and intelligent man and that you want peace."[69]

What exactly gave Metzenbaum that sense of Saddam is not clear. But the rest of the visit was uneventful and the delegation returned to the United States with a mixed view of the Iraqi president. Within a month of his return, Metzenbaum argued against imposing stiff sanctions on Iraq's government. Saddam Hussein is a leader and could take important steps toward peace, he told the Senate. "He is in a particularly good position to be a spokesperson for peace in the Middle East," Metzenbaum said.[70] The same senator who thought Gadhafi should be eliminated viewed Saddam Hussein as a "spokesperson for peace." By July Metzenbaum had changed his mind. He backed a package of sanctions and voted the next month to cut other economic ties after Iraq invaded Kuwait. Recent events convinced him, Metzenbaum said, that the Iraqi ruler could not be persuaded to work for an end to hostilities. Saddam, it seemed, had become a spokesperson for war, not peace.

Two days after Iraq's August 2, 1990, invasion of Kuwait, Metzenbaum hurried an amendment through the Senate giving the president more power to enforce a blockade. Added to the defense bill, it allowed Bush to restrict imports of oil or other goods from countries that continued doing business with Saddam Hussein's government. Metzenbaum did not play a large part in the subsequent debate over the merits of economic sanctions versus waging an air and ground war against Iraq. But in one curious outburst, he lit into France, an ally in the Gulf War, saying the country "never can be counted upon." France, it seemed, wanted to tie the coalition's war effort to a new peace initiative in the Middle East. Metzenbaum apparently did not want undue pressure put on Israel. "Few nations have been more remiss, more turning their back on their obligations to the world community, and their responsibilities as far as their relations with this country are concerned than the French," he said.[71]

He eventually voted with the losing side against a military strike. But as fighting started, he said, "Congress will solidly support our forces in the Middle East. Our thoughts tonight are with those troops in the desert and their families back home."[72] He was not a vocal critic of the ensuing conflict, which was won quickly and with relatively few American casualties. Metzenbaum called the war effort "magnificent," yet he complained that the Persian Gulf War had not brought democracy to the region. "It's pitiful that we came out of this war, having sacrificed American lives, and to what end? Kuwait and Saudi Arabia haven't moved an inch toward democratizing their countries."[73]

Years later, the naïveté of Metzenbaum and his Mideast traveling mates, prior to Desert Storm, still rankled some of their Senate colleagues. "It was embarrassing," said Indiana Republican senator Richard Lugar, a respected foreign policy expert. "They were falling all over Saddam Hussein—[Saddam's] understanding and compassion and so forth."[74]

Metzenbaum rebounded, as usual. And with the Bush presidency nearing an end and his Senate career winding down, his motor kept running. As he passed seventy-five years, he refused to take a break, ease up on his staff, or go along with legislation that was not in the public interest. Instead of acting like a man on the last leg of a long journey, he worked at a pace that suggested he would run for reelection after all. His top aides didn't rule it out.

"I think where he does not get enough credit—and people realized it at the time, people on the inside—is how much power he had. How much stuff he actually got done, as a result of his willingness to say no, and tell his friends no, and tell his enemies no," said administrative assistant Joel Johnson.[75] Metzenbaum would keep saying no, right down to his final year in the United States Senate.

＿＿ ⚜ ＿＿

CHAPTER 9

Fighting to the Finish

Advise and Dissent

From his first day in the Senate through his final year in public service, Howard Metzenbaum took seriously his constitutional duty
to advise and consent. Metzenbaum was free with his advice on White
House nominations to positions of prominence. It was the "consent"
part that came hard. With a majority, he had voted against President
Reagan's choice of conservative Robert Bork for the Supreme Court
vacancy created by the retirement of Justice Lewis Powell. Metzenbaum
came out against Bork even before the confirmation hearings began.

Bork, intellectual to a fault, was a strict constructionist and outspoken critic of judicial activism. As Richard Nixon's solicitor general,
he agreed to fire Watergate special counsel Archibald Cox when no
one else would. Metzenbaum said Bork was too far out of the mainstream for a lifetime appointment to the Supreme Court. He cited a
1984 decision when Bork ruled that a New Jersey company was within
its rights in advising female employees in a lead-tainted workplace they
could undergo sterilization or lose their jobs. "I must tell you it is such a
shocking decision," Metzenbaum said to Bork, seated across from him
in the Judiciary Committee hearing room. "I can't understand how you
as a jurist could put women to the choice of work or be fired." Bork,
who had been part of a three-judge panel issuing a unanimous decision, said he merely upheld the judgment of the Occupational Safety

and Health Administration (OSHA).[1] Metzenbaum called the opinion "inhumane." With liberal interest groups piling on, Bork lost ground during a grueling five days of testimony before the committee.

His rejection, first in committee and then by the full Senate, infuriated Republicans because Democrats all but conceded Bork's ideology, not his résumé, brought him down. Labor unions, the ACLU, Common Cause, the NAACP, and other like-minded organizations spent millions of dollars stopping Bork in 1987. After his nomination fell, Beltway insiders began using the term "borked" to describe a strategy of attacking a nominee's political philosophy or personal foibles, notwithstanding qualifications for the job at hand. But Metzenbaum understood that not every questionable nominee could or should be "borked." In the early 1990s, he would wrestle with three Supreme Court appointments that left him ambivalent, and in one case, deeply embarrassed.

It started with the inscrutable David Souter. Metzenbaum didn't know what to make of President Bush's selection in 1990 of the rail-thin New Hampshire jurist. It was cast as a "stealth nomination" because little was known about the man or his record. New Hampshire senator Warren Rudman, a leading Republican moderate, championed Souter's nomination for the seat left open by the retirement of William Brennan, a hero to the political left. Many Democrats suspected that sober, stoic Souter was a conservative in a moderate's clothing. They tried to draw him out on the Supreme Court's 1973 *Roe v. Wade* decision, which legalized abortion. Metzenbaum, sitting on the Judiciary Committee, was impressed by Souter but wanted more specifics before recommending confirmation to the full Senate. "Most of the time, I know I'm right," Metzenbaum told aides. "But this time, I don't know." He decided to confront Souter directly on the abortion question during a confirmation hearing. Rudman described a tense scene.

> Howard Metzenbaum asked David if he thought he understood, not as a lawyer, but as a human being, how a woman felt when she had an unwanted pregnancy. David hesitated for a moment before he replied:
>
> "Senator, your question comes as a surprise to me. I was not expecting that kind of question and you have made me think of something that I have not thought of for 24 years.

"When I was in law school, I was on the board of freshman advisors at Harvard College. I was a proctor in a dormitory. One afternoon, one of the freshmen who was assigned to me—I was his advisor—came to me and he was in pretty rough emotional shape. And we shut the door and sat down, and he told me that his girlfriend was pregnant and he said she is about to have a self-abortion and she does not know how to do it. He said she is afraid to go to the health services, and he said, 'will you talk to her?' So I did.

"I know you will respect the privacy of the people involved, and I will not try to say what I told her. But I spent two hours in a small dormitory bedroom that afternoon listening to her and trying to console her to approach her problem in a way different from what she was doing, and your question has brought that back to me.

"I think the only thing I can add to that is, I know what you were trying to tell me, because I remember that afternoon."

The room was hushed. David hadn't said what he told the young woman—whether to have an abortion or to have the child—but no one could doubt his concern or his compassion.[2]

Souter's dramatic answer, ringing with authenticity, may have been decisive. He got Metzenbaum's vote and was confirmed 90–9 on April 27, 1990. Souter turned out to be a mildly liberal justice who often voted with Democrats on the Court and showed no inclination to overturn the abortion ruling.

"God is my judge, not you, Senator Metzenbaum"

Metzenbaum called his part in the debacle over Clarence Thomas's Supreme Court nomination the following year one of his worst performances in the United States Senate. The same could be said for the Senate Judiciary Committee and its handling of the confirmation hearings and late-breaking charges that Thomas sexually harassed a woman named Anita Hill.

Metzenbaum had gone into the Thomas hearings on a roll after speaking forcefully against Bush's choice to run the Central Intelligence Agency and also battling to limit the bailout of collapsed savings and loans. The failure of shady savings institutions eventually cost taxpayers several hundred billion dollars as the government tried to soften the losses of bilked customers. Metzenbaum subpoenaed business executives and browbeat federal watchdogs in a bid to put more of the burden on the thrifts. He had only modest success. He did push through an amendment forcing the Resolution Trust Corporation (RTC), the bailout agency, to reexamine a series of 1988 deals that Metzenbaum viewed as overly generous to bankrupt savings and loans. When the agency failed to follow through, he blocked its budget with a filibuster. Eventually, RTC's bureaucrats agreed to give the early bailouts a second look. Metzenbaum also prodded the regulators to abandon the notion of not suing officers of delinquent savings banks with a net worth of less than $5 million. Why should those guys be left off the hook? New Jersey senator Bill Bradley said Metzenbaum's agitation was worth the effort because he gave a voice to helpless investors and to ordinary citizens, the innocent bystanders in the scandal. He "fought to keep taxpayers from paying too heavy a price," Bradley said.

Metzenbaum could count. He knew the odds were against him when he took on a multibillion-dollar industry or a well-connected White House nominee. But he thought he could score points and perhaps shame his powerful adversaries, making them more sensitive to the issues he raised. He would send them a message.

With Bush's CIA nominee, Robert Gates, he just seemed to be spoiling for a fight. Metzenbaum dismissed Gates as a "see-no-evil, hear-no-evil, speak-no-evil" bureaucrat and tried to implicate him in the Iran-Contra affair. The arms-for-hostages foreign policy fiasco, carried out by Oliver North and others, scarred Ronald Reagan's second term. And Metzenbaum was more than willing to resurrect it during the Bush presidency. "Many of us wonder how, in an organization [the CIA] whose motto boasts, 'know the truth,' you as a top official could know so little of it," he told Gates, the CIA's deputy director during Iran-Contra.[3] Gates insisted he acted honorably but conceded he should have done more to uncover the secret dealings with Iran and the aid to antigovernment fighters in Nicaragua.

Gates was confirmed, despite his critic's aggressive line of attack. But

Metzenbaum didn't look like a loser. He was in demand on ABC's *Nightline, The McNeil-Lehrer News Hour,* and other television news programs. "There's probably an element of the last hurrah in this," University of Virginia political scientist Larry Sabato said. "If you're not running for reelection, you're liberated. And he's never been afraid to defy the odds."[4]

Metzenbaum was already leading the charge against Thomas, a conservative African American appeals court judge, when the explosive claim of sexual harassment was leaked to National Public Radio and the New York newspaper *Newsday.* Bush had nominated Thomas to succeed Thurgood Marshall, who retired as the Supreme Court's first black justice. But NPR and *Newsday* reported that the Judiciary Committee possessed an affidavit accusing Thomas of badgering Hill with date requests and "dirty talk" when he was her boss at the Education Department and later at the Equal Employment Opportunity Commission. Her story dated back eight to ten years, and Hill continued working for Thomas after the alleged incidents.

There had been no hint, to that point, that the panel intended to call Hill as a witness. Now, with his hand forced, Judiciary chairman Joe Biden scheduled thirty hours of hearings on her complaints, running right through an idyllic autumn weekend in 1991. With most of the proceedings aired live on television, Thomas vehemently denied everything; Hill reiterated her grievance. And Metzenbaum, in his clumsy questioning, looked like an aging baseball pitcher who "lost his fastball," *Plain Dealer* columnist Brent Larkin wrote.[5]

Metzenbaum had already challenged Thomas's positions on affirmative action, age discrimination, and abortion. When he brusquely told Thomas that sexual harassment should not be swept under the rug, the beleaguered witness rose up in indignation, his cup of anguish filled, as one commentator put it. "God is my judge, not you, Senator Metzenbaum," Thomas said.[6] Metzenbaum called out another witness, reading aloud a transcript of a phone conversation between John Doggett and committee staffers who confronted him with unsubstantiated harassment charges. Doggett, a pro-Thomas Texas lawyer, angrily told Metzenbaum, "Your comments about this document are one of the reasons our process of government is falling apart."[7]

Even a lame attempt at humor failed. As the tawdry process dragged through the weekend—replete with references to pubic hair and porn stars—Metzenbaum said the committee was making "a valiant effort to justify to the American people why we got a salary increase." Clunk. He never could tell a joke. "I think the senator regrets having brought that up," his press secretary said.[8]

Thomas was confirmed 52–48 after the lurid committee testimony proved inconclusive. An apology to Doggett and an admission on the Senate floor that "the past several days have been some of the most difficult that I've experienced" were not enough to get Metzenbaum off the hook.[9] Metzenbaum, Ted Kennedy, and Illinois senator Paul Simon were variously fingered as the sources of the media leak of Hill's troubling story. Metzenbaum's legal aide, James Brudney, a Yale Law School classmate of Hill's, was identified as a go-between.[10] Metzenbaum and Brudney denied it. "I am confrontational and willing to get into a battle and have no embarrassment about standing up and fighting for positions I believe in, even when they are unpopular. But I don't lie," Metzenbaum said.[11] He was furious when he thought Orrin Hatch publicly singled him out as the source of the sexual harassment information. "One of my colleagues, whom I considered a friend, on the other side of the aisle—with absolutely no evidence—is telling reporters that I am responsible for leaking Anita Hill's story to the press. . . . He owes me a public apology."[12] Hatch backpedaled.

A subsequent investigation failed to solve the mystery of the disclosure. "We may never know who leaked Anita Hill's allegations," special counsel Peter Fleming said. Metzenbaum, shaken, went into damage control mode. Larry Sabato said the senator came across on TV as "harsh and mean"[13] during the hearings. Metzenbaum himself said, "I was off my game." He did not want his last term and Senate legacy tarnished by a sordid soap opera. "I am certainly concerned that this is probably a low point for me, maybe in my entire political career," he said in a mea culpa.[14]

It was a rare public admission of embarrassment. He seldom let on that setbacks bothered him. But conscious that his time was growing short, he became more sensitive to the feelings of others and did worry, at times, whether his actions were "seemly." His personal secretary, Juanita Powe, believed the senator mellowed during his last term.

But the mellow Metzenbaum had a limited shelf life. Jump ahead to the Clinton presidency and Metzenbaum's last two years in the Senate. Stephen G. Breyer, a Clinton nominee, was a federal appeals court judge of decidedly liberal persuasion. But he just rubbed Metzenbaum the wrong way. His distaste for Breyer spoke volumes about Metzenbaum's views of life and of his fellow human beings. The wealthy Boston Brahman was an accomplished lawyer and experienced judge, picked by the White House with the expectation that his impeccable record would assure a smooth confirmation as a replacement for Justice Harry Blackmun.

Metzenbaum saw a different side: a judge with holdings in Lloyd's of London and an insurer that offered liability coverage to clients who could come before him in environmental cases. He also detected a pattern of antitrust rulings that favored big business over smaller companies and consumers. Sixteen times during his fourteen years on the federal bench, Metzenbaum said, Breyer voted against alleged victims in antitrust cases. "Antitrust is just an old-fashioned word for fair competition," said Metzenbaum.[15]

He had fought throughout his time in the Senate for tougher anti-trust laws and enforcement. The Sherman Antitrust Act, the work of Ohio Republican John Sherman, outlawed monopolies. But Metzen-baum believed it was also a buffer against capitalism run amok. Despite his persistence, he had only modest success in strengthening procompe-tition statutes. His repeated attempts to repeal the McCarran-Ferguson Act, exempting the insurance industry from most antitrust laws, were in vain. In 1994, he passed the International Antitrust Enforcement Assistance Act. That made it easier for the Justice Department and the Federal Trade Commission to go after foreign cartels by giving them clear authority to exchange evidence with counterpart agencies overseas. "When he is speaking on antitrust, you want to listen," Alan Simpson advised Breyer.[16] Breyer listened. He had to. But his nomina-tion was never in jeopardy. Metzenbaum was in the distinct minority on this one. He didn't care. He was seventy-seven. This would be one of his last fights—one he knew he could not win—and it would get ugly before it was over.

Breyer was virtually sainted by the president, other Democrats, and some in the media. He was a Harvard law professor, a gourmet cook, a bird watcher, a doting parent, a Stanford graduate, an Eagle Scout— yes, a Renaissance man. "He is tri-lingual. . . . He reads Proust in the original French, and he even has studied architecture," gushed Senator John Kerry.[17] Metzenbaum didn't read a lot of Proust, or spend time observing the bird world. He was unimpressed and said he might vote against Clinton's nominee.

It may not have been apparent to other senators or reporters in the committee room, but a July 12 confirmation hearing exposed the core of Metzenbaum's being. Breyer, a big shot by position and birth, wasn't sensitive in his legalistic rulings to the plight of the little guy, Metzenbaum believed. In his way of thinking, lawmakers and judges were supposed to protect "little guys" from getting stepped on by powerful interests. He was fending off a virus and had seen his prolabor striker-protection bill go down to defeat in the Senate that same day. He knew fellow Democrats were singing the praises of the man he was going to try to discredit. But he had done his homework and made up his mind: there would be no free ride for "St. Stephen."

Metzenbaum was all over him on a steamy Tuesday in July. He said he hoped as a consequence of his hard questions, "Maybe the milk of human kindness will run through you and you won't be so technical" in Breyer's rulings on the high court. That was too much for Judiciary chairman Joe Biden of Delaware. "Senator, I'm sure at the first conference after the first case, he'll turn to Judge [Antonin] Scalia and say, you know, let's think how Metzenbaum would do this," he said sarcastically and the room broke out in laughter. But before Metzenbaum was finished, he had given Breyer a thorough scolding about cases he decided "where the little guy gets squeezed out." Metzenbaum said, "You're more inclined to follow some esoteric theory of law, or maybe some regulatory approach to the law than . . . the whole question of protecting that small business person." Breyer could hardly get a word in edgewise. "One after the other, Judge Breyer is not sensitive to the fact that the little guy doesn't have a chance, except for the antitrust laws. . . . In too many cases, time after time, as the *Fordham* [*Law Review*, citing sixteen opinions against antitrust claims] article indicates, you hold against the little guy, the small business person, the consumer."[18]

Two days later in the same hearing room, Metzenbaum pounded with such tenacity that he infuriated political ally Ted Kennedy. When Metzenbaum quoted an ethics expert as saying it was "imprudent" for Breyer to have investments with a firm offering liability insurance, Kennedy interrupted. He insisted Metzenbaum distorted the comments of University of Pennsylvania law professor Geoffrey C. Hazard. The professor said, "There was no violation of ethics" on Breyer's part, Kennedy quoted, only that it was "possibly imprudent" for a judge to have such an investment because of the potential for a conflict. "Well, I didn't think that I was in a debate with my colleagues on this committee," said Metzenbaum, chastened by Kennedy's rebuke.[19] "Let's get with it," Senator Orrin Hatch snapped. The Utah Republican, like

Kennedy, thought Metzenbaum had unfairly edited the law professor's statement.

Accepting the inevitable, Metzenbaum voted for Breyer as the committee approved the nomination, but he wasn't through. On July 29, the full Senate opened final debate on Breyer. Metzenbaum knew he could not finally oppose Clinton's choice, not after going along with the nominations of Souter, Scalia, and Justice Sandra Day O'Connor. Hatch called Breyer a "man of integrity." Mitchell said his decisions showed "both compassion and intellect."[20] But Metzenbaum, with full knowledge he would anger his friends, couldn't resist a parting shot at a man he viewed as an elitist. Perhaps Biden was right. Maybe he *did* feel he could affect Breyer's behavior as a sitting Supreme Court justice.

"I don't think this was a great appointment for our president. I think Judge Breyer is far less of a jurist than we should accord a position on the Supreme Court."[21] In a lengthy speech to the Senate, he said Breyer's record "has not been impressive for a judge who is supposed to have a big heart." The senator from Ohio said he was "sorely tempted" to vote against the nomination. "It is with serious reservation and a heavy heart that I will vote for him. But, it is not a vote that makes me particularly proud."[22] Breyer was confirmed 87–9.

A New President

It pained Metzenbaum to challenge a Democratic president's wisdom because he had waited a long time for a leader like Clinton. Metzenbaum always had misgivings about Jimmy Carter's presidency and he lacked enthusiasm for Democratic standard-bearers Walter Mondale and Michael Dukakis. But Metzenbaum found his man in Arkansas governor Bill Clinton. After a twelve-year chill from a Republican-held White House, he had welcomed Clinton's inauguration in January 1993 with unbridled enthusiasm.

Earlier in the decade, before Bill Clinton came to Washington, Metzenbaum had serious reservations about the southern governor and his crowd. He had no use for the Democratic Leadership Council (DLC), a group of moderate, probusiness Democrats that helped Clinton develop many of the programs that formed a rationale for his campaign. Clinton had served as president of the DLC, which was derided by Jesse Jackson as "Democrats for the Leisure Class." That was pretty close to Metzenbaum's view. In May 1990, in the midst of an ideological struggle for control of the Democratic Party, Metzenbaum founded his own group: the Coalition for Democratic Values. "I am tired of seeing more and more of my colleagues become shadow Republicans," he told the *Washington Post*'s David Broder. Metzenbaum, Broder wrote, "has not been a significant player in national party affairs," but he used $50,000 in leftover 1988 campaign funds to launch the organization and recruited more than three dozen congressmen as charter members.[23] Among the joiners were some of the better-known liberals, including senators Tom Daschle, Chris Dodd, and Alan Cranston, and Ohio representatives Don Pease, Tom Sawyer, Louis Stokes, and Ed Feighan.

Going on the offensive, Metzenbaum publicly upbraided Senate majority leader Mitchell for being too conciliatory toward moderates and conservatives. "Sometimes he isn't strong enough. Mitchell often bends over backward to accommodate the reactionaries in our own party."[24] The coalition's manifesto said the nation did not need two Republican parties. The "future of the Democratic Party does not lie in fine-tuning Reaganism," the liberals said.[25] The idea was to unite grassroots activists, progressive thinkers, and Democratic businessmen. Together, they would make a case for traditional liberal policies on defense cuts, health care, and social services.

Metzenbaum's group organized a few conferences, aired a couple of television ads, and put out some policy papers, offering an alternative viewpoint to the DLC's positions. With an economic slump gripping the country, the liberal group devised an antirecession plan. Metzenbaum's coalition sought to raise taxes on the wealthy and trim the Pentagon's budget. The savings would pump $100 billion into public works, rebuilding of bridges, highways, and water systems.

After the Democratic Leadership Council announced it would hold its annual meeting in Cleveland in 1991, Metzenbaum refused to join other Ohio Democrats at a Washington fund-raiser to help underwrite the home-state event. "I am always intense, so what else is new?" he said of his reported combativeness on the matter.[26] Instead of aiding the DLC, he held his own conference in Des Moines on the same May weekend that the moderates met in Cleveland. Purely coincidental, of course.

But when Clinton emerged as a credible candidate in late 1991, Metzenbaum decided it was time to get acquainted, even if the young governor was a DLC stalwart. He invited Clinton to speak at a meeting of his rival coalition, and the presidential hopeful immediately called to accept. Clinton's informal manner captivated Metzenbaum, a midwesterner with no tolerance for pretense. He was impressed that Clinton didn't mind rubbing elbows with unreconstructed liberals at the risk of offending his moderate and conservative followers. Clinton resigned as chairman of the DLC after officially announcing his bid for president. The candidate likely "saw Metzenbaum as a back channel to the party's left," said Metzenbaum aide Joel Johnson.[27]

During the 1992 campaign, Metzenbaum was usually at Clinton's side during his frequent visits to Ohio. He also served as surrogate for the candidate in meetings with union groups. Son-in-law Joel Hyatt hosted a fund-raiser for Clinton during the heat of the primary season. Metzenbaum and Clinton's relationship continued after Inauguration Day. Now, at last, his phone calls were returned, his advice heeded, and his presence welcomed at bill-signing ceremonies and social events at the White House.

Life was good. Metzenbaum was enjoying himself at both ends of Pennsylvania Avenue—and it showed. His attire was a tip-off. Still a natty dresser as a septuagenarian, he took to wearing wild novelty ties featuring crazy quilts, animals, and whimsical motifs. One of his favorites depicted Cleveland's signature Terminal Tower skyscraper. He inspired sartorial risk-taking among colleagues such as Biden, a cuff-linked dandy in his own right. "Well, I think everyone's entitled to be a Metzenbaum once in their life," Biden said, smiling broadly during a break on the Breyer nomination. "I'm a Metzenbaum today—that's why I'm wearing this tie." Showing off neckwear emblazoned with cartoon characters, Biden said that Washington State Democrat Patty Murray, one of seven female senators, had teased him for his conservative attire. "'Joe, I must tell you, you are very dull' and then [she asked] why couldn't I be more like Howard Metzenbaum. . . . So I went out and got a Metzenbaum tie."[28] Metzenbaum said his wife, Shirley, had urged him to "go with it" when he hesitated before purchasing one of his flashy and expensive ties. "I just think the only way we males have an opportunity to get dressed up a little bit is with our ties," he said.[29]

Maybe it was his wardrobe, or more likely a shrugging acceptance of his role as the Senate contrarian, but Metzenbaum's rough treatment of Breyer didn't isolate him from the White House. By and large, he worked well with the new administration. A *Congressional Quarterly* analysis in December 1993 found Metzenbaum sided with Clinton 92 percent of the time in Senate voting. In the entire Ohio congressional delegation, only John Glenn was more loyal to the president.[30] As Metzenbaum became ever more enamored with the Clinton presidency, his Coalition for Democratic Values faded and by mid-decade disappeared. The short-lived coalition's activities were meant more as a shot to the bow of the party's moderate faction than as a bid to create a policy group or sustain an effective money-raising apparatus. After Clinton's first hundred days in office—a time of turmoil for the president—Metzenbaum said, "He has faced tough issues and he has spoken out candidly. He has not ducked. He has not equivocated."[31]

Battles Won and Causes Lost

Metzenbaum's own legislative legacy, going into his last term, was a work in progress. "The three-term Ohio Democrat is a gut fighter who, as always, will be involved in a number of high visibility fights as the 103rd Congress draws to a close," the *Wall Street Journal* predicted.[32] One thing was clear in these high-visibility scraps: he loved to regulate—everything that moved, or could be moved, from bicycle helmets to buckets. On the first day of the new Congress in 1993, he introduced eleven bills, seven involving some type of regulation of individuals or businesses. He included one to force bike riders under the age of sixteen to wear helmets (he was still unnerved by his wife's accident). Later that year, he wrote legislation requiring warning labels on industrial-size plastic buckets used for cleaning solutions. Tiny tots were falling into them, he said. About thirty toddlers drowned each year in the five-gallon vats, the *Cleveland Plain Dealer* reported in 2000.[33] Neither bill passed.

He was passionate about product labeling, or truth in advertising, as consumer advocates called it. His 1990 Nutrition Labeling Act required processed foods sold in grocery stores to show how their calories, fat, cholesterol, and the like fit into the context of a recommended daily diet. Low-fat, high-fiber, and "light" designations now had to fall within federally imposed definitions. Regulation comes at a cost. Verifying nutrition claims on food labels, in keeping with the law, cost the Ohio Agriculture Department $174,000 a year, an unfunded mandate on state government. But the idea caught on with the public. In subsequent years, food product labeling would be taken for granted, something diet-conscious consumers came to expect.

Metzenbaum was still looking out for the interests of organized labor by resisting attempts to weaken OSHA enforcement, trying to strengthen union organizing laws, and helping strikers. His last gasp was a bill blocking companies from hiring permanent replacement workers to take the jobs of strikers. It was a critical issue for American business leaders who believed the bill would invite more strikes since workers hitting the bricks would keep their job security even without a contract. Metzenbaum called it a "moral question," essential to the survival of the labor movement. The battle continued through 1993 and 1994, his last two years in the Senate. Without a meaningful right to strike, he said, collective bargaining is "little more than collective begging."[34]

The Democratic-run House passed the bill 239–190. But the progressive *Washington Post* editorial page came out against it, saying it "would go too far and strip management of a right that it, too, must have if the system is to function fairly," and that "it's one thing to try to keep the collective bargaining system functioning fairly [and] quite another to get into the business of trying to ordain results."[35] The management side recruited actor Charlton Heston to lobby against the bill with undecided senators. He called it "the push-button strike bill" and said it "was probably the most important labor vote in this administration so far."[36]

At the urging of the chamber of commerce and other employer lobbies, Republican foes filibustered, attempting to prevent a final vote through nonstop debate. "I say to Republicans in the United States Senate, let this measure go, let the members of the Senate vote on it up or down and it will pass," said Metzenbaum, who didn't like it one bit when others used the very tactics he perfected.[37] He was also trying to get the Clinton administration to lobby harder for a striker replacement law. But as he nagged his friends in the White House to do more for him, he was beating up their Supreme Court nominee, Breyer, in the confirmation process. Twice during July 1994, Metzenbaum attempted to choke off the GOP's filibuster. Twice he failed, each time by seven votes. It was a big disappointment. Labor's best friend in the Senate had been unable to deliver the unions' top legislative priority. It wasn't Metzenbaum's failing so much as a sign of organized labor's declining influence.

The AFL-CIO would also come up short in its struggle to kill the North American Free Trade Agreement, despite help from Metzenbaum, Glenn, Kennedy, and others. They were convinced the open borders promised by NAFTA would increase incentives for U.S. companies to close plants and move jobs to Mexico. There, the manufacturers could pay lower wages and deal with fewer environmental regulations. Metzenbaum traveled to Matamoros, Mexico, in 1992 to tour the American-owned *maquiladoras* (assembly plants along the border that took advantage of cheap labor and lax regulation) and the wretched *colonias* where many workers lived. The senator, in shirtsleeves and tennis shoes, said American firms were opening plants in Mexico to "live off the fat of the land—there's not much fat—low wages, poor environment, lack of labor standards. They are taking advantage of the situation."[38] But Clinton wanted the pact, and the unions didn't have enough clout to bury it. "Too often the focus of the union leaders is narrow—the threat of potential job loss, for instance, outweighs the greater economic good, as in the NAFTA battle," the *Plain Dealer* wrote. "Their position is not selling on Capitol Hill."[39]

Metzenbaum also went down swinging on another labor issue—albeit an unusual one, as this union's members were elite professional athletes averaging more than $1 million a year in salary. Metzenbaum, once part owner of the Cleveland Indians, wasn't bothered by the fact that baseball players were far removed from the Joe Lunch-pail types he typically defended. He knew their bosses—knew what kind of people ran major league baseball. With help from his friend Ted Bonda, he had raised some campaign money among baseball owners. But the beer barons, developers, and real-estate magnates that operated the big-league clubs were not his type. Most were Republicans and from moneyed families. Despite his wealth, Metzenbaum had resented guys like them his whole life. So when he sensed fan frustration over the 1994 baseball strike, he went after the owners with a vengeance. His target was their antitrust exemption, baseball's immunity from a law he spent a career trying to enforce.

He first introduced the bill in 1993 after the owners ousted commissioner Fay Vincent, a reformer who was considered sympathetic to the concerns of players and fans. Without the exemption, baseball would be vulnerable to players' lawsuits. The big leagues would lose their ability to limit the number of teams and prevent franchises from moving at whim from one city to another. Chaos would reign, some critics predicted, with constant expansion and teams popping up in small markets that couldn't support baseball. Metzenbaum was not an avid fan of professional sports. In a good year, he couldn't name the Tribe's starting lineup. After all, he had lost money on his Indians investment. He went to the occasional game but was not one to scrutinize box scores or turn the radio dial looking for game results. He preferred to participate, swimming seventy-six laps on his seventy-sixth birthday in 1993.

His bill was defeated in the Judiciary Committee in June, even after he reluctantly narrowed it so it would apply only to labor relations. He revived it after the players struck later that summer, in part because the owners wanted to impose salary caps on their clubs' payrolls.

The owners, of course, were looking out for their own interests. But Metzenbaum seemed blind to the intransigence of the powerful players' union, putting the entire blame for the walkout on management. Admitting he was taking sides, he said his bill should "relieve players' fear that they need to strike in order to prevent a salary cap from being shoved down their throats."[40]

The U.S. Supreme Court allowed the antitrust exemption in its 1922 opinion that baseball had unique status as a sport, distinct from everyday commerce. It was upheld in 1972 when the court rejected Curt Flood's bid for free agency after he was traded from the St. Louis Cardinals to the Philadelphia Phillies. Once the strike began, Metzenbaum sought to add his legislation as a rider on other bills whenever the opportunity arose. He was blocked on September 14 when he tried to call it up, but he tried again at the close of the 1994 session.

A week before adjournment, he attempted to amend a big spending bill with the antitrust repealer. Congress was trying to wrap up its business in an election year. Many legislators wanted to go home and campaign. "I do not care to be an obstructionist," Metzenbaum said as other senators implored him not to bring up the amendment on September 27. "Let me plead with the senator from Ohio to offer his amendment on another vehicle," his friend Dale Bumpers said to him. "I have to strenuously object, or ask the senator from Ohio to please withhold his amendment on this bill," Senator Tom Harkin of Iowa chimed in. "I know he is very sincere. I do not quarrel with his motives.

But I believe it is the wrong time, and I will do everything that I can to oppose this," said Senator Jim Exon of Nebraska.[41]

This didn't stop him. Metzenbaum eventually introduced the antitrust amendment and then tied up the Senate for two hours on September 30 in a futile debate. Senator George Mitchell of Maine, a Red Sox fan, opposed taking away the exemption, as did majorities on both sides of the aisle. "Here today, on a Friday afternoon, one week from adjournment, I am adamantly opposed to the federal government jumping into a baseball strike," Republican senator Phil Gramm of Texas told Metzenbaum.[42] Kansas Republican Nancy Kassebaum called Metzenbaum's scheme "an unprecedented attempt to affect the outcome" of a labor dispute by giving one side an advantage.[43] After refusing to take no for an answer on a bill he knew wouldn't become law that year, "the senator from Ohio" angrily withdrew the amendment, but only after exasperating his colleagues one last time.

This was Metzenbaum at his worst, a sore loser in a game he never had a realistic chance of winning. "The owners don't give a damn," he complained after taking the amendment down. "They're arrogant— they're rich."[44] The strike killed the second half of the 1994 season, canceling the World Series and the hopes of the Indians, who may have been the American League's best team. But contrary to Metzenbaum's gloomy prediction that the dispute would wipe out another summer of baseball, the strike ended later that year and the 1995 season opened on schedule without the dreaded salary cap.

The Last Bill

Metzenbaum didn't mind being wrong once in a while. He never lost heart or worried much about his won-lost record. He worked hard all the way up to the closing gavel. His last major achievement, the transracial adoption law, would prove bittersweet. It started with his love of children and his pursuit of a noble cause. He wanted to find parents for minority youngsters taken from abusive homes or orphaned for other reasons. "Senator Howard Metzenbaum is a persistent pain in the neck. As a result, thousands of little kids are likely to have a better life," the *Wall Street Journal*'s Al Hunt wrote.[45]

Metzenbaum wanted adoption agencies to stop standing in the way of placements of black children with white families. Minorities made up about 40 percent of the 20,000 children awaiting adoption.[46] But black social workers resisted transracial adoptions, insisting that African American parents should raise black children, even if the kids had to languish in foster homes while waiting for the right match. Metzenbaum agreed that the race of the parents should be considered when all other factors in an adoption were equal. But he said adoptions should not be delayed or denied in other cases—that is, when black parents could not be found for kids, yet willing white couples were turned away. "This is one of those bills that has no constituency— there is no political mileage in this kind of a bill," he said.[47] Not only that, but Metzenbaum was rejecting political correctness, the idea that black children could only preserve their cultural sense of "blackness" if brought up by black parents.

With the help of African American cosponsors, he won approval in 1994 for a bill barring any agency that received federal money from making adoption decisions based solely on race, color, or national origin. It gained 77–20 passage as part of a broader education bill in early October and was signed into law by Clinton. "It is one of the proudest moments of my Senate career, that transracial adoptions will be permitted," Metzenbaum said.[48]

But his pride would soon turn to anger. Even in winning, he had lost. Metzenbaum was snookered. His language was not tight enough to fend off an interpretation by the Department of Health and Human Services (HHS) that undermined his legislative intent. A fact sheet issued by the bureaucrats the following April agreed that Metzenbaum's law prohibited adoptions based "solely" on race. But the department said the act "permits an agency to consider both a child's cultural, racial and ethnic background . . . as one of a number of factors in determining whether a placement is in the child's best interests." It also said placement agencies could consider "the capacity of the foster or adoptive parents to meet the needs of a child of a specific background."[49]

Metzenbaum, by then in private life, was enraged. Critics said the guidelines would make transracial adoptions even more difficult by codifying racial preference as an acceptable consideration. The law, with its unintended consequences, unraveled. "Some bastards at HHS intervened and did the bill great harm," citizen Metzenbaum said.[50]

With his approval, it was repealed in 1995 and replaced with more restrictive language denying federal money to any agency that discriminated by race in placing children in adoptive homes. "I'm more interested in getting children adopted than I am in having my name on a law," he said.[51]

As a private citizen, Metzenbaum could no longer threaten to hold up the Health and Human Services budget. But as a senator, his elasticity and brassiness were boundless. In August 1994, when Senate leader George Mitchell threatened to hold all-night sessions to wear out a Republican filibuster on a health care bill, Metzenbaum complained that "a filibuster by any other name is a filibuster."

"All I hear is talk, talk, talk and the American people say, 'What are they doing there on the floor of the U.S. Senate?' They are not doing much," he said. Then turning to the Republican side, he lectured, "If you have the votes then vote it up or down . . . What you are doing here is playing games—we are playing political games."[52]

The games were coming to an end for Metzenbaum. On June 29, 1993, he had announced that he would "conclude my service as a member of the United States Senate" at the adjournment of the 103rd Congress. It was a day that his staff and friends knew was coming but dreaded nonetheless. In his campaign against Voinovich, he had said that if reelected his third term would likely be his last. But after he got back to business in the Senate, he was coy about his prospects. At one point, some top aides thought there was a fifty-fifty chance he would run again. His longtime associate Harold Stern urged him to go for it. "He has said he is keeping his options open," press secretary Nancy Coffey said in late 1990. "[He] wouldn't want to make any lobbyists happy. No one is going to dance on his grave until his heart stops."[53]

His wife, Shirley, had mixed feelings, honoring his work in the Senate but wanting him to spend more time with her and their seven grandchildren. Metzenbaum, then seventy-six, always worked hard. But he wasn't a hopeless "workaholic" by the unforgiving standards of Washington's Beltway. He had a life. He loved to travel with his family. He played tennis and swam, and he often went out socially with Shirley. He enjoyed an occasional beer or a glass of Dewars Scotch and a meal at a good restaurant. "I love my job in the Senate, but I love other things in my life more," he said as he told colleagues he was retiring.[54] No doubt, he was sincere.

But there was also a subtext to his decision. Joel Hyatt, bitterly disappointed when "Howard" chose to run again in 1988, was pressing hard for the announcement so he could begin planning a 1994 Senate campaign of his own. "My political plans are the subject for another day. This is Howard Metzenbaum's day," Hyatt said as word of the retirement spread.[55] Hyatt soon created an "exploratory committee" and raised $800,000 to contest the seat he had coveted for a dozen years or more. Many of Metzenbaum's aides believed if Hyatt had not been in the picture, the senator would have run for a fourth term. Some of them pleaded with him to reconsider.

Hyatt was a frequent presence in the Senate office, to the chagrin of some staffers who did not appreciate his back channel to the boss. But Metzenbaum, the father of four daughters, regarded him almost as a son and valued his input. He once suggested that Joel and Susan Hyatt install a second phone in their bedroom so he could talk to them simultaneously during late-night consultations. Without question, Metzenbaum wanted Joel to succeed him when the time came to leave. And yet he was ambivalent about giving up a job he loved.

More battles loomed ahead; Metzenbaum still had eighteen months to go. He offered no apologies or regret to colleagues, many for "whom I've made life difficult." That was not his way. Instead he handed out familiar, unsolicited advice. "We don't look beyond one day's news cycle, unless it's to envision the next election's attack ad. We therefore find ourselves ducking tough choices, postponing the inevitable, passing the buck . . . Let's try to work together to distinguish this Congress as one that steps up, accepts actual responsibility, suffers necessary pain, and makes real progress." He acknowledged, "Easy for me to say, I suppose, as I won't face the voters next fall. But if I have learned one thing here, it is that you can sometimes take positions that don't sit well with the majority of your constituents and still thrive politically."[56] No one—not even his worst enemies—could dispute this last point as it applied to his career. One by one, senators came to the floor to give the old tiger his due: Don Riegle of Michigan, Paul Simon of Illinois, Carl Levin of Michigan, Kennedy, Mitchell, Bradley, and Orrin Hatch. Metzenbaum had earned their respect, in some cases their friendship, even if he drove them nuts with his tactics.

"If his last name had been shorter, it might well have become one of those made-in-Washington verbs," the *Plain Dealer* editorialized. "As a verb, to 'metzenbaum' would mean to 'stand in the way of, to form a barrier, to intimidate by any means available.'" His hometown paper went on to say that Metzenbaum "may have been more liberal than most Ohioans, but he managed skillfully to come across more as a populist than an ideologue."[57] *Newsweek* praised his liberalism. "Metzenbaum is that rare species, a powerfully effective senator, and a powerfully effective liberal."[58]

The tributes, accolades, and festive banquets rolled through his final eighteen months in office. When his old circle in Cleveland roasted and toasted him, the printed program for the dinner had the heading, ONE PERSON CAN MAKE A DIFFERENCE . . . ONE PERSON DID. In his Senate valedictory on that summer day in 1993, Metzenbaum began his slow fade with grace. He told friends and foes he had few regrets, many treasured memories, and a love of combat that "is undiminished," conceding, "I've won my share of battles, and fought my share of lost causes."[59]

—— Ⅼⅼⅼ ——

CHAPTER 10

An Unthreatened Man

Shirley Metzenbaum always told her husband that he tilted at real dragons, not illusionary windmills. It was worth the effort, she said, even if his jousts were often in vain. He slew his share. Metzenbaum thought about those battles while visions from his past and present drifted by in a surreal waltz on May 28, 1998, four years after his retirement. Senate colleagues, civil rights leaders, the attorney general of the United States, even Republicans joined him for a monumental day in Cleveland. Behind him was a turn-of-the-century courthouse where he had once practiced law as a young man, unable to get a job with the city's prestigious firms. The five-story neoclassical building went up in the heart of Cleveland's downtown seven years before he was born in a modest Jewish neighborhood a few miles away. And now it was to be renamed in his honor. In the background, a choir sang his favorite song: "To dream the impossible dream, to fight the unbeatable foe . . . to run where the brave dare not go."

In the end, his was an American story—the upwardly mobile struggle, the victor over discrimination and near poverty, and a lifelong affinity for the less fortunate. It was a triumph for the never-say-die, hard-work-will-pay-off, and win-at-all-costs philosophy. "I never learned to sing the song, but I did get to fulfill my dream," he said in a moment when all of his dragons were, at last, silenced.[1] On this sunny spring day, he heard others sing his praises as a fighter "for those in the dawn, the twilight, and the shadows of life."[2]

A fighter, yes. Relentlessly, Metzenbaum fought. "He is always fighting," President Clinton said of him during a visit to Cleveland in 1994. "He doesn't always win, but he always fights."[3] "It is the highest compliment that can be said about a public official," said Senator Mike DeWine, the Republican who won Metzenbaum's seat in 1994. "No matter where you travel across this state, there is one word that is always used, and that word is 'fighter.'"[4]

On other occasions, choosing his own words, Metzenbaum explained his style and also revealed a key to his electoral success. "I've never believed that anyone was sent here to take a computerized opinion poll on every issue. Nor do I believe that you should check with the special interest groups before deciding how to vote. You should vote your conscience, speak your mind, and fight on the side you believe to be right. Most importantly, you should let your constituents know exactly where you stand."[5]

In a state that voted Democratic in only four presidential contests over the second half of the twentieth century, an ultraliberal, partisan Democrat named Metzenbaum flourished. He transcended ideology and party labels, but not with the charisma of Jack Kennedy or the bipartisan appeal of John McCain. He did it with grit, determination, and a combativeness that convinced voters that he was on their side. "He had a sixth sense about what people were concerned about—and jumped on it," said George Voinovich, who rebounded from his loss to Metzenbaum by winning election in 1998 to the Senate seat vacated by John Glenn. "He knew issues that people cared about, and he exploited those issues."[6]

Metzenbaum, the fighter for the consumer, the working person, the minority, the underdog, and the left-behind, would challenge the ruling class whatever the odds. He would tell the powers-that-be that they were not going to get away with it—the big shots were not going to trample on the weak and powerless. No one was immune. Judge James G. Carr, chief justice for the U.S. Northern District in Ohio, got a going-over and some insight into the Metzenbaum mind-set when the senator interviewed him for a federal court vacancy. Metzenbaum worked furiously on other matters throughout their meeting in his

Senate office. "I think I would have gone the other way on that one," he remarked bluntly after reviewing Carr's written opinions as a magistrate. Ultimately, however, he recommended Carr for nomination to the Northern District bench. When he called to give him the good news, Metzenbaum said to him, "Remember this rule: promise me you will remember the little people."[7]

That's the prototypical Metzenbaum, thought Peter Harris. "If you could see a map of his DNA, it would be there. There are big guys and little guys, and the little guys get run over, and it is up to him to bring some balance."[8]

It is easier, of course, to block legislation than to pass it. But even those who disagreed with Metzenbaum grudgingly gave him credit for being a formidable hell-raiser. He was fearless and, most of the time, positive that he was right on the issues, even when those he respected told him he was wrong. He was so antiestablishment that some Ohioans took him for a grumpy conservative, ranting against bureaucrats, big government, and the intelligentsia. Public opinion polls consistently confirmed this mistaken impression. His demeanor came across more like a dour Jesse Helms—the Senator No of the right—than an ebullient Ted Kennedy.

Metzenbaum aide Dick Woodruff observed that "they didn't know he was liberal; they didn't know he was Jewish."[9] But they knew he was a straight-talker. Dale Butland, a press secretary to both Metzenbaum and John Glenn, said the "key to Howard Metzenbaum's success in Ohio was that he always ran five points better in Republican counties than other Democrats did. He didn't talk out of both sides of his mouth."[10]

But intellect, image, and determination were not the whole story. GOP consultant Roger Stone credited "luck and money" to Metzenbaum's ability to prevail in a Republican-leaning state.[11] Metzenbaum didn't deny that he was the recipient of good fortune or that his fund-raising helped propel him to victory after victory. He didn't deny he had some good bounces—and he made the most of them. "I have been a very lucky guy—very lucky. I have been lucky in politics," he said at a dinner marking his eighty-fifth birthday. "I am no Frank Sinatra, but I did it my way."[12]

Metzenbaum was never outspent in a major campaign, although Voinovich held him to a virtual draw, with each man hauling in well over $8 million. And like many Democrats, Metzenbaum benefited from the

Watergate scandal and won election to a full term in 1976 against a foe that appeared wishy-washy on the question of Nixon's impeachment. In 1982 his opponent, conservative John Ashbrook, died in the midst of the campaign. His successor was a little-known and underfunded state senator named Pfeifer. Metzenbaum ran a masterful campaign in 1988, yet his rival, Voinovich, made several unforced turnovers.

Fortune, then, may have been on his side, but there was another key ingredient in the mix: Metzenbaum was more influenced by his Jewish faith and heritage than he let on. Without apology, he thought of himself as a secular man, yet he was never far from his roots. In Ohio, Rabbi Arthur Lelyveld, a civil rights activist and head of Fairmount Temple in Beachwood, said that "principled, prophetic Judaism" guided Metzenbaum, even though he paid little heed to ritual. Metzenbaum, a Fairmount member, got his values "from his family and what he learned in the synagogue," said Lelyveld, who knew him for more than forty years.[13] During his years in the Senate, Metzenbaum and Shirley attended ecumenical Bible classes conducted on Capitol Hill by an Israeli-born author and ethicist. Metzenbaum once said, "Anti-Semitism is a reality for that group of bigots who live in this country and elsewhere throughout the world. To deny its existence would be to deny the facts. But having said that, it's a real testimonial to the lack of anti-Semitism that a Metzenbaum can be elected in a state that had only 2 percent or 2.5 percent members of the Jewish faith."[14]

Senator Carl Levin, a Michigan Democrat, believed his friend's principles were forged by years of fighting discrimination against Jews and others. Levin ascribed Metzenbaum's compassion for the underprivileged to the Jewish principle of "tsedaka," the Hebrew word that usually translates as charity and signifies the obligation to contribute to the betterment of society.[15] Tsedaka is related to another Hebrew word meaning justice. Mark Talisman, a lobbyist and Jewish-American activist in Washington, said the Torah is "street language" for Jews and meant to be applied in daily life. Metzenbaum "used it as a sort of directory of operations," he said.[16]

But did Metzenbaum see a contradiction between his aggressive accumulation of personal wealth and his concern for the poor? "Certainly that went through my mind at times," he said. "But I don't think there are many of us who will say, I am going to give up all of my money and live a very strict life, a monastic life. Maybe one out of 10,000—I am not that one."[17] Byron Krantz, a corporate lawyer who says he is further to the left than his mentor, rejected the suggestion that Metzenbaum was a limousine liberal. "I reconcile his wealthy lifestyle very easily. Look to his heritage. If you look within the Jewish religion, you will find a lot of very, very tough businessmen, and you will find a group of people who are historically very liberal. Jews are still Democrats. It makes no sense economically that Jews are Democrats. But they are. And it makes no sense that Jews are liberals, based on their socioeconomic positions. But they are. It is a heritage, a long heritage. It is the biblical mandate—charity. It is your obligation to share. It is your obligation to give to charity. It is your obligation to provide for people."[18] In the Bible, God admonished Isaiah to "feed the hungry, clothe the naked, shelter the homeless."

The poor were an important part of Metzenbaum's constituency, but so were middle-class workers, especially those in unions. Voinovich said Metzenbaum's strong political base in the labor movement was central to his electoral success in Ohio, a state among the highest in union members per capita in the nation. "He understood who his constituency was, and they knew it, and he represented their interests quite well here in the Senate. And he was smart enough as those years went by to pick issues where he reached out to the independents and the moderate person in Ohio. He was looked upon as kind of a spokesman for the little guy."[19]

In the closing days of his career, Metzenbaum fought to the finish line. "We wanted Metzenbaum to be Metzenbaum until the end," said Nancy Coffey. Senior aides did not want him diminished as a lame duck or distracted by a would-be-successor looking over his shoulder. A year before he retired, the *Almanac of American Politics* described him as "prickly, persistent and at times irritating. . . . Tactically, Metzenbaum often accomplishes his goals through his deft use of Senate rules and his willingness to antagonize his colleagues when necessary. He capitalizes on senators' desire to start a scheduled recess by threatening filibusters and other delays. . . . His desire to eliminate what he considers unwarranted tax breaks and other special benefits for wealthy individuals and corporations has earned him a nickname from quick-witted Republican Leader Robert J. Dole of Kansas: 'the commissioner.'"[20]

At a retirement party for Metzenbaum, Dole recounted, "I remember once when I was the majority leader Senator Metzenbaum said, 'That's all we are going to do today. I am going home.' I said, 'Where are you going?' He said, 'I am going home to Ohio.' And that was all we did that day."[21]

Senator Tom Harkin, who always thought Metzenbaum would seek a fourth term, still got excited when his old friend took command of the Senate floor during his last term. He exulted when Metzenbaum gave liberals an edge in a dustup over threatened cuts to Medicare. "There was that old flash. That old fire was there again. And I told Ruth [Harkin's wife], 'Howard is in there again. He is in there, doing it again.' And I said, 'Boy, I tell you, it was so great what he did on that to make sure we prevailed.'"[22]

"He could be vitriolic, blustery and reckless even with retirement looming at the age of 77," said the *Plain Dealer*'s exit piece. "He was a curmudgeon, the last angry liberal," but also, "his instincts for good art, a good deal, and good politics seldom failed him."[23] Commentator Dick Feagler, who covered Metzenbaum for the *Cleveland Press* in the years before his Senate career, referred to him as the "last of the New Deal Liberals."

"There are people that hate me with a passion," Metzenbaum admitted, "but when I do meet them, I laugh and kid them. And I tell them, I absolutely defend their right to be wrong."[24] He, however, was seldom wrong, or so he thought. His legislative legacy is substantial yet not the stuff of greatness for a career that spanned three decades. The bills he passed did not always have the impact he anticipated. A year after enactment, his plant-closing law wasn't giving business leaders the heartburn some of them feared. In truth, the law appeared to have little effect on the job picture. In Ohio, state officials reported 160 notices were issued affecting 23,000 workers who had lost jobs or were laid off. "Even supporters acknowledge that although the law provides two months paid notice, it can't provide long-term help to workers in areas where no other jobs are available," the Associated Press reported.[25] His 1988 worker-retraining law filled in some of those gaps.

The Brady Law stayed in effect, requiring background checks of handgun buyers. However, the waiting period no longer applied by the turn of the century since computerized records could be checked instantly at the point of sale. In 2002, Metzenbaum was surprised to learn that pro–gun rights attorney general John Ashcroft, in a court proceeding, used his Senate arguments for restricting firearms. Ashcroft wanted to buttress the government's case when he was forced to defend the assault weapons law. "I guess this goes to prove the old adage: if you live long enough, you might see anything," Metzenbaum said.[26] But the assault weapons ban expired in 2004 after Congress refused to renew it. Ashcroft's Justice Department lawyers were merely doing what was required of them.

But the people in the trenches always remembered Metzenbaum's long struggle for gun control. Sarah Brady, calling him "my beloved Senator Metzenbaum," said the country was safer because of his efforts. "The entire nation owes Howard Metzenbaum a great debt of gratitude," she said. "Because of him the debate over gun violence and public safety will never, ever be the same again."[27]

In all, Metzenbaum was responsible for thirty-seven bills becoming law, a record he once inelegantly referred to as a "shithouse full" of successful legislation. They ranged from symbolic memorials to breakthrough federal financing for Alzheimer's research and the development of "orphan drugs" to treat rare diseases. He was an original cosponsor of bills banning age discrimination in the workplace and restoring tenets of civil rights laws overturned by the Supreme Court. The 1991 Civil Rights Act made it harder for businesses to systematically exclude minorities or women from the workplace, and it expressly authorized voluntary affirmative action. Metzenbaum believed the highlights of his legislation were nutrition labeling for products on grocery shelves, the Brady Bill, infant formula standards, and pension protection. "Laws like nutrition labeling do not fit easily on a bumper sticker," said Joel Johnson, but they make a difference in people's lives.[28]

In 2000, the *Washington Post* reported that "study after study shows that a majority of Americans—in some cases huge majorities—routinely use Nutrition Facts to help them decide what to eat. Food companies have developed thousands of new, reduced-fat products since the labels were mandated by [Metzenbaum's] law in 1994." Sadly, the report said, Americans were fatter than ever, a fact that no doubt distressed weight-conscious Metzenbaum.[29] Worthwhile efforts, to be sure, yet his name is seldom associated with landmark legislation in the manner of the Gramm-Rudman or McCain-Feingold laws. Rather, Metzenbaum's lasting legacy is that of a stopper—the killer of special interest deals, the bane of boondoggles. From his efforts to halt wasteful water projects and railroad giveaways to his determination to avoid sticking taxpayers with the tab for the savings and loan bailout, he was the unquestioned gatekeeper. His ploy of introducing dozens of amendments before cloture votes—used to quash filibusters—prompted the Senate to limit postcloture debate to 100 hours, and eventually to thirty.[30]

John Glenn once called Metzenbaum a "great big traffic light on the Senate floor that stops things from getting through on a buddy-buddy basis with nobody watching."[31] Other senators learned it was wiser to clear their little schemes in advance with Metzenbaum rather than get jammed up in front of that "big traffic light." Between 1970 and 1994, there were 194 filibusters, more than eight times the number conducted in the entire nineteenth century. Beginning in 1974, Metzenbaum had a hand in many of those originating on the Democratic side.[32] The mere threat of a filibuster by him was enough to cause the Senate to change course and move to a less contentious bill. "He was certainly the master of obstruction. His staff was incredibly well informed," said Sarah Binder of the Brookings Institution. "Did he have a positive effect? There's no doubt that Metzenbaum extracted concessions from opponents, due to his legislative tactics. It's also likely that anticipation of objections from Metzenbaum led senators to alter legislation to avoid a Metzenbaum hold or filibuster."[33]

Senator Kennedy had no doubt that Metzenbaum had a "positive effect." The "Metzenbaum Mark" on legislation was comparable to the "Good Housekeeping Seal of Approval," he said.[34] "If President Kennedy were writing another book, *Profiles in Courage,* there would be a chapter on Howard Metzenbaum," Kennedy said on another occasion.[35] Louis Stokes, Ohio's first black congressman, said Metzenbaum was a fighter for the "voiceless" as far back as his days in the Ohio legislature. "Many times, he alone championed issues that others feared," said Stokes. "Always consistent and never wavering, he has steadfastly represented the state of Ohio, women, minorities, and the unrepresented with zeal and passion."[36]

In his last term, Metzenbaum again turned his attention to the north, as he stood in the way of a proposed handover of 18,000 acres in Alaska's Tongass National Forest to a mining company. The federal government was supposed to get subsurface rights to 10,000 acres on Admiralty Island in exchange for the larger plot, which had strong potential for gold and other minerals. "It appears to be another example of a wasteful government giveaway," Metzenbaum said, questioning why the mining company, Sealaska Corporation, and its partner wanted the land. Like any good lawyer, he knew the answer. "I'll tell you why in one word—gold," he told the Senate.[37] In 1995, the Tongass deal went through with Metzenbaum on the sidelines in retirement. However, he had made his point, and the federal government gave up only 7,500 acres to the mining interests.

"To the end, we were still holding up things," Nancy Coffey said in 1994. But finally, wistful at the dwindling of his Senate days, Metzenbaum relented. In his last week, as staff was still monitoring bills and recommending holds, he would say, "let it go."[38] "We start a new career, raise a little more hell," he said at a Senate going-away party. "I would have sung, 'I Did It My Way,' but I can't carry a tune."[39] Seven years after his departure, Metzenbaum was still missed in the closing hours of legislative business, Senator Harkin said. That's when items, beneficial to a handful of folks but not to the country as a whole, slip into legislation. "Every year at the end of a session, people are saying, where's Metzenbaum? When he was here the public interest was protected," Harkin said. "There will never be in my lifetime a person who fought harder for the public interest than Howard Metzenbaum."[40]

His detractors, those questioning his "positive effect," would amend Harkin's statement to say Metzenbaum fought for the public interest *as he saw it*. In 1993, the nonpartisan National Taxpayers Union rated him the fourth biggest spender in the Senate, based on the estimated cost of legislation he sponsored that year. He called himself a fiscal conservative but applied his penny-pinching selectively. He was eager to stop wasteful Defense Department outlays, energy company projects, or pork-barrel projects alien to his own political sensibilities. He was eager to spend government money on issues he believed in—"people programs," as he called them.

Special interest? In 1992, he approached Senate finance chairman Lloyd Bentsen about preserving a tax credit going to employers that offered prepaid legal-service plans to employees. Joel Hyatt's company provided such plans to several large firms, covering about one million workers. Business would have suffered had the tax credit expired. "Metzenbaum has often railed against deals that he perceives are done for specific corporate clients. He vigorously opposes generous settlement terms for ailed savings and loan owners as well as breaks for corporations seeking tax abatement for cities and states," an Ohio newspaper reported at the time.[41] Hyatt said, sure, he wanted to preserve the credit but had not spoken to Metzenbaum about it. The tax relief stayed put.

Metzenbaum did not exactly go out a winner, but then again he probably didn't expect to. In his last year in office, he was on the losing side
in the baseball antitrust argument, the failed striker-replacement bill,
and the General Agreement on Tariffs and Trade. Only twelve other
senators joined him in voting against ratification of GATT, an international trade deal. In addition, he made little headway in attempts to
discredit Justice Breyer, and the White House ignored his call for the
firing of CIA director James Woolsey.

In retirement, the old tiger was restless. He became chairman of
the Consumer Federation of America. The part-time job made him
an occasional lobbyist and front man for a nonprofit association of
240 consumer groups. In 2001, *The Hill,* a capitol tabloid, named him
among the top "grassroots/nonprofit lobbyists."[42] He held a news conference now and then, testified on Capitol Hill, and published op-ed
pieces, but it wasn't the same. He knew his impact was limited, and it
bothered him. "There's a hell of a difference between being in the U.S.
Senate and being a has-been in the U.S. Senate," he said.[43] "I want to
fight with somebody and there's no one to fight with right now."[44] He
regretted not being able to run for another term, although he knew he
had no choice but to step aside for Joel Hyatt. As the 1994 campaign
took shape, a columnist suggested, "Hyatt would do well to model
himself after his father-in-law, who, in the judgment of many Ohioans,
including those who have voted for him, is an SOB, but doggone it, he
is our SOB."[45]

But that was not Hyatt's strategy. He "has not been invited to campaign on Hyatt's behalf and has no present plans to get involved in any
way," the senator told reporters in October during the Hyatt-DeWine
campaign. "I would like to be involved, but I respect his wishes. He
has told me over and over again that he feels he has to win this election on his own."[46] Metzenbaum was disappointed at being left out.
Could Metzenbaum beat DeWine if he were the candidate? "Sure," he
answered.[47]

The bravado faded as he settled into retirement. Hyatt lost to
DeWine, even after promising he would be "on your side" during the
last weekend of the campaign. Four years later Voinovich claimed
Glenn's seat. Metzenbaum and Shirley eventually sold their homes in
Washington and Lyndhurst and lived full-time in Aventura, Florida,
where they owned a comfortable high-rise condominium overlooking
a golf course and, just beyond it, the Atlantic.

Perhaps for the first time, Metzenbaum became introspective. "Maybe I was a little too rough sometimes on people," he said over a meal at Washington's University Club, where he was treated with deference as "Senator Metzenbaum."[48] He admitted apologizing to Justice Ruth Bader Ginsberg for coming on too strong during her confirmation to the Supreme Court. He came to respect DeWine, who was grateful when he was able to claim Metzenbaum's first-floor suite in the Russell Office Building. Metzenbaum did little for DeWine's hapless Democratic opponent, Ted Celeste, in the 2000 election.

Juanita Powe and Joel Johnson—confidants as close to Metzenbaum as any—believed the rough edges softened in his last term. "He is not the same man who came here nineteen years ago. He had a chip on his shoulder. He was demanding and impatient and wanted to accomplish a lot," Johnson said in 1994. "He changed. He grew and matured. In his last term, he seemed very comfortable with his . . . place in history and the institution. He had already sort of created this mythical 'Senator No,'" and "one thing he never did is stop. He never gave up."[49]

Out of office, Metzenbaum savored rare moments in the limelight. At the 2000 Democratic National Convention, the *Cincinnati Enquirer*'s Howard Wilkinson wrote:

At 83 years old, Howard Metzenbaum, former U.S. senator from Ohio, still knows how to work the crowd. With his shock of white hair and horn-rimmed glasses, the man a generation of Ohio Republicans loved to hate strode to the lectern at the Ohio delegation breakfast like an octogenarian rock star. Mr. Metzenbaum, scourge of the utility companies, bane of conservative Supreme Court nominees, and curmudgeon extraordinaire, gave Ohio delegates what they have been looking for. "Of all the Republicans in the world, how is it that George W. Bush ended up choosing somebody like Dick Cheney?" Metzenbaum asked the delegates.[50]

In 2004, Metzenbaum's political instincts failed him. In Cincinnati, he endorsed liberal front-runner Howard Dean, a man he barely knew, over former Senate colleagues like John Kerry and Joe Lieberman. After Dean's presidential campaign collapsed, Metzenbaum belatedly backed Kerry, the eventual nominee. Metzenbaum didn't worry much about the enemies he made. But in an unforgiving city like Washington, the offended ones have long memories and keep daggers at the ready. His old foe, Senator D'Amato, called Senate majority leader George Mitchell the Senate's toughest negotiator. Then D'Amato took his revenge with relish: "And no doubt, the meanest, was former Senator Howard Metzenbaum from Ohio. I clashed with him because it was always Metzenbaum's way or no way. He would stop all bills from moving forward and threaten to filibuster if he didn't get what he wanted. I'm happy to say that I was able to do the same to him."[51]

Ohio Republicans also got in their licks. "We don't have any contact with Metzenbaum—none," said Congressman David Hobson of Springfield. "You know what people say to me? 'That's Howard.'"[52] Bill Saxbe, whose appointment as attorney general opened up the Senate seat in 1973, always thought Metzenbaum's personality hurt him. "The problem is that Metzenbaum has got no following because he is such an asshole when it comes to dealing with people."[53] And Roger Stone, celebrating the Republican takeover of the Senate in 1994, said, "I hope it galls him [Metzenbaum] that all the left-wing stuff he did in the Senate over the years is now going to be canceled out and his seat will be taken over by a conservative Republican."[54] In a losing reelection campaign, Georgia Democrat Wyche Fowler complained that Metzenbaum's name was synonymous with liberal extremism in the South. "[Republican Paul] Coverdell's press conference today was just 'Fowler, Kennedy, Metzenbaum.' You would think, wouldn't you, that he could find some way to put a little more positive face than that for the voters."[55] Fowler wound up losing to Coverdell.

In Ohio, the business community remembered Metzenbaum's hostility to its interests. "Howard Metzenbaum seemed to go out of his way to antagonize business," said Jack Reimers, president of the Ohio Chamber of Commerce in early 1990s. "He was the epitome of the anti-business politician. He thrived, savored, and sought to be viewed that way."[56] Metzenbaum won back some enemies with his steadfast pursuit of the public interest. To the astonishment of Buddy Rand's friends, even Rand came around to Metzenbaum's side, admiring his political acumen and Senate service. Rand donated $1,000 to Metzenbaum after a chance encounter with him in 1988 outside the Theatrical Restaurant in downtown Cleveland. The good in Metzenbaum outweighed the bad, Rand said in an interview.[57] Senator Orrin

Hatch, perhaps Metzenbaum's most frequent Senate sparring partner, called him "a great senator for three reasons. He always believed the cause was greater than himself. He had a superior command of the legislative process and, I think, wrote the book on guerilla legislative tactics. And for all his ferocity in committee and on the Senate floor, he was a gentle man and a good friend."[58]

Shirley Metzenbaum said her husband's deepest desire as he entered his seventh decade of life was for a peaceful future. "Becoming grandparents has affected both of us. I think [we would hope for] a better world for our kids, a world without fears," she said when asked about the couple's desire for the future.[59]

Nearing eighty, Metzenbaum finally learned how to type and picked up some computer skills so he could carry on email correspondence with his grandchildren. "I'm taking typing lessons," said the man who could crunch numbers in his head so fast that aides wondered if he was using a calculator. "All the better," Metzenbaum suggested, "to cruise the Internet in search of cyber windmills to tilt against, new rights to wrong, and maybe even to make a few bucks."[60]

Few politicians get the recognition they think they deserve in their lifetime. Metzenbaum, a polarizing figure, got his courthouse but faded to the fringes of Washington by the turn of the century. The Republicans running Congress and the White House were too busy deregulating and naming things after Ronald Reagan to consider honoring someone who battled with the iconic fortieth president, and also the forty-first, George Herbert Walker Bush. At DeWine's instigation, the NASA research facility in Cleveland was renamed after John Glenn, as were sundry schools and auditoriums. Robert Taft Sr. was honored with a memorial bell tower in the shadow of the Capitol. Larger-than-life statues of James A. Rhodes adorn the atrium of a state office tower in Columbus and the plaza of another government building in Toledo. But there was no Metzenbaum high school, no Metzenbaum highway, no Metzenbaum bust glowering through horn-rimmed glasses on a pedestal.

Ohio representative Dennis Kucinich, a political soul mate, though not close to Metzenbaum personally, wanted a statue of the senator to replace or join the obscure Republican, William Allen, in the Capitol's Statuary Hall. Against long odds, he made the case at the courthouse ceremony in 1998. "Howard, I'll tell you this—in my time that I hope to spend in Congress—I hope some day when I walk out of that lobby from the House of Representatives, I'll be able to see an additional honor granted you. That you would be placed in Statuary Hall—and I am serious—as one of the great Americans. We have to put this in perspective. Just because we know someone, there is a tendency to think . . . well, he is not all that great. Howard Metzenbaum was a great United States senator."[61] On a more modest scale, an environmental-consumer group, Ohio Citizen Action, named an award after Metzenbaum following his retirement as an "example of principled tenacity."[62] One of the first recipients was Baldemar Velasquez, the folk-singing president of the Toledo-based Farm Labor Organizing Committee, which represented the migrant workers Metzenbaum visited in the heat of his 1988 campaign.

In 2000, six years removed from the Senate, Metzenbaum offered advice to new lawmakers and talked about principle and what made him tick. Maintain your independence and don't worry about the political consequences, he said. Vote your convictions, and you'll keep the support of the people, as long as you show them "your decisions are being made on the basis of what you think is right or wrong, and not being influenced by lobbyists."[63]

Maybe he wasn't pure, but he surely was consistent. Metzenbaum *made* a difference. Joel Johnson went to work for Democratic leader Tom Daschle and later Bill Clinton after his old boss left the scene. Often in tight spots, he heard Democratic senators sigh, "If we only had Metzenbaum for this one."[64] It was in "the nitty-gritty, detail-laden battle[s]" that his absence was most obvious, wrote a *Newsweek* reporter, adding, "No one can really replace Howard Metzenbaum." His friendly rival, Alan Simpson, who called him "the old Cat," said, "We all go around saying it [criticism] doesn't bother us, then we go home at night and practically suck our thumbs," but not Metzenbaum—"he's an unthreatened man."[65]

Few politicians get the recognition *they think* they deserve in their lifetime. Metzenbaum, a polarizing figure, got his courthouse but faded to the fringes of Washington by the turn of the century. One of his last public appearances came at a rededication ceremony for the old federal courthouse in Cleveland 2005, three years before his death.

In Washington, the Republicans running Congress and the White

House during most of his retirement years were too busy deregulating and naming things after Ronald Reagan to consider honoring a man that battled with the iconic fortieth president, and also "41," George Herbert Walker Bush.

At DeWine's instigation, the NASA research facility in Cleveland was renamed after John Glenn, as were sundry schools and auditoriums. Robert Taft Sr. was honored with a memorial bell tower in the shadow of the Capitol. Larger-than-life statues of James A. Rhodes adorn the atrium of a state office tower in Columbus and the plaza of another government building in Toledo. But there was no Metzenbaum high school, no Metzenbaum highway, no Metzenbaum bust glowering through horn-rimmed glasses on a pedestal.

Epilogue

Unlike so much of his public life, the last act for Howard Metzenbaum was subdued and lacking in dramatic punch—or shouted objections from the floor for that matter.

He was ninety, and he had lived well. But his quality of life deteriorated badly during the last months of his life. His death was no surprise to the loved ones who gathered near him the evening of March 12, 2008, in an assisted living condominium on the twenty-second floor of a high-rise in suburban Miami. Yet Metzenbaum wouldn't be remembered that way—frail, unsteady, his appetite gone, his memory almost erased, and his words trailing off.

Susan Hyatt, the most political of his four daughters, had vivid memories of a dynamic six-footer leaping from a stage near the end of a speech and wading into shocked audiences.

"Get off your butts," he would tell them. "If you see something wrong, you've got to do something about it."[1]

When Ted Kennedy learned of Metzenbaum's death, he said of his old ally: "He was the conscience of the Senate, who never shied away from the difficult fights and never apologized for standing up for workers. He was a master of using every rule of the Senate."[2]

That was the man *Plain Dealer* columnist Dick Feagler knew. "Metzenbaum grew up poor and Jewish and listening to the sculpted, hopeful phrases of FDR on the radio. He made himself rich but hung on to his boyhood politics. He was the last of the ferocious New Deal liberals, and the country is closing that book, and he's getting out at a good time.

Feagler wrote those words when Metzenbaum retired from the Senate in 1994, and his appraisal was reprinted after the senator's death. "My politics are not Metzenbaum's," he added, "but I'll tell you this: You knew where he was. You knew what he was going to do. In an age of hacks who trade their convictions for poll results, he would have none of that. And that alone is damn refreshing."[3]

Refreshing but hard-edged too.

"The liberal lion could be a grouch. Howard Metzenbaun was tough by nature, rough and gruff, and his mind was always whirling away, crunching numbers or sorting facts, plotting strategies for his multiple battles," the *Plain Dealer* reported in an assessment of his career.[4] Amy Metzenbaum, his youngest daughter, always wondered about those critiques. That was not the patient, good-natured, loving father she knew.

"I said, 'Amy, I'm sorry but it's true,'" Metzenbaum's longtime personal aide Juanita Powe said. "He was tough. But he had a heart of gold."[5]

About 250 people showed up for Metzenbaum's funeral at the Anshe Chesed Fairmount Temple in Beachwood, Ohio, on the Sunday after his death in Florida. There were few tears and more than a few empty seats. Perhaps they should have held the service at Public Square in downtown Cleveland so the harried consumers, steelworkers, pensioners, environmentalists, minority citizens, and migrant workers who Metzenbaum helped over the years could have paid their respects.

His hometown newspaper covered the funeral, and a lone television crew set up outside the synagogue. "Uh-oh. Only one camera. He wouldn't have liked that," said Joel Johnson, one of his administrative assistants, recalling the boss's penchant for publicity.

In an era of multimedia twenty-four-hour news cycles, the public's attention span is short, said James Wagoner, another one of Metzenbaum's top aides. "We are in warp speed. You leave the public eye for a year and it seems like ten years. He has been off the scene for some time."[6]

In Washington, the U.S. Senate, where Metzenbaum served for sixteen years, noted the senator's death by unanimously passing a resolution honoring him. "Howard Metzenbaum's forte has been his passion," said Senator Robert Byrd of West Virginia, one of several who took to the floor to memorialize their old colleague.[7]

One U.S. senator, Ohio Democrat Sherrod Brown, attended the funeral, along with Ohio lieutenant governor Lee Fisher and congressman Dennis Kucinich. Former senator and onetime vice president Al Gore was there, and two dozen or so former Senate staffers filed into the temple—Johnson, Powe, Wagoner, Harold Stern, Candy Korn, Nancy Coffey, Ellen Bloom, Linda Bouchard, Sherry Sweitzer, Mimi Johnson, Mike Mastrian, and Roger Berliner, among others. Most had been chewed out at one time or another by the senator, and they shared stories about his outbursts on the ride to a snow-covered cemetery in Cleveland Heights. Following the family members, they took turns dropping shovels of dirt on his casket.

At the funeral, Al Gore was thinking about the guy who could tie the Senate up in knots without breaking a sweat. "He would boom the phrase. I can hear him now, saying, 'I object!' And I assure you all men did not speak well of him when he objected. People knew he spoke the truth as he saw it and would not flinch. And they admired that courage even if they disagreed with him."[8]

"An innocent bystander Howard was not," agreed Susan's husband, Joel Hyatt. "He admired doers."[9]

His daughters said one of the things that was amazing about their father "was his ability to be incredibly effective working on 'big picture' policy changes and, at the same time, be touched by the problem of one person. . . . Dad always remembered, whether fighting for a law or helping someone whose sad story he had read about in the paper, that hard work is not always enough."[10]

James Wagoner could attest to Metzenbaum's broad effectiveness and also his ability to focus on the individual. Veterans on the staff "took pride" in the times they were bawled out by the boss, he said, because if he wasn't on your case, it meant you were not doing your job. "He had enormously high standards and expectations," said Wagoner, who, over time, developed a deeply personal "mentor to student, father-son" relationship with the senator. "Working by Howard's side was incredibly formative," Wagoner said. "He really taught me not to bring a handshake to a political campaign when a knife could be more effective. Your ideas and ideals are worth fighting for."[11]

At Metzenbaum's request, a Robert Goulet recording of "The Impossible Dream" was played at the close of the ceremony in the temple.

"At the age of 40 he took singing lessons so he could learn to sing 'To Dream the Impossible Dream,'" his family said. "We always teased him about it because not only did he not improve his singing, he could never remember the words."[12]

Maybe not, but he always had the quest in mind. He was not a dreamer but a doer on a journey to the dragon's lair. He had fought the unbeatable foe.

Notes

Preface

1. Susan Hyatt, telephone interview with author, Mar. 13, 2008.

Introduction: The Early Years

1. Tom Diemer, "Howard's End," *Cleveland Plain Dealer,* Dec. 4, 1994.

2. Joseph D. Rice, "Good Government Is Really Nothing More Than Good Business," *Plain Dealer,* Jan. 17, 1977. The Union Club in downtown Cleveland was an exclusive men's club when Howard Metzenbaum (HM) made his remark. It has since dropped an exclusionary policy against Jews and blacks. The Greater Cleveland Growth Association is a civic organization similar to a chamber of commerce.

3. *Cleveland Press,* Dec. 21, 1973.

4. NRA Political Victory Fund letter, May 1988, in author's possession.

5. Cleveland Press Archives, July 24, 1969, Cleveland State University (CSU). This was Metzenbaum dogma. He often made remarks similar to the quote used here.

6. James Schiller, interview with author, Sept. 28, 1995.

7. Unsigned memo to HM, ca. 1982, Metzenbaum Senate Papers (MSP), Western Reserve Historical Society (WRHS).

8. Milton Wolf, interview with author, Aug. 28, 1995.

9. *Plain Dealer,* Nov. 4, 1976.

10. *Washington Times,* Nov. 9, 1994.

11. *Plain Dealer,* Jan. 17, 1977.

12. Ibid., Oct. 20, 1982.

13. *Wall Street Journal,* June 29, 1988.

14. Thomas J. Brazaitis, "The Final Campaign," *Plain Dealer Sunday Magazine,* Jan. 3, 1988.

15. Ibid.

16. *Wall Street Journal,* June 29, 1988.

17. Jolie Solomon, "Fighting at the Finish," *Newsweek,* Aug. 1, 1994, 43.

18. *Plain Dealer Sunday Magazine,* Sept. 24, 1961.

19. HM, interview with author, Oct. 13, 1994.

20. All of Irwyn Metzenbaum's comments are from an interview with author, Sept. 1995.

21. Ted Bonda's comments in this chapter, unless otherwise noted, are drawn from interviews on Sept. 15, 1995, and Nov. 19, 1997. Bonda died on Oct. 22, 2005, at the age of eighty-eight.

22. Diemer, *Plain Dealer,* Dec. 4, 1994.

23. HM, telephone interview with author, Oct. 13, 1994. In researching HM's time at Ohio State University, the author relied on his own reporting, but also drew heavily from Dick Feagler's July 24, 1969, story in the *Cleveland Press,* "Work Is Metzenbaum's Way of Life," and from Thomas J. Brazaitis's Jan. 31, 1969, article "The Final Campaign," *Plain Dealer Sunday Magazine.*

24. HM, interview with author, Oct. 13, 1994.

25. Similar to Bill Clinton three decades later, Metzenbaum understood the importance of maintaining political viability.

26. Arthur Lelyveld, interview with author, Sept. 6, 1994.

27. *Plain Dealer,* Dec. 4, 1994.

28. HM, telephone interview with author, Mar. 3, 1997.

1. Starting Up in Politics

1. All of Irwyn Metzenbaum's comments are from an interview with author, Sept. 1995.

2. Vanik's comments throughout this chapter are from an interview with author, Aug. 18, 1995.

3. Cleveland Press Archives, Aug. 20, 1932, CSU. (HM was fifteen years old when this was published, and, presumably, the well-read youngster was paying attention.)

4. *Plain Dealer,* Feb. 12, 1935.

5. Ibid.

6. *Columbus Citizen,* Dec. 23, 1935. At that time, legislators did not have separate offices and worked at their desks on the floor of the Senate or House.

7. Cleveland Press Archives, Feb. 5 or 15, 1938 (date is illegible), Cleveland Plain Dealer Library.

8. "Metzenbaum Joins Magic Names," *Cleveland Press,* Jan. 18, 1949.

9. Bob Seltzer, *Cleveland Press,* Oct. 2, 1959.

10. "Love Lives On, Won't Touch Wife's Estate," *Cleveland Press,* Dec. 4, 1935.

11. N. R. Howard, "Brilliant Metzenbaum Lived Melancholy Life," *Plain Dealer,* Jan. 7, 1961.

12. "James Metzenbaum School Board Member," *Cleveland Press,* Aug. 20, 1933.

13. *Plain Dealer,* Jan. 7, 1961.

14. Ibid., Jan. 9, 1959.

15. *Plain Dealer Sunday Magazine,* Jan. 31, 1988.

16. Unless otherwise noted, Metzenbaum's comments about his first contest for public office throughout this section are drawn from an April 8, 1997, interview with author. After covering Senator Metzenbaum for sixteen years for the *Plain Dealer,* the author continued to interview him from time to time during his retirement. The author and Metzenbaum would meet at the University Club and other Washington-area restaurants. Although the retired senator and his family did not authorize this book, he was enthusiastic about it and freely answered questions about his career during these meetings.

17. "H. Metzenbaum Charges Clark Erred on School," *Cleveland Press,* Dec. 6, 1947.

18. Peyton Ford to HM, published in the *Plain Dealer,* Oct. 1, 1970.

19. *Cleveland Press,* Oct. 13, 1970.

20. HM, interview with author, Oct. 12, 1994.

21. *Here in Ohio,* Oct. 1949, newsletter published in Elyria, Ohio, by Joseph E. Neuger.

22. HM, interview with author, Oct. 12, 1994.

23. Cleveland Press Archives, Feb. 4, 1949, CSU.

24. *Cleveland Union Leader,* May 6, 1949.

25. *Here in Ohio,* Oct. 1949.

26. "The Senator's First Lady," *Cleveland Press,* Scripps Howard News Service, May 21, 1980.

27. HM, interview with author, Apr. 8, 1997.

28. HM, interview with author, Apr. 8, 1997.

29. Shelley Metzenbaum, email to author, June 13, 2006.

30. Terry Metzenbaum, interview with author, Sept. 1, 1995.

31. Cleveland Press Archives, Mar. 14, 1950, CSU.

32. Ibid., Aug. 1, 1950.

33. Ted Bonda, interview with author, Sept. 15, 1995. Irwyn Metzenbaum died in a nursing home in Aurora, Ohio, on January 8, 2002, at the age of eighty-nine.

34. HM, telephone interview with author, Mar. 3, 1997.

35. *Plain Dealer,* Sept. 15, 1931.

36. *Cleveland Press,* Aug. 20, 1932.

37. *Cleveland Union Leader,* May 6, 1949.

38. HM, interview with author, Oct. 13, 1994.

39. Alvin Silverman, *Plain Dealer,* Dec. 9, 1948.

40. HM, interview with author, Oct. 13, 1994.

41. *Plain Dealer,* Dec. 9, 1948, Library of Congress.

42. Susan Metzenbaum, email to author, Aug. 23, 2005.

43. *Plain Dealer Sunday Magazine,* Jan. 31, 1988.

44. HM, interview with author, June 5, 1995.

45. *Cleveland Press,* May 21, 1980.

2. *Making Money*

1. HM, interview with author, Apr. 15, 1997.

2. HM, interview with author, Feb. 8, 1998. Metzenbaum told the same story to *Cleveland Press* reporter Dick Feagler in a July 24, 1969, story, "Work Is Metzenbaum Way of Life."

3. Ted Bonda, interview with author, Sept. 15, 1995.

4. *Cleveland Press,* July 24, 1969.

5. HM, interview with author, Apr. 15, 1997.

6. "Pioneer Company in the Field," *New York Times,* Jan. 17, 1965.

7. Ted Bonda, interview with author, Nov. 19, 1997.

8. David Skylar, interview with author, Sept. 21, 1995.

9. Ted Bonda, interview with author, Nov. 19, 1997.

10. HM, interview with author, May 14, 1998.

11. Wilson Hirschfeld, "Metzenbaum's Other Side," *Plain Dealer,* Oct. 19, 1970.

12. HM, interview with author, May 14, 1998.

13. Wilson Hirschfeld, "Metzenbaum and Unionism," *Plain Dealer,* Nov. 10, 1969.

14. Ted Bonda, interview with author, Sept. 15, 1995.

15. *Plain Dealer,* Oct. 10, 1965.

16. *New York Times,* Jan. 17, 1965.

17. Harold Stern, interview with author, Aug. 29, 1995.

18. Byron Krantz, interview with author, Nov. 18, 1997.

19. Harold Stern, interview with author, Aug. 29, 1995.

20. Joe Rice, interview with author, Aug. 29, 1995.

21. HM, interview with author, June 5, 1995.

22. Harold Stern, interview with author, Aug. 29, 1995.

23. Harold Stern, "My Political Journey" (unpublished manuscript, 2002), 1.

24. HM, interview with author, Apr. 15, 1997.

25. Harold Stern, interview with author, Aug. 29, 1995.

26. Susan Metzenbaum, interview with author, Sept. 28, 1995.

27. Julian Krawcheck, "Metzenbaum Assails Lodges' Negro Ban," *Cleveland Press,* Nov. 17, 1967.

28. Byron Krantz, interview with author, Nov. 18, 1997.

29. Candy Korn, interview with author, Sept. 30, 1995.

30. Years later Metzenbaum would work on gun control legislation in Washington with Michael Feighan's nephew, Congressman Edward Feighan, but the two were not close.

31. Ray Dorsey, "Miller's Gag Rule Draws Blast from Metzenbaum," *Plain Dealer,* Apr. 15, 1960.

32. "Ward Club Bars Burke, Metzenbaum," ibid., Apr. 27, 1960.

33. Moses Krislov, interview with author, Sept. 29, 1995.

34. Thomas J. Brazaitis, unpublished interview with Metzenbaum, ca. Dec. 1987. Used with permission.

35. Susan Metzenbaum, interview with author, Sept. 28, 1995.

3. The Activist

1. *Cleveland Press,* June 21, 1949.

2. Ibid., Sept. 30, 1949.

3. Rand's comments, unless otherwise noted, are from an interview with author, Aug. 30, 1995.

4. Western Reserve University merged in 1967 with Case Technical Institute and was renamed Case Western Reserve University.

5. *Cleveland Press,* July 10, 1952.

6. David Skylar, interview with author, Sept. 21, 1995.

7. "Metzenbaum Firm Buys Berea Paper, 8 Others," *Cleveland Press,* July 17, 1969.

8. David Skylar, interview with author, Sept. 21, 1995.

9. HM, interview with author, June 5, 1995.

10. *Cleveland Press,* July 11, 1962.

11. *Plain Dealer,* Aug. 26, 1957.

12. Moses Krislov, interview with author, Sept. 29, 1995.

13. Byron Krantz, interview with author, Nov. 18, 1997.

14. Byron Krantz, interview with author, Nov. 18, 1997.

15. George Condon Jr., interview with author, Jan. 20, 1977.

16. HM, interview with author, May 14, 1998.

17. William F. Miller, "Guild Seeks ComCorp Recognition," *Plain Dealer,* May 25, 1971.

18. "Metzenbaum Target of New Guild Drive," *Cleveland Press,* May 27, 1971.

19. David Skylar interview, Sept. 21, 1995.

20. David Skylar interview, Sept. 21, 1995.

21. Ted Bonda, interview with author, Aug. 30, 1995.

22. HM, interview with author, Feb. 8, 1998.

23. John E. Bryan, "Metzenbaum Is Rejected for Society Board Seat," *Plain Dealer,* Apr. 11, 1968.

24. Ibid.

25. HM, interview with author, Feb. 8, 1998.

26. "Metzenbaum on Society Board," *Cleveland Press,* Apr. 12, 1968.

27. Moses Krislov, interview with author, Sept. 29, 1995.

28. Video of Metzenbaum's seventy-fifth birthday tribute, June 1, 1992, courtesy of Candy Korn. Metzenbaum's birthday is June 4.

29. Harold Stern, interview with author, Aug. 29, 1995.

30. "End of Private Golf Demanded at Manakiki, Sleepy Hollow," *Cleveland Press,* Dec. 1, 1955.

31. HM, interview with author, Feb. 8, 1998.

32. Susan Metzenbaum, interview with author, Sept. 28, 1995.

33. HM, interview with author, Mar. 1, 1998.

34. Jack Torry, *Endless Summers: The Fall and Rise of the Cleveland Indians* (South Bend, Ind.: Diamond Communications, 1995), 137.

35. *Cleveland Press,* Feb. 28, 1959.

36. HM, interview with author, Sept. 18, 1995.

37. That DiSalle was chosen came as no surprise to Metzenbaum, since a governor from the same party customarily heads the presidential campaign in his state. However, DiSalle's support for John Kennedy did not come easily. As Robert Dallek writes in *An Unfinished Life: John F. Kennedy, 1917–1963* (New York: Little, Brown, 2003), Ohio required especially tough negotiations with Gov. Mike DiSalle, who wanted to run as a favorite son and then barter his state's delegates at the convention. But the Kennedys—threatening to back Cleveland Democratic leader Ray Miller, DiSalle's chief rival, as the head of the Ohio delegation—forced DiSalle into a public endorsement of Kennedy in January. At a meeting between Kennedy and DiSalle in an airport motel in Pittsburgh, DiSalle says that Kennedy told him, "You're either going to come out for me, or we are going to run a delegation against you in Ohio, and we'll beat you." When Kennedy's threat did not settle matters, Bobby Kennedy, accompanied by party chairman John Bailey, went to Ohio to force the issue. Bailey, a veteran politician who does not shock easily, told Ken O'Donnell later that "he was startled by the going-over Bobby had given DiSalle" (247).

38. Dick Feagler, "The Sun Goes Down on a Dream," *Cleveland Press,* June 8, 1968.

39. Harold Stern, interview with author, Apr. 26, 2005.

40. "H. Metzenbaum Quits ITT Post for Civic Work," *Cleveland Press,* Sept. 18, 1968.

41. Dick Feagler, "A Politician's Politician: Metzenbaum Has Knack for Making This Work," ibid., July 25, 1969.

4. Glenn Wars I

1. *Ohio State Alumni Magazine,* Oct. 2004. Bricker died in 1986 at ninety-two.

2. Alexander P. Lamis and Mary Anne Sharkey, eds., *Ohio Politics* (Kent, Ohio: Kent State Univ. Press, 1994), 202.

3. Harold P. Stern, "My Political Journey" (unpublished manuscript, 2002), 1. Bricker ran for vice president in 1944 with Thomas Dewey. The Republican ticket lost to Franklin D. Roosevelt but narrowly carried Ohio.

4. HM, interview with author, June 5, 1995.

5. Harold Stern, telephone interview with author, Sept. 13, 2005.

6. Richard O. Davies, *Defender of the Old Guard: John Bricker and American Politics* (Columbus: Ohio State Univ. Press, 1993).

7. Harold Stern, interview with author, Sept. 13, 2005.

8. HM, interview with author, May 30, 1995.

9. Byron Krantz, interview with author, Nov. 18, 1997.

10. Scott Montgomery and Timothy R. Gaffney, *Back in Orbit: John Glenn's Return to Space* (Atlanta, Ga.: Longstreet Press, 1998), 89, 90.

11. Frank Van Riper, *Glenn: The Astronaut Who Would Be President* (New York: Empire Books, 1983), 179.

12. Ibid., 184.

13. Ibid., 183.

14. Walter Anderson, "Celebrity Profiles in Courage," *Family Circle,* Oct. 21, 1986, 126, 128.

15. Ibid., 126.

16. Richard L. Maher, "Metzenbaum Raps Veil Around Glenn," *Cleveland Press,* Mar. 5, 1964.

17. Van Riper, *Glenn,* 196.

18. Ibid., 198.

19. Chuck Baker, letter to HM, Aug. 20, 1964, MSP, WRHS.

20. Chuck Baker, letter to HM, Aug. 22, 1964, MSP, WRHS.

21. Harold Stern, interview with author, Apr. 26, 2005.

22. Chuck Baker, letter to HM, Aug. 17, 1964, MSP, WRHS.

23. Byron Krantz, interview with author, Nov. 18, 1997.

24. Harold Stern, interview with author, Aug. 25, 1995.

25. Harold Stern, interview with author, Aug. 25, 1995.

26. Byron Krantz, interview with author, Nov. 11, 1997.

27. Barbara Metzenbaum, interview with author, Oct. 4, 2005.

28. Susan Metzenbaum, interview with author, Sept. 14, 2005.

29. Barbara Metzenbaum, interview with author, Oct. 4, 2005.

30. James N. Naughton, "Ohio: A Lesson in Changing Politics," *New York Times*, May 10, 1968.

31. William B. Saxbe with Peter D. Franklin, *I've Seen the Elephant: An Autobiography* (Kent, Ohio: Kent State Univ. Press, 2000), 78, 79.

32. "Metzenbaum Pledges Senate Raise Support," *Cleveland Press*, Sept. 17, 1969.

33. Feagler, *Cleveland Press*, July 25, 1969.

34. Harold Stern, interview with author, Aug. 29, 1995. Glenn, in a telephone conversation on Jan. 10, 2006, said, "I really don't have any recollection of that meeting, but that isn't to say it didn't happen."

35. Harold Stern, interview with author, Aug. 29, 1995.

36. Bob Dykes, interview with author, Sept. 28, 1995.

37. Van Riper, *Glenn*, 230. The accounts of the 1970 and 1974 primary contests between Glenn and Metzenbaum are drawn from Van Riper's book, author's files and notes, and Richard F. Fenno, "The Presidential Odyssey of John Glenn," *Congressional Quarterly*, 1970.

38. "Upset Time," *Time*, May 18, 1970.

39. "Metzenbaum, Glenn Disagree on Viet Massacre Blame," *Cleveland Press*, Dec. 4, 1969. Cleveland Press Archives, CSU.

40. Richard L. Maher, "Metzenbaum Spurt Credited to Young," *Cleveland Press*, Apr. 30, 1970.

41. Montgomery and Gaffney, *Back in Orbit*, 93.

42. Ibid.

43. Joseph Dirck in conversation with the author, Nov. 1, 1982.

44. Van Riper, *Glenn*, 225, 226.

45. John Glenn with Nick Taylor, *John Glenn: A Memoir* (New York: Bantam Books, 1999), 324.

46. Joe Rice, interview with author, Aug. 29, 1995.

47. Fenno, "Presidential Odyssey," 14.

48. *Cleveland Press*, May 2, 1970. CSU Archives.

49. Glenn, *Memoir*, 325.

50. Thomas J. Brazaitis, unpublished interview with Metzenbaum, Dec. 17, 1987. Used with permission.

51. HM, interview with author, May 30, 1995.

52. *Plain Dealer*, Jan. 11, 1998.

53. Roy Meyers, interview with author, June 16, 1997.

54. Bob Dykes, interview with author, Sept. 28, 1995.

55. Van Riper, *Glenn*, 239; author's notes.

56. H. R. Haldeman, *The Haldeman Diaries: Inside the Nixon White House* (New York: G. P. Putman's Sons, 1994), 175, 176.

57. Richard L. Maher, *Cleveland Press*, Oct. 30, 1970.

58. Ibid.

59. Richard L. Maher, "Poll Shows Taft Cuts into Dem Margin Here," *Cleveland Press*, Oct. 20, 1970.

60. HM, interview with Thomas J. Brazaitis, Dec. 17, 1987.

61. "Metzenbaum's Aim Akin to JFK's, Shriver Says," *Plain Dealer*, Oct. 29, 1970.

62. Ibid.

63. HM, interview with author, Oct. 13, 1994.

64. Shelley Metzenbaum, email to author, Oct. 13, 1994.

65. Susan Metzenbaum, email to author, Aug. 23, 2005.

66. Amy Metzenbaum, email to author, Aug. 5, 2005.

67. *Plain Dealer*, Oct. 29, 1970.

68. Harold Stern, interview with author, Aug. 29, 1995.

69. *Cleveland Press*, Oct. 30, 1970.

70. *Plain Dealer*, Dec. 25, 1977.

71. Ibid., May 1, 1972.

72. *Plain Dealer* Readers' Forum, May 6, 1972.

73. Ibid.

5. Glenn Wars II

1. John Gilligan, interview with author, Apr. 1, 2006.

2. James Schiller, interview with author, Sept. 28, 1995.

3. James Friedman, interview with author, Sept. 21, 1995.

4. Van Riper, *Glenn*, 236.

5. Walter Anderson, *Courage Is a Three-Letter Word: Celebrity Profiles in Courage* (New York: Random House, 1986), excerpted in *Family Circle*, Oct. 21, 1986.

6. Van Riper, *Glenn*, 24.

7. Richard F. Fenno Jr., *Senators on the Campaign Trail: The Politics of Representation* (Norman: Univ. of Oklahoma Press, 1996), 26.

8. Joe Rice, interview with author, Aug. 29, 1995.

9. Van Riper, *Glenn*, 249.

10. *Cleveland Press*, Apr. 17, 1974.

11. Montgomery and Gaffney, *Back in Orbit*, 95.

12. Bud Karmin, interview with author, June 19, 1995.

13. Bud Karmin, interview with author, June 19, 1995.

14. HM, interview with author, Sept. 24, 1999.

15. *Cleveland Press*, Apr. 26, 1974.

16. *Plain Dealer*, Feb. 9, 1974.

17. Glenn, *Memoir*, 329.

18. *New York Times*, Apr. 21, 1974.

19. James Schiller, interview with author, Sept. 28, 1995.

20. Charles R. Babcock, "Fame as an Astronaut Launched Glenn to Wealth," *Washington Post,* Jan. 30, 1984.

21. *Plain Dealer,* Apr. 18, 1974.

22. *Cleveland Press,* May 1, 1974, Library of Congress.

23. Ted Joy, "Howard Metzenbaum's Place in the Sun," *Cleveland Magazine,* July 1974, 74–76.

24. Ibid., 75.

25. *Plain Dealer,* Mar. 28, 1974.

26. Ibid., Mar. 26, 1974.

27. Tom Diemer, "Jackie Onassis Spoke Up for Glenn," *Plain Dealer,* May 28, 1994. Former Glenn press secretary Steve Avakion directed the author to this source.

28. *Cleveland Press,* May 3, 1974, Library of Congress. The *Cleveland Press* analysis regarding Glenn's "political philosophy" is from May 1, 1974.

29. Coyne, called the "Irish Godfather," survived the bad advice he gave Metzenbaum and served another twenty-five years as mayor of Brooklyn, a 4.3-square-mile suburb of 11,000. He commanded city hall for fifty-two years and was the longest-serving mayor in the United States before losing in 1999 to neophyte Kenneth E. Patton. He was also Cuyahoga County Democratic chairman for twelve years.

30. *John Glenn: A Memoir,* 330.

31. John Glenn, interview with author, Jan. 10, 2006.

32. Van Riper, *Glenn,* 265, 266.

33. Ibid., 226; author's notes.

34. John Glenn, interview with author, Jan. 10, 2006.

35. HM, interview with author, May 30, 1995.

36. HM, interview with author, Sept. 24, 1999.

37. Abe Zaidan, "Glenn May Be Headed for a Job," *Akron Beacon Journal,* May 12, 1974.

38. *Plain Dealer,* May 6, 1974.

39. John Glenn, interview with author, Jan. 10, 2006.

40. Robert Crater, "Metzenbaum Is Active Despite Primary Loss," *Cleveland Press,* July 18, 1974. Metzenbaum resigned two days before Christmas, giving Glenn barely a week's worth of seniority before the next session of Congress opened.

41. *Cleveland Press,* May 16, 1974.

42. *Congressional Record* (Apr. 10, 1974): 10,422–26.

43. Crater, *Cleveland Press,* July 18, 1974.

44. James Schiller, interview with author, Sept. 28, 1995.

45. HM, letter to James Schiller, May 14, 1974, courtesy of James Schiller.

46. HM, interview with author, July 1999.

47. "SENATOR Metzenbaum," *Cleveland Press,* Apr. 23, 1975.

6. The Senate Years I

1. HM, interview with author, Sept. 24, 1999.

2. Harold Stern, "My Political Journey" (unpublished manuscript, 2002), 14.

3. Jim Friedman, interview with author, Sept. 21, 1995.

4. Bob Dykes, interview with author, Sept. 28, 1995.

5. Stephen L. Kadish to Senator Floyd Haskell, May 1, 1975, MSP, WRHS.

6. Cleveland Press Archives, Apr. 14, 1975, CSU. The newspaper's observation that the loss to Glenn could mean the end of Metzenbaum's political career is from May 8, 1974, and is on microfilm at the Library of Congress.

7. *Dayton Journal-Herald,* Oct. 27, 1976.

8. Jim Friedman, interview with author, Sept. 21, 1995.

9. *Plain Dealer,* Jan. 8, 1994.

10. Carl B. Stokes, *Promises of Power: A Political Autobiography* (New York: Simon and Schuster, 1973).

11. Joseph D. Rice, "Metzenbaum, Stanton Run into Apathy in Senate Race," *Plain Dealer,* May 3, 1976.

12. Ibid.

13. George E. Condon Jr., "Veil of Embarrassment Falls on Candidate," *Plain Dealer,* May 30, 1976.

14. Thomas Chema, interview with author, Sept. 20, 1995.

15. George P. Rasanen, "No Regrets Over Gamble, Stanton Says," *Plain Dealer,* Oct. 1, 1976.

16. James Stanton, conversation with author, ca. 1994.

17. HM, interview with author, May 14, 1998.

18. Thomas Chema, interview with author, Sept. 20, 1995.

19. Thomas Chema, interview with author, Sept. 20, 1995.

20. James Schiller, interview with author, Sept. 28, 1995.

21. Bob Dykes, interview with author, Sept. 28, 1995.

22. *Plain Dealer,* June 9, 1976.

23. *Toledo Blade,* Oct. 24, 1976, Library of Congress.

24. Bob Dykes, interview with author, Sept. 28, 1995.

25. HM, interview with author, May 27, 1998.

26. HM speech to Cleveland Club of Washington, Apr. 16, 1997.

27. Joel Hyatt, interview with author, Aug. 31, 1995.

28. Condon, *Plain Dealer,* May 30, 1976; Condon, interview with author, May 30, 1976.

29. Bill Carlson, telephone interview with author, July 21, 2005.

30. Barry Direnfeld, interview with author, Oct. 12, 1994.

31. Thomas Chema, interview with author, Sept. 20, 1995.

32. Alexander P. Lamis and Mary Anne Sharkey, eds., *Ohio Politics* (Kent, Ohio: Kent State Univ. Press, 1994), 211.

33. Tom Diemer and Bill Sloat, "Robert Taft Jr. Dead, Served in U.S. Senate," *Plain Dealer*, Dec. 8, 1993.

34. George P. Rasanen, "Metzenbaum Takes Calls from Public in Person Daily," *Plain Dealer*, Feb. 14, 1977.

35. "Metzenbaum Announcement Draws Criticism by Glenn," *Plain Dealer*, Apr. 1, 1977.

36. "Politics in America," *Congressional Quarterly*, 1984.

37. HM, interview with author, June 16, 2003.

38. Sarah Binder, email correspondence with author, Jan. 25, 2005. Binder said post-cloture filibusters became an issue only after a 1975 change in Rule 22, lowering the threshold for cutting off debate from a two-thirds vote of the Senate to a three-fifths majority. Binder and Steven S. Smith authored *Politics or Principle? Filibustering in the United States Senate* (Washington, D.C.: Brookings Institution, 1996).

39. *New York Times*, Sept. 29, 1977.

40. Thurmond, who served in the Senate past his one hundredth birthday, held the record for length of filibuster, according to the *Washington Post*, April 26, 2001.

41. HM diary, Oct. 11, 1977, on loan to author.

42. HM diary, Oct. 11, 1977.

43. HM diary, Oct. 11, 1977.

44. "Filibuster Collapses, Gas Price Vote Today," *Plain Dealer*, Oct 4, 1977.

45. Mary McGrory, *Washington Star*, Oct. 11, 1977.

46. "Metzenbaum Filibusters All Night," UPI, *Cleveland Press*, Sept. 28, 1977.

47. Robert H. Snyder, "No Longer Ohio's Other Senator," *Plain Dealer*, Oct. 2, 1977.

48. Ibid.

49. *Cleveland Press*, Oct, 7, 1977.

50. Ibid.

51. "Politics in America," *Congressional Quarterly*, 1984, 1,164.

52. Ibid., 1,164–84.

53. James Abourezk, *Advise and Dissent: Memoirs of South Dakota and the United States Senate* (Chicago, Ill.: Lawrence Hill Books, 1989).

54. *Congressional Record* (May 17, 2000).

55. Barry Direnfeld, interview with author, Oct. 12, 1994.

56. HM, memo to senior staff, ca. 1982, MSP, WRHS.

57. Barry Direnfeld, interview with author, Oct. 12, 1994.

58. *Plain Dealer*, July 30, 1978.

59. HM diary, Apr. 25, 1977.

60. HM to George M. White, Mar. 14, 1980, in MSP, WRHS.

61. HM diary, Apr. 30, 1977.

62. HM diary, May 16, 1977.

63. Joel Johnson, interview with author, Nov. 24, 2004.

64. HM diary, Apr. 30, 1977.

65. HM diary., Oct. 11, 1977.

66. Thomas J. Brazaitis and Judy Grande, unpublished interview with John Glenn for the *Plain Dealer,* Aug. 8, 1981.

67. HM diary, Apr. 30, 1977.

68. HM diary, Apr. 26, 1977.

69. Brazaitis and Grande, Aug. 8, 1981.

70. HM diary, Feb. 20, 1979.

71. Unpublished interview with the *Plain Dealer,* ca. Sept. 1981.

72. Thomas J. Brazaitis and Judy Grande, "No Love Lost or Found Between Ohio's senators," *Plain Dealer,* Sept. 29, 1981.

73. Ibid.

74. Ibid.

75. Unpublished interview with Glenn advisor, Brazaitis, and Grande.

76. HM diary, Feb. 20, 1979. Metzenbaum considered it "an accepted fact" that Kennedy would beat Carter in the Democratic primary, but, in fact, Kennedy lost to Carter in 1980.

77. Byron Krantz, interview with author, Nov. 18, 1997.

78. Joel Johnson, interview with author, Nov. 24, 2004.

79. HM diary, May 24, 1977.

80. HM diary, Feb. 20, 1979.

81. Thomas J. Brazaitis, "Metzenbaum Halts Big Project, Then Retreats," *Plain Dealer,* July 22, 1979.

82. HM diary, Mar. 15, 1979.

83. HM diary, June 16, 1980.

84. HM diary, June 16, 1979.

85. HM, interview with author, Aug. 8, 1998.

86. Roy Meyers, interview with author, June 16, 1997.

87. Tom Diemer, "Metzenbaum for Haig, Bigger Military," *Plain Dealer,* Jan. 17, 1980.

88. *Plain Dealer,* Jan. 17, 1981.

89. HM, remarks to Cleveland Club of Washington, Apr. 16, 1997.

90. HM, memo to advisors, Nov. 19, 1981, MSP, WRHS.

91. Unsigned staff memo, ca. 1981, MSP, WRHS.

92. *Plain Dealer,* Jan. 7, 1979.

93. Stern, "My Political Journey" (unpublished manuscript, 2002).

94. HM, letter to Robert Byrd, Dec. 2, 1980, MSP, WRHS.

95. "Politics in America," *Congressional Quarterly,* 1984, 1,164.

96. Video of Metzenbaum's seventy-fifth birthday tribute, June 1, 1992,

courtesy of Candy Korn. Humorist Will Rogers was known for saying, "I never met a man I didn't like."

97. Judy Burke, "Metzenbaum, Oil Firm Executive Trade Barbs," *Plain Dealer,* June 19, 1980.

98. "Politics in America," *Congressional Quarterly,* 1984, 1,165.

99. Senator Richard Durbin, remarks made at the June 19, 2002, Consumer Federation of America annual dinner. In succeeding years, Durbin followed Metzenbaum's advice, often getting under the skin of Senate Republicans with his flip remarks.

100. Joel Johnson, interview with author, Nov. 11, 2004.

101. Edward S. Greenberg and Benjamin I. Page, *The Struggle for Democracy* (New York: Harper Collins College Publishers, 1993), 395.

102. "Politics in America," *Congressional Quarterly,* 1984.

103. *Plain Dealer,* Sept. 30, 1982.

104. *Washington Post,* Dec. 20, 2005.

105. Barry Direnfeld, interview with author, Oct. 12, 1994.

106. Anonymous source, ca. Mar. 1995.

107. Marcy Kaptur, remarks made at the June 19, 2002, Consumer Federation of America annual dinner.

108. Harris memo, Dec. 19, 1979, MSP, WRHS.

109. Amos Kermisch, "Glance at Voting Record Surprises," *Plain Dealer,* Jan. 16, 1983.

110. Metzenbaum memo to political advisors, Nov. 9, 1981, MSP, WRHS.

7. The Senate Years II

1. *Congressional Quarterly,* 1983.

2. "Ohio Senate Battle Looms for 1982," 79.

3. Author's notes. Bob Hughes often used this phrase in conversation with reporters.

4. "Ohio Senate Battle Looms for 1982," 79.

5. Petroleum Club–Midland invitation, Apr. 13, 1982, MSP, WRHS.

6. Joseph D. Rice, "Metzenbaum Rides High for '82," *Plain Dealer,* Feb. 25, 1981.

7. Unsigned memo, ca. 1981, MSP, WRHS.

8. Rick Sloan's memos of July 5, 1981, and Dec. 12, 1981, are both included in MSP, WRHS.

9. Dick Woodruff, interview with author, June 4, 1997.

10. Barry Direnfeld, interview with author, June 4, 1977. Both Direnfeld and Woodruff (above) were interviewed at a Capitol Hill event honoring Metzenbaum's eighty-second birthday.

11. A statement drafted for the 1982 race, ca. 1981, MSP, WRHS.

12. Undated draft brochure, MSP, WRHS.

13. Rhodes often used the phrase, "Congress giveth, Congress taketh away." Earl Barnes told the "Burning Tree" story to reporters in 1981.

14. *On Principle,* anniversary edition of the newsletter of the Ashbrook Center for Public Affairs, 1999. Unless otherwise noted, the Ashbrook material presented in this chapter is from Ashbrook Center sources at Ashland University, Ashland, Ohio.

15. Jack Kemp, introduction to *No Left Turns: A Handbook for Conservatives Based on the Writings of John M. Ashbrook* (Fairfield, Ohio: Hamilton Hobby Press, 1986).

16. Lee Edwards, "The Conscience of the Movement," *On Principle* (Feb. 1999): 6.

17. William G. Batchelder, "John M. Ashbrook: A Personal Reminiscence," *On Principle* (Feb. 1999).

18. July 1, 1982, MSP, WRHS.

19. Apr. 14, 1982, MSP, WRHS.

20. Ibid. Ted Bonda died on Oct. 22, 2005, at the age of eighty-eight. "He lacked the money to attend college yet served as president of the Cleveland school board and Ohio Board of Regents. He used his own money to keep Major League Baseball in Cleveland. . . . He began his career as a clerk in a shoe store and a parking lot attendant," the *Plain Dealer* said in an obituary.

21. Milton Wolf, interview with author, Aug. 29, 1995.

22. Ashbrook's congressional papers, his ideas, and a reconstruction of his Capitol Hill office are preserved at the Ashbrook Center at Ashland University. He was an inspiration to a cadre of young Ohio conservatives, including Batchelder, who became a common pleas judge, and the late Tom Van Meter, a state legislator from Ashland.

23. HM, interview with author, Aug. 1, 1998.

24. HM, interview with author, Aug. 1, 1998.

25. Undated document, ca. 1982, MSP, WRHS.

26. "Metzenbaum Crime Votes Criminalized," *Columbus Dispatch,* July 21, 1982.

27. Brent Larkin, "Metzenbaum Vindicated by Victory," *Plain Dealer,* Nov. 3, 1982.

28. John Green, interview with author, July 11, 1994.

29. Joel Hyatt, interview with author, Aug. 31, 1995.

30. Rhodes lost the governor's race in 1986. He died March 4, 2001, at the age of ninety-one, having outlived most of his political contemporaries. Although he reportedly never apologized publicly for the Kent State shootings, he once told the author, "It was the most sorrowful day of my life."

31. HM diary, Dec. 24, 1982.

32. Ward Sinclair, "Thank God for Metzenbaum!" *Washington Post,* Dec. 12, 1982.

33. HM diary, Dec. 24, 1982.

34. Shirley Metzenbaum, interview with *Plain Dealer* reporter Thomas J. Brazaitis, ca. winter 1987.

35. "Politics in America," *Congressional Quarterly,* 1984, 1,164.

36. Ibid.

37. John Green, interview with author, July 11, 1994.

38. "Senate Must Act to Save Itself," *Washington Post,* reprinted in *Plain Dealer,* Feb. 19, 1983.

39. Joel Johnson, telephone interview with author, Aug. 1, 1995.

40. Juanita Powe, interview with author, July 16, 2006.

41. Nancy Coffey, interview with author, Oct. 20, 2004.

42. Martin Tolchin, "The Metzenbaum Art Gallery," *New York Times,* Mar. 29, 1985.

43. Thomas J. Brazaitis, unpublished interview with Shirley Metzenbaum, Dec. 18, 1987.

44. Thomas J. Brazaitis, unpublished interview with HM, Dec. 17, 1987. Used with permission of *Plain Dealer.*

45. *Plain Dealer Sunday Magazine,* Jan. 31, 1988.

46. Nadine Corodas, *Congressional Quarterly,* July 18, 1987.

47. Steven S. Smith, *Call to Order: Floor Politics in the House and Senate* (Washington, D.C.: Brookings Institution, 1989), 113.

48. Attached to memo from Metzenbaum to Harris, May 20, 1985, MSP, WRHS.

49. Paul Simon, news release offered as a column, Nov. 24–30, 1985.

50. June 28, 1983, MSP, WRHS.

51. HM, interview with author, Apr. 15, 1997.

52. Joel Johnson, interview with author, Nov. 24, 2004.

53. HM, interview with author, Oct. 13, 1994.

54. Jeffrey Friedman, telephone interview with author, Sept. 27, 1995.

55. Jeffrey Friedman, telephone interview with author, Sept. 27, 1995. For more information, see Amos Kermisch, "Metzenbaum Gets $250,000 Finder Fee," *Plain Dealer,* May 16, 1984.

56. Juanita Powe, interview with author, July 16, 2004.

57. *Plain Dealer Sunday Magazine,* Jan. 31, 1988.

58. Jeffrey Friedman, interview with author, Sept. 27, 1995.

59. HM, interview with author, Sept. 7, 1995.

60. Author's notes from courthouse renaming ceremony, May 27, 1998.

61. HM press release, author's files, Aug. 29, 1986.

62. Don Sweitzer, telephone interview with author, Oct. 2, 1994.

63. HM press release, June 13, 1986.

64. Marcus Gleisser, "Ohio Senators Disappointing, Grace Contends," *Plain Dealer,* Jan. 10, 1986. Reagan cut back on legal aid and also implemented other commission recommendations, with mixed success. Grace died in 1995 but left behind an influential watchdog group, Citizens Against Government Waste, an organization he cofounded.

65. Mary McGrory, "Reynolds' Rights Portfolio," *Washington Post,* June 6, 1985.

66. *Washington Post.,* May 13, 1986.

67. Pension-system newsletter of Asset International Inc., 1998.

68. "Water Project in Arizona Spurs Metzenbaum Inquiry," *Dayton Daily News,* July 7, 1985.

69. Smith, *Call to Order,* 154.

70. Diemer, "Metzenbaum Says Khadafy Ought to Be Eliminated," *Plain Dealer,* Jan. 9, 1986.

71. Thomas J. Brazaitis, unpublished interview with Shirley Metzenbaum, Dec. 18, 1987.

72. *Washington Times,* June 7, 1984.

73. HM press release, Aug. 4, 1987, in author's possession.

74. Diemer, "Together at Last Glenn, Metzenbaum Bury the Hatchet," *Plain Dealer,* Aug. 25, 1985.

75. Jacqueline Calmes and Ron Gurwitt, "Power in the 100th Congress," *Congressional Quarterly,* Jan. 7, 1987, 6.

76. HM news release, Nov. 21, 1986, in author's possession.

77. Joel Johnson, interview with author, Nov. 24, 2004.

78. Peter Harris, interview with author, Aug. 2, 2004.

79. Joel Johnson, interview with author, Nov. 24, 2004.

80. "1988 Senate Ratings," *Cook Political Report,* Aug. 25, 1988.

81. Peter Harris, interview with author, Aug. 2, 2004.

82. John Green, interview with author, July 11, 1994.

83. Juanita Powe, interview with author, July 16, 2004.

84. "Legislative Accomplishments," Metzenbaum press release, Oct. 24, 1988.

85. *Congressional Quarterly,* July 18, 1987.

86. Newsletter of Asset International Inc., 1998.

87. Peter Harris, interview with author, Aug. 2, 2004.

88. HM news release, May 18, 1988.

89. Diemer, *Plain Dealer,* Dec. 4, 1994.

90. Republican National Senatorial Campaign document, July 23, 1987, MSP, WRHS.

91. Steve Luttner and Brent Larkin, "GOP Plan Targets Metzenbaum's Communist Friend," *Plain Dealer,* July 29, 1987.

92. John Glenn press release, July 29, 1987.

93. HM campaign document, July 29, 1987, WRHS.

94. Eric Breihdel, "Metzenbaum Storm: But It's All True," *New York Post,* Aug. 1, 1987.

95. Milt Wolf, interview with author, Aug. 28, 1995. Wolf died May 19, 2005, at the age of eighty. He was the son of a police detective who worked under Eliot Ness when the famed gang-buster was Cleveland safety director. In his multifaceted life, Wolf was a builder, diplomat, philanthropist, humanitarian, political fund-raiser, and U.S. Army meteorologist during World War II. His favorite politician was John Glenn.

8. The Final Campaign

1. Samuel C. Patterson and Thomas W. Kephart, "The Case of the Wayfaring Challenger," *Congress and the Presidency,* 8, no. 2 (Autumn 1991): 107.

2. Tom Diemer, "Voinovich Recalls His Democratic Roots," *Plain Dealer,* Sept. 17, 1998.

3. Ibid., June 22, 1980.

4. Peter Harris, interview with author, Sept. 13, 2004.

5. Brazaitis, *Plain Dealer Sunday Magazine,* Jan. 31, 1988.

6. John E. Yang, "Metzenbaum Amasses Power in the Senate by Blocking Action," *Wall Street Journal,* June 29, 1988.

7. Ibid.

8. Video of HM's seventy-fifth birthday tribute, June 1, 1992, courtesy of Candy Korn.

9. *Plain Dealer,* Sept. 21, 1986.

10. Tom Diemer, "Metzenbaum, Voinovich Race Is Second Costliest," *Plain Dealer,* Aug. 11, 1988.

11. Keith C. Epstein, "Outsiders Fund Battle for U.S. Senate Seat," *Plain Dealer,* July 23, 1988.

12. *Plain Dealer,* Apr. 14, 1988.

13. Ibid., Apr. 15, 1988.

14. George Voinovich, interview with author, Oct. 11, 1994.

15. Joe Frolik, "With Big Lead in Polls, Voinovich Has Little Interest in Debates," *Plain Dealer,* Oct. 10, 1998.

16. Video of HM's seventy-fifth birthday tribute, June 1, 1992, courtesy of Candy Korn.

17. Peter Harris, interview with author, Aug. 2, 2004.

18. *Beacon Journal,* Apr. 7, 1991.

19. Howard Wilkinson, "Senate Race Loses Out to Space," *Cincinnati Enquirer,* Jan. 18, 1998.

20. Jonathan Riskind, "Mailing Rehashes Communist Charges Against Metzenbaum," *Lake County News-Herald,* Aug. 22, 1988.

21. Original documents, ca. summer 1988.

22. Joe Wagner, interview with author, Feb. 23, 2000.

23. Judy Grande, "Mayor Not Among Co-sponsors of Ohio Porn Bill," *Plain Dealer,* Sept. 9, 1988.

24. Steve Luttner, "Voinovich Amplifies Kid Porn Allegation," *Plain Dealer,* Sept. 8, 1998.

25. Peter Harris, interview with author, Aug. 2, 2004.

26. Dick Feagler, "TV Campaign Consultants Are Political War Criminals," SouthCoastToday.com, Oct. 14, 1997, http://archive.southcoasttoday.com/daily/10–97/10–14–97/b040p065.htm (accessed Oct. 2, 2007).

27. George Voinovich, interview with author, Nov. 15, 2004.

28. Dale Butland, interview with author, Aug. 1998.

29. NRA Victory Fund mailer, Apr. 1988.

30. Tom Price, "Colleagues Now Calling Metzenbaum Senator Can-Do Instead of Senator No," *Dayton Daily News,* Oct. 30, 1998.

31. Peter Harris, interview with author, Aug. 2, 2004.

32. George Voinovich, interview with author, Nov. 15, 2004.

33. Samuel C. Patterson and Thomas W. Kephart, "The Case of the Wayfaring Challenger," *Congress and the Presidency: A Journal of Capital Studies* 18, no. 2:118.

34. George Voinovich, interview with author, Nov. 15, 2004.

35. Robert Bennett, interview with author, May 12, 1999.

36. Tom Diemer, "Fiery Metzenbaum Goes On the Offensive," *Plain Dealer,* May 14, 1989.

37. Ibid.

38. David E. Rosenbaum, "Back-stabbing Brings Blood on Senate Floor," *New York Times,* July 11, 1993.

39. *Toledo Blade,* July 9, 1989.

40. *Congressional Record* (June 14, 1990): 7,928.

41. Text of Senate speech, June 26, 1990, in author's possession.

42. *Congressional Record* (Sept. 23, 1993).

43. The 58–42 vote on June 26, 1990, provided a majority for the amendment but was nine short of the required two-thirds.

44. Prepared statement for Senate speech, June 26, 1990, in author's possession.

45. HM, interview with author, Apr. 25, 2000.

46. Tom Diemer, "Shoot-out Over Handgun Control Shifts to Assault Weapons," *Plain Dealer,* Apr. 9, 1989.

47. Richard M. Aborn, "The Battle Over the Brady Bill and the Future of Gun Control Advocacy," *Fordham Urban Law Journal* 22 (1995): 417.

48. *New York Times,* citing Bureau of Justice Statistics, Nov. 11, 1993.

49. HM news release, Feb. 24, 1993, in author's possession.

50. Joel Johnson, interview with author, Nov. 24, 2004.

51. Richard Cohen, "Can't Save This Bill," *Washington Post*, Aug. 15, 1994.

52. "Proposal to Curtail Spread of Assault Weapons," *Washington Post*, Nov. 20, 1993.

53. *Congressional Record* (Mar. 25, 1993): 53,768.

54. Feinstein news release, Nov. 17, 1993, in author's possession.

55. Text of Metzenbaum's speech to Senate, Aug. 24, 1994, in author's possession.

56. Craig's Senate floor speech, *Congressional Record* (Aug. 25, 1994).

57. *Washington Post*, Sept. 13, 2004.

58. Prepared statement for Senate floor speech, June 12, 1992, author's files.

59. Twelve years later, without embarrassment, Vice President Cheney would acknowledge his lesbian daughter, although he took offense when John Edwards mentioned her in the vice presidential debate in 2004. Cheney did not serve in the armed forces.

60. HM Senate floor statement, June 12, 1992.

61. John Glenn, interview with author, ca. 1993.

62. HM news release, July 28, 1992, author's files.

63. HM, testimony before Senate Armed Services Committee, May 7, 1993.

64. HM speech, Apr. 21, 1993.

65. *Columbus Dispatch*, May 21, 1995.

66. Martha Pope, letter to HM, MSP, WRHS, ca. 1991.

67. Alan K. Simpson, *Right in the Old Gazoo* (New York: William Morrow, 1996), 113, 114.

68. Jake H. Thompson, *Bob Dole: The Republicans' Man for All Seasons* (New York: Donald I. Fine, 1994), 190.

69. Jack Anderson and Dale Van Atta, "Metzenbaum and Innocence Abroad," *Washington Post*, Aug. 8, 1990.

70. Michael Kranish, "Invasion Changed Views of Five Senators Who Met Hussein," ibid., Aug. 12, 1990.

71. HM's comments on France were published in the Jan. 21, 1991, *Plain Dealer* under the boldface title, "Quel est le mot pour 'tirade'?"

72. HM issued his statement promising congressional support for Desert Storm on Jan. 16, 1991.

73. Thomas J. Brazaitis, "Thrill of Victory a Fading Memory, Triumph Tainted by Saddam's Survival," *Plain Dealer*, Jan. 12, 1992.

74. Richard Lugar, remarks to reporters at the Sperling Breakfast, Washington, D.C., June 12, 1998.

75. Joel Johnson, interview with author, Nov. 24, 2004.

9. Fighting to the Finish

1. United Press International, Sept. 18, 1987.

2. Warren Rudman, *Combat: Twelve Years in the U.S. Senate* (New York: Random House, 1996), 187, 188. The chapter title, "Advise and Dissent," is borrowed from former senator James Abourezk, who wrote the book *Advise and Dissent: Memoirs of South Dakota and the U.S. Senate.*

3. Tom Diemer, "Gates Says He Should Have Asked Questions," *Plain Dealer,* Sept. 17, 1991.

4. Tom Diemer and Keith C. Epstein, "Headline Howie's Still Knocking Them Dead," *Plain Dealer,* Sept. 20, 1991.

5. Brent Larkin, "Senator feels sting," *Plain Dealer,* Oct. 17, 1991.

6. Jack Torry, "Metzenbaum Says He Was 'Plain Stupid,' Apologizes to Witness," *Toledo Blade,* Oct. 16, 1991.

7. Ibid.

8. Staff and wire reports, "Metzenbaum Rethinks His Pay Raise Quip," *Plain Dealer,* Oct 15, 1991.

9. HM Senate speech, Oct. 15, 1991.

10. *Congressional Quarterly,* Oct. 12, 1991, 2,963. Brudney soon left Metzenbaum's staff to take a teaching position at Ohio State University.

11. *Plain Dealer,* Oct. 18, 1991.

12. Tom Diemer, "Only Metzenbaum Knows for Sure," *Plain Dealer,* Oct. 10, 1991.

13. Tom Diemer, "Metzenbaum 'Off My Game' at Thomas Hearings," *Plain Dealer,* Oct. 17, 1991.

14. Brent Larkin, "Senator Feels Sting," *Plain Dealer,* Oct. 17, 1991. Metzenbaum's "low point" comment was reported in Larkin's column on the editorial page.

15. Metzenbaum opening statement for Judiciary Committee confirmation hearings on Breyer, July 12, 1994, author's files.

16. Transcript of Senate Judiciary Committee hearing, July 12, 1994.

17. "The Beatification of St. Stephen," *Time,* July 25, 1994.

18. Transcript of Senate Judiciary hearing, July 12, 1994.

19. Neil A. Lewis, "Clash Punctuates Nomination Hearing," *New York Times,* July 15, 1994. Associated Press, "Metzenbaum Grills Breyer," *Plain Dealer,* July 15, 1994.

20. Tom Diemer, "Senate Confirms Breyer for the Court," *Plain Dealer,* July 30, 1994.

21. Ibid.

22. Ibid.

23. David Broder, "Hills Liberals Launch Democratic Coalition," *Washington Post,* May 14, 1990.

24. John Harwood, "Sen. Mitchell to Play Pivotal Role in Determining How Effectively Congress Will Work with Clinton," *Wall Street Journal*, Dec. 17, 1992.

25. Coalition for Democratic Values statement, May 14, 1990, author's files.

26. Tom Diemer, "Energy Plan Provokes Stumbling in Congress," *Plain Dealer*, Feb. 25, 1991.

27. Joel Johnson, interview with author, Dec. 2, 2005.

28. Al Kamen, "Panetta in the Morning," *Washington Post*, July 18, 1994.

29. Diane Duston, Associated Press wire copy, "Senators Loosen Up in Choice of Neckties," July 17, 1994.

30. DeWine for U.S. Senate news release with chart, Dec. 28, 1993, published by the *Columbus Dispatch* and citing *Congressional Quarterly*, author's files.

31. HM, author's files, Apr. 27, 1993. The intraparty argument reignited in 2004 after Senator Kerry's defeat in the presidential election. Failed presidential candidate Howard Dean said his party was driven to a "false centrism" as a way to please major contributors. "The Democratic Party has for some time failed to live up to its mission of being a party for ordinary people," Dean said in *You Have the Power: How to Take Back Our Country and Restore Democracy in America* (New York: Simon and Schuster, 2004), 163, 55.

32. Albert Hunt, "Metzenbaum Breaches Adoption Color Barrier," *Wall Street Journal*, July 14, 1994.

33. Karl Turner, "Second Toddler Drowns in Bucket," *Plain Dealer*, June 6, 2000.

34. "Labor Bill Filibuster Disgusts Metzenbaum," *Plain Dealer*, July 13, 1994.

35. "The Striker Replacement Bill," editorial, *Washington Post*, Apr. 27, 1993.

36. Tom Diemer, "'Strike Bill' Foes Marshal Forces to Strike Back," *Plain Dealer*, May 21, 1994.

37. Tom Diemer, *Plain Dealer*, July 13, 1994.

38. Tom Diemer, "Metzenbaum Meets with Mexican Workers," *Plain Dealer*, Oct. 16, 1992.

39. Tom Diemer, "Labor Movement Short on Muscle," *Plain Dealer*, July 16, 1994.

40. HM statement introducing Baseball Fans Protection Act of 1994, Aug. 11, 1994, author's files.

41. *Congressional Record* 140, no. 137 (Sept. 27, 1994): S 13,425–27.

42. Ibid. (Sept. 30, 1994): S 13,785.

43. Tom Diemer, "Metzenbaum Drops Bid to Intervene in Baseball," *Plain Dealer*, Oct. 1, 1994.

44. *Plain Dealer*, Oct. 1, 1994.

45. Albert Hunt, *Wall Street Journal*, July 14, 1994.

46. Department of Health and Human Services Multiethnic Placement Fact Sheet, undated, acquired by author Apr. 26, 1995; *Wall Street Journal*, July 14, 1994.

47. Tom Diemer, "Metzenbaum Predicts Passage of His Transracial Adoption Bill," *Plain Dealer,* Mar. 30, 1994.

48. Tom Diemer, "Metzenbaum wins on adoption bill," *Plain Dealer,* Oct. 6, 1994.

49. Department of Health and Human Services Multiethnic Placement Fact Sheet, undated, acquired by author Apr. 26, 1995; *Wall Street Journal,* July 14, 1994.

50. Martha Brant, "Storming the Color Barrier," *Newsweek,* Mar. 20, 1995, 29.

51. News release, undated, Consumer Federation of America, "Metzenbaum Law Repealed." After retirement from the Senate, Metzenbaum worked part time as chairman of the Consumer Federation, which issued the news release on his behalf.

52. Author's notes, Aug. 1994.

53. Thomas J. Brazaitis, unpublished notes, October 1990, used with permission from the *Plain Dealer.*

54. HM retirement statement to U.S. Senate, June 29, 1993, author's files.

55. Joel Hyatt statement, June 29, 1993, issued after Metzenbaum retirement announcement.

56. HM retirement statement, June 29, 1993, author's files.

57. "Farewell to a Fighter," editorial, *Plain Dealer,* Jan. 1, 1995.

58. Jolie Solomon, "Fighting at the Finish," *Newsweek,* Aug. 1, 1994, 42.

59. HM retirement statement, June 29, 1993, author's files.

10. An Unthreatened Man

1. Tom Diemer, "Courthouse Renamed to Honor Metzenbaum," *Plain Dealer,* May 28, 1998. The song "The Impossible Dream" is from the 1972 stage production of *Man of La Mancha,* written by Mitch Leigh and Joe Darion.

2. This quote is from Dale Butland, who, representing John Glenn at the courthouse event, said, "Metzenbaum sought justice through law not for the rich and powerful who are capable of taking care of themselves, but for those in the dawn, the twilight, and shadows of life who are too often left behind and in need of help and hope. He may not have won every battle, but he never gave up and he never gave in, no matter how long the odds."

3. Author's notes from President Clinton speech, July 31, 1994.

4. Diemer, *Plain Dealer,* May 28, 1998.

5. Howard Metzenbaum, "Ignore Polls," *Washington Times,* Nov. 9, 1994.

6. George Voinovich, interview with author, Nov. 15, 2004.

7. James G. Carr spoke at the rededication of the Howard Metzenbaum U.S. Courthouse on Sept. 20, 2005. The courthouse, which is on the National Register of Historic Places, underwent a $51 million renovation between 2002 and 2005. Metzenbaum, in good spirits but appearing frail, did not speak at the event.

8. Peter Harris, interview with author, Sept. 13, 2004.

9. Dick Woodruff, interview with author, June 4, 1997.

10. Dale Butland, interview with author, Jan. 25, 2005.

11. Diemer, *Plain Dealer*, Dec. 4, 1994.

12. HM's comments at Consumer Federation of America event, honoring him in Washington, D.C., June 19, 1992.

13. Arthur Lelyveld, interview with author, Sept. 6, 1994.

14. HM, interview with author, ca. Dec. 1987.

15. Carl Levin campaign letter on Metzenbaum's behalf, undated, but provided to author on Aug. 13, 1987.

16. Mark Talisman, telephone interview with author, Oct. 12, 1994.

17. HM, interview with author, Mar. 1, 1998.

18. Byron Krantz, interview with author, Nov. 18, 1997.

19. George Voinovich, interview with author, Nov. 15, 2004.

20. Michael Barone, *Almanac of American Politics* (Washington, D.C.: National Journal Group, 1993).

21. Tom Diemer, "Metzenbaum Says Farewell," *Plain Dealer*, Oct. 8, 1994.

22. Tom Diemer, "Metzenbaum On the Way Out but Won't Go Quietly," *Plain Dealer*, July 4, 1993.

23. Diemer, *Plain Dealer*, Dec. 4, 1994, reprinted in the *Congressional Record* 141, no. 40 (Mar. 3, 1995).

24. Diemer, *Plain Dealer*, Dec. 4, 1994.

25. Associated Press, wire copy, Mar. 6, 1990.

26. Bill Sloat, "It's Ashcroft-Metzenbaum vs. NRA," *Plain Dealer*, Apr. 20, 2002.

27. Text from Sarah Brady speech, May 28, 1998, Cleveland, Ohio, author's notes.

28. Joel Johnson, interview with author, Nov. 24, 2004.

29. *Washington Post*, Jan. 3, 2000.

30. Gregory R. Thorson and Tasina Nitzschke, "When the Majority Party Won't Listen: The Use of the Senate Filibuster by the Minority Party," undated, www.morris.umn.edu/~gthorson/filibuster.pdf (accessed Oct. 5, 2007).

31. Tom Price, *Dayton Daily News*, Oct. 30, 1988.

32. "Gridlock Stops Senate," *The Hill*, May 31, 2000, 10.

33. Sarah Binder, email exchange with author, Jan. 25, 2005.

34. Tom Diemer, "Metzenbaum on Way Out," *Plain Dealer*, July 4, 1993.

35. Diemer, *Plain Dealer*, Oct. 8, 1994.

36. *Plain Dealer*, July 4, 1993.

37. HM, speech to the Senate, June 12, 1990, author's files.

38. Nancy Coffey, interview with author, Oct. 20, 2004. Although Metzenbaum did not seek reelection in 1994, his term did not end officially until early January 1995, when DeWine was sworn in.

39. *Plain Dealer,* Oct. 8, 1994.

40. Harkin's speech to the Consumer Federation of America, May 21, 2001, author's notes.

41. Rodney Ferguson, "Metzenbaum Sought Tax Break," *Plain Dealer,* Apr. 29, 1992.

42. Melanie Fonder, "Star Rainmakers," *The Hill,* Mar. 20, 2002.

43. HM, interview with author, Apr. 4, 1997.

44. Ibid., Sept. 7, 1995.

45. Thomas J. Brazaitis, "It's DeWine's Race to Lose," *Plain Dealer,* July 17, 1994.

46. Tom Diemer, "Metzenbaum will chair consumer federation," *Plain Dealer,* Oct. 13, 1994.

47. Ibid.

48. HM, interview with author, Nov. 14, 1996.

49. Diemer, *Plain Dealer,* Dec. 4, 1994; Joel Johnson, interview with author, Nov. 24, 2004.

50. Howard Wilkinson, "Metzenbaum Blasts Bush's Choice of Cheney," *Cincinnati Enquirer,* Aug. 16, 2000.

51. Alfonse D'Amato, "Ask Senator Al," *George* magazine, July 2000.

52. Tom Diemer, *Plain Dealer,* Dec. 4, 1994.

53. Bill Saxbe, telephone interview with author, ca. 1992.

54. Roger Stone, interview with author, Dec. 1, 1994.

55. Richard F. Fenno Jr., *Senators on the Campaign Trail,* 212.

56. Tom Diemer, *Plain Dealer,* Dec. 4, 1994.

57. Buddy Rand, interview with author, Aug. 30, 1995.

58. Statement issued by Hatch, May 26, 1998, author's files.

59. Thomas J. Brazaitis, unpublished interview with Shirley Metzenbaum, ca. Dec. 1987, used with permission.

60. William Hershey, "A Veteran Views the '98 Political Landscape," *Beacon Journal,* Feb. 24, 1997.

61. Dennis Kucinich, remarks made at the courthouse renaming ceremony in Cleveland, Ohio, May 27, 1998.

62. *Ohio Citizen Action,* Summer 2001.

63. Liza Heron, "Life After Congress," *Roll Call,* June 29, 2000, 42.

64. Tom Diemer, "Metzenbaum Left Senate Behind, but Not Causes," *Plain Dealer,* May 28, 1998.

65. Jolie Solomon, "Fighting at the Finish," *Newsweek,* Aug. 1, 1994, 42–43.

Epilogue

1. Susan Metzenbaum remarks at Metzenbaum funeral, Mar. 16, 2008.

2. Ted Kennedy statement, Mar. 13, 2008.

3. Dick Feagler, "It's So Long for a Friend, and a Passing Era, Too," *Plain Dealer,* Nov. 9, 1994. Posted on the *Plain Dealer* website, Mar. 13, 2008.

4. Stephen Koff, Elizabeth Auster, and Sabrina Eaton, "Metzenbaum Was 'Watchdog at the Gate,'" *Plain Dealer,* Mar. 13, 2008.

5. Ibid.

6. Interview with author, Apr. 2, 2008.

7. *Congressional Record* (Mar. 13, 2008): S 2035, S 2036.

8. Al Gore remarks at Metzenbaum funeral, Mar. 16, 2008.

9. Joel Hyatt remarks at Metzenbaum funeral, Mar. 16, 2008.

10. Metzenbaum family members, *Plain Dealer* website, Mar. 13, 2008.

11. Interview with author, Apr. 2, 2008.

12. Metzenbaum family memories, *Plain Dealer* website, Mar. 13, 2008.

Index